D1400613

Design   Lazin & Katalan, NYC
Cover Photography   Emily Eldridge
Printed in the United States of America

Library of Congress Cataloging in Publication Data

Behr, Marion
    Women working home.

Includes bibliographies.
    1. Self-employed women—United States.
2. Home labor—United States.   I. Lazar, Wendy
II. Title.
HD6072.6.U5B44   658′.041   81-2110
                                        AACR2
ISBN 0-939240-00-9

Women Working Home

The Homebased Business
Guide and Directory

Written and compiled by Marion Behr and Wendy Lazar

First Edition

WWH Press
New Jersey

Acknowledgements

Women Working Home is a tribute to the many women working from their homes who have taken time from their busy schedules to define their work and describe their business environments.

From the beginning of our study, organizations and individuals have enthusiastically responded to our project. This book could not have existed without the help of those who offered us the use of their networks on local and then national levels because of their belief in our attempt to uncover an economically potent, formerly invisible, work force.

Since our inquiry began in New Jersey, we wish to thank the following for their initial assistance and encouragement: the Art Center of New Jersey; Associate Alumnae of Douglass College; Division of Women, New Jersey Department of Community Affairs; Women Helping Women; and the New Jersey chapters or offices of the National Association of Social Workers, Designer Craftsmen, League of Women Voters, Printmaking Council, U.S. Small Business Administration, and Women's Caucus for Art.

We specifically thank Clara Allen for her wisdom and encouragement; Adele Kaplan, Michael Moylan, and Al Sinisgalli for pointing us in the right direction; Lynn Miller, whose assistance was invaluable in the beginning stages of our study; Alyssia Lazin and Jak Katalan for the design of the book; Marie MacBride and Adele Mohr for their help in proofreading; Pat Morris for her insight; Beth Preiss for her expertise as statistician; and Arleen Priest for sharing her energy and good judgment. For the hours spent behind their typewriters, we are indebted to Jo-Anne Green and Carolyn Rodefeld. Our first step to national recognition came through Susan Costello of *Enterprising Women,* and we thank her for that. Our gratitude also goes to Terri Tepper who has permitted us use of her photographs and has shared her nationwide research with us.

If the best is truly left for last, then our closing remarks must be reserved for our families: to our children, Dawn, Darrin, and Dana Behr and Jodi and Kim Lazar, who were enthusiastic though our time was not always their own; to Omri Behr, who believed in our idea and our abilities and gave generously of his secretaries' services; and to Martin Lazar, for his patience and good humor that kept him smiling while the phone kept ringing!

Our project is not finished with the publication of this book, for it represents a starting point for us and a determination that each succeeding directory will be greater than the previous one.

Contributors

Sylvia Allen
Owner of Allen Communications, with extensive background as audio-visual user, producer, marketer, and consultant. Author of *A Manager's Guide to Audiovisuals* and *How to Prepare a Production Budget for Film and Videotape*. Editor and majority owner of *Monmouth Magazine*.

Jan Anderson
Assistant Director for Research and Project Support in Princeton University's Office of Research and Project Administration with responsibility for assisting faculty members in targeting appropriate funding sources, both federal and private, for research projects.

Kaye Andres
Psychotherapist in private practice in Upper Montclair, New Jersey, working with individuals, couples, and on-going groups. Consultant to major corporate and professional groups on interpersonal management skills. Teaches creative uses of conflict and process skills of expert communication.

Dora Back
Owner of part-time After 6 Secretarial Service, offering extensive typing and dictation services. Employed full-time as secretary in chemical company. Preparing for full-time After 6 with retirement in two years.

Katherine F. Bailey
Senior Sales Director for Mary Kay Cosmetics.

Dr. Omri M. Behr
Patent attorney—Law office of Omri M. Behr—Princeton, New Jersey. Licensed 1967—New Jersey, New York, U.S. Patent Office. Fellow: Royal Society of Chemistry. Member: American Patent Law Association. Practice includes all aspects of intellectual and industrial property law. Specialization: pharmaceutical, biological, and foreign patent law. Author of articles on trademarks, copyrights, and laws concerning patent protection for microbiological inventions of foreign origin.

Peg Carey
Newspaper in Education Consultant for *Trenton Times* Newspapers. Conducts training workshops for teachers, newspaper personnel, and students. Presented Newspaper in Education concept to educators at conference of Reading Association of Ireland in Dublin.

Isabel Bogorad Fleiss
Executive Director of WomanSurance Advisory Services, Wayne, New Jersey. Founder and director of The Phone Power School of Insurance for People with Disabilities. Marketing consultant to insurance industry. Publisher of consumer-oriented newspaper series.

Arnold L. Glickman
Certified Public Accountant—licensed in New York, New Jersey, and Texas. Founder and President of seven-member accounting firm of Glickman & Co. in Closter, New Jersey. Conducts professional and executive development courses in finance and accounting for major businesses. Member: American Institute of CPAs, New York State Society of CPAs, New Jersey State Society of CPAs.

Martin Lazar
Psychotherapist in private practice in Norwood, New Jersey and New York City, working with adults, families, children, and groups. Psychiatric Social Work Supervisor, New York Department of Mental Hygiene, doing psychotherapy with children and families. Adjunct Professor of Social Work, Rutgers University. Developer of programs for the underachieving youngster. Lecturer and consultant in workshops and seminars in interpersonal relations and communications for private foundations, schools, and industry.

Elizabeth T. Lyons
Chief executive of Elizabeth T. Lyons & Associates, offering business, organizational, and management consultation, and E.T. Lyons Placement Service in New Brunswick, New Jersey. Serves as New Jersey and Region II representative to National Unity Council, chair of Coalition of New Jersey Small Business Organizations, president of New Jersey Association of Women Business Owners. Conducts workshops and seminars on management and entrepreneurship.

Marie MacBride
Free-lance writer, copy editor, and indexer. Author of *Orange Pages: A Directory of News Media for Bergen County* and *Step by Step: Management of the Volunteer Program in Agencies.* Served as volunteer in many parts of United States and Girl Scout professional worker in program and public relations for ten years.

Lynn F. Miller
Multimedia Services Librarian, Rutgers University Libraries.
Compiled Slide Registry of New Jersey Women Artists and
Directory of New Jersey Women Artists. Founding coordinator
of Women Artists Series and New Jersey Women Artists Group
Show. Co-author of *Lives and Works: Talks with Women Artists*
and *Contemporary American Theater Critics.* Member: Board of
Directors, Women Helping Women.

Pat Morris
Painter and printmaker interested in feminist movement in art.
President of New Jersey Chapter of Women's Caucus for Art.

Beth Preiss
Economist with Department of Housing and Urban Development's Office of Policy Development and Research. Ph.D. can-
didate at Princeton University—dissertation research concerns sex
discrimination in credit market.

Emily Rosen
Former copy writer and greeting card verse writer turned
"serious closet poet." Co-owner of Witty Ditty, singing telegram service, in Scarsdale, New York.

Nancy Rubin
Freelance writer, specializing in sociological trends and education. Articles in *The New York Times* and in various other periodicals, magazines, and newspapers. Currently completing a
book about suburban women to be published by Coward,
McCann and Geoghegan in 1982.

Sonia Schlenger
Director of Organizational Systems in Fair Lawn, New Jersey, a
consulting service designed to help busy individuals become better organized. Lectures on subjects of organization and success.

Adrienne Zoble
Chief executive of Adrienne Zoble Advertising in Martinsville,
New Jersey. Member of Board of Trustees of Raritan Valley
Chamber of Commerce. A founder of LINK, a business and
professional organization of top executives and entrepreneurial
women, and a founder of New Jersey Association of Women
Business Owners. Teaches workshops on marketing and advertis-
ing at Brookdale Community College and Rutgers University.

Contents

Preface

Women Working Home: The Homebased Business Guide and Directory is the first attempt to discover, identify, and assist women who are pursuing gainful work in their homes, rather than in "conventional" places of business. The book is intended to encourage and aid women who work at home and obtain for them the recognition due an economically useful and socially desirable mode of employment. The income generated by these businesses range from the modest to a level equivalent to the salaries of all but the most highly paid executives in major industries. In this book, information has been collected and categorized from several hundred women who have filled in questionnaires and written letters defining and describing their occupations. The information has been classified by name, occupation, and geographic area.

My business is in my head—a few files here and there are helpful, but mostly for show.... I had a building, seven gals on staff, all marvelously talented and gone on to bigger and better things ... sold the building because I was paying everyone every Friday but me! Also, the housing slump was scary. To my surprise, I find I do as well growth-wise from home, and better, much better, net-wise."

Public Relations Consultant

The letters present a fascinating insight into the attitudes of women with homebased businesses. Many quotes from these letters have been included throughout the book. They provide information, advice, or simply reveal greater insight into women who have developed, nurtured, and run a business from home.

The book has also been amplified by articles written by individuals whose expertise allows them to deal with certain topics in a confident, direct, and efficient manner. These have been included both to help the woman who has a homebased business and, equally, to simplify problems and encourage those who wish to begin such a business. We have introduced the general approaches for establishing a homebased business and have attempted to include as much information as possible. If there are specific problems beyond what is covered here, please consult the experts.

Since our study started in New Jersey, some of the information is New Jersey oriented, however even these items contain information which will be useful regardless of geographic location. In 1979, a craftsperson wrote to us, "you are opening a door to progress that is at present unseen. The need to help the woman in business at home, to throw a light of respect on her, and to credit her with the importance she deserves, is very much overdue." We do wish, of course, to keep this door open. Future editions will cover larger areas. A questionnaire has been included in the back of this book. Please fill it in and return it, reproduce it, or give it to a friend so that the expanding network of women who work at home can continue to spread across the country.

WOMAN LEARNS TO BE BLACKSMITH, BUT SAYS MOTHERHOOD IS WOMAN'S PROFESSION!

TUNA A. HAWK.

Ames, Ia., Aug. 11. — Miss Tuna A. Hawk probably is the only college-graduated woman blacksmith in the country.

She has taken a course in the black-smith department of Iowa State college and carries a diploma stating that she is eligible to work at the trade.

In college Miss Hawk has taken her turn at the forge, handled white-hot iron, welded, riveted and repaired just like men.

But her idea of the profession for women is wifehood and motherhood.

Here are the woman blacksmith's views of life:

"All the issues of a woman's life are centered in the home.

"Is it any more than fair that a woman should be permitted to ask the man of her ideals to help her found and operate that home?

"Must women, because of custom, wait only to be chosen by some man who is not her ideal or else never enter her life profession?

"Every woman, if she is to live up to her ideals must do one of two things—get the special man she desires or live an unmarried life!

"Marriage is an episode in a man's life. Marriage is a woman's life.

"As the situation stands today a girl may see the man who is her ideal, but must stand in line and hope and pray he will come and choose

"If he doesn't, she must accept the man who does come or never enter her chosen profession—wifehood and motherhood.

Introduction

I work at home because it pays better, because I have more freedom creatively, because there is some flexibility in scheduling time for working, and because I find satisfaction in the self-discipline working at home demands. I feel that, by building up my own at-home business, I will have found a perfect (at least for me) way of blending career and motherhood when we have children. I believe that in this way I can work it out to have the best of both worlds.''

Advertising Consultant

Legend tells us that one day in mid-eighteenth century England James Hargreaves knocked over his wife's hand-operated spinning machine, dislodged the wheel, and watched it continue to revolve on the dirt floor of their humble Lancashire cottage, thus discovering the principle of the spinning jenny. The Hargreaves invention, which allowed wool to be spun eight times faster than by earlier methods, revolutionized the British textile trade, destroyed the cottage system of fabric production, and hastened the rise of the Industrial Revolution that sent millions of people from jobs in their country homes and farms to the urban mills of Great Britain and North America.

Now, nearly two hundred years after the beginning of the Industrial Revolution, the wheel has turned again, as thousands of women discover that it is once more possible to remain at home and establish profitable enterprises that have an impact upon the mainstream of American economic life. Some of these women are engaged in traditional home industries—sewing, cooking, fabric design, the crafts, and such child-oriented endeavors as day care centers, after-school programs, and educational instruction. Others have developed businesses as disparate as market research, landscape design, editing services, cat breeding, professional party planning, and industrial psychology.

While there has not yet been a federal study conducted on the number of women entrepreneurs operating businesses from their homes, there are several indications that the phenomenon is occurring with staggering frequency. According to the 1979 figures of the Bureau of Labor Statistics, there were 1.9 million self-employed women in the United States, a 43% increase in self-employed women since 1972. In that year, one out of every five self-employed individuals was a woman; by 1979 that figure had increased to one out of every four.

The U.S. Census Bureau reveals a similar growth pattern. According to the 1977 figures, which are based on corporate tax returns and do not include women with large corporations, there were 702,000 women-owned businesses in the United States in 1977, with almost half of those enterprises believed to be conducted from the home. Those businesses accounted for $41.5 billion in receipts and represent a 30% increase in women-owned firms and a 72% increase in receipts since 1972.

The reasons many women have chosen to establish businesses at home rather than in traditional office settings are as complex and varied as the enterprises they have created, but

11

there are several unifying themes. They include: the low cost of maintaining a home office, the proximity of young children and the flexibility it affords those faced with the demands of running a household, the distaste for commuting to work, the need to seek additional income beyond a regular nine-to-five job, the quest for a second career after retirement. Many began businesses as a result of a special talent or interest. A few started businesses casually, as "one step beyond a hobby," and then watched their sales volume expand as their products became surprisingly popular.

Economists, business advisors, labor specialists, and government officials have suggested other reasons why women have also become increasingly attracted to homebased entrepreneurship, not the least of which includes higher educational attainments among women, improved work skills and job expertise, disappointment with the corporate setting as an avenue for creativity, flexibility, and promotion, and an augmented sense of independence about their own lives.

"A hundred years from now people will look back to this age as the beginning of a generation of great women entrepreneurs," predicts Beatrice Fitzpatrick, chief executive officer of the American Women's Economic Development Corporation, a Manhattan educational, training, and counseling organization for women entrepreneurs. She maintains that there is now a "fortuitous confluence" of women's social and historical roles, an increasingly service-oriented economy, and a vast reservoir of unmet needs in our society that will give rise to a new breed of businesswomen unlike any others in recorded history—women who will have begun many of their businesses at home.

Other specialists, like Clara Allen, Director of the New Jersey Division on Women, have characterized the possibilities for women working at home as limitless avenues—not only for those experienced women now in the work force, but for the millions of other women who have skills and talents but perceive themselves still as "unmarketable" housewives. Still other experts, like Michael Wachter, labor economist professor at the University of Pennsylvania, predict vast changes in the labor force of the 1980s to accommodate working women, especially those with children, and maintain that working at home may well be an important mechanism of that change.

Undoubtedly there is a revolution underway, a groundswell of female entrepreneurial activity born of dreams, disappointment, and determination. Like other social changes it has begun quietly, among women working at home in their attics, laundry rooms, basements, and backyards. Yet there is little doubt a new movement has begun, a massive silent effort by women who have chosen to remain at home but are equally committed to making an economic impact upon their communities. Some have succeeded easily; others have continued to struggle from year to year; and a few, regrettably, have given up.

12

EVERY GIRL SHOULD SPEND ONE YEAR IN FATHER'S OFFICE, SAYS TITLED DIRECTRESS

Lady Macworth, Daughter of Lord Rhondda, in New British Cabinet, Says Business Woman Will Make Better Wife Than Clinging Vine!

LADY MACWORTH.

BY LADY MACWORTH.
(In an Interview With Mary Boyle O'Reilly.)

CARDIFF, Wales, Feb. 3. — Every girl should spend a year in her father's office or shop after she leaves school and before she enters society.

Once woman takes her independent place in the world, there will be a strengthening in the partnership of the family!

WAR CHANGES VIEWPOINT.

Most fathers train their sons; their daughters were expected to develop business acumen by the light of nature. I say "WERE" because the war has changed men's point of view.

The protected English girl of 1914 was pathetically like the well-born American girl of 1860; two years of war has wrought a revolution.

Before the war the ordinary English girl never expected to work for money; today she has tried it, and she is not likely to revert.

DAUGHTERS TRUSTED NOW.

Before the war few British fathers were ready to trust their daughters; now, for poignantly pathetic reasons, thousands of girls must become qualified to carry on.

But business is a curious thing. Its intricacies do not come by inspiration. Whether prosperous or poor, business women must be trained. And for such training no teacher can equal a girl's father, no school surpass his office.

Every father who has broken his son to business will appreciate the pleasure of training his daughter. For the average girl does not smoke or drink; she is always neat and clean; she is usually deft and quick, with a genuine liking for detail if not for the actual work. And, subconsciously, a father realizes that a trained woman holds the key to most situations and has the brains to use that key.

MUST EARN BREAD NOW.

Nowadays, neglect to train a girl to business is unfair to the girl and unfair to her family.

Women who never worked before must today earn their daily bread.

Women have replaced men in scores of industries—note that I say "replaced," and not "surplanted."

No one can foretell the length of the war or the conditions that will be precipitated by the great peace.

One thing, however, IS certain: the girl trained to business in her father's office is prepared for most emergencies. That experience will go far to make her a happier spinster or a more trustworthy wife.

MARRIAGE FINER THING.

Marriage, with the independent woman of the future, will be a far finer thing than was marriage with the clinging vine of the past. There are some people so misguided as to imagine that the practical business woman will be less lovable and less loving than the unpractical wife of yesteryear.

I concede as quite likely that the new business girl will not be so ready to accept the first man who asks her.

Why should she? She can afford to wait!

Her waiting will mean more love marriages, which are, after all, the only marriages worth while. For the business girl who marries will have deeper understanding, more forbearance and far greater sense of comradship. Such qualities are warranted to wear. She may prove less easy to bluff, but as for being a shrew or a petty tyrant→NEVER.

This book is dedicated to the women who have persevered in their efforts, who have maintained their equilibrium in the face of fiscal, familial, and social obstacles. This is their story, one that deserves to be shared with other women who have already begun businesses in their homes or who may plan to do so in the future—entrepreneurs who have dared to ask the same questions, have entertained similar dreams, and are in search of the movement's most comprehensive answers.

Choosing a Home Business

Success means many things to many people—money, fulfillment, self-esteem. But for most, the base line is money and happiness (and not necessarily in that order). The ideal would seem to be feeling happy about what you're doing while the money rolls in! If a person achieves that, then one's occupation is not work but fun. It's a rare combination! How many people do you know who really enjoy their work?

Choosing a home business, then, begins with an analysis of your skills and interests. What do you enjoy doing? Certain activities will make you feel good. List all sorts of activities and experiences, work-related or not, from which you can identify skills. Do you enjoy being with children—playing the stock market—planting a garden—shopping—cooking—speaking a foreign language—traveling? Have you a green thumb—a good ear—a discerning eye? Look for skills that overlap in several activities. What appeals to you? Creating? Taking risks? Communicating? Problem solving? Teaching? Persuading? Do you prefer to work alone or with others, under pressure or in a relaxed atmosphere? Analyze values. What's really important to you: making money or making a name for yourself, filling free time or filling a need, proving yourself or helping others? To thine own self be true! Be honest! If you don't like being with kids in a noisy room, a child care center is not for you! If you hate to cook, selling homemade food items is silly! When this exercise is completed, you should have a pretty good idea of who you are, which activities and values are most important to you, your skills, and the kind of work setting you prefer. Think about these long and hard. Perhaps there are several job descriptions that would cover the items on your list.

Think positively! If woman cannot exceed her grasp, then what's a heaven for? Think big! Anything is possible—and if it's impossible, it will take just a little longer to achieve!

Speak with people in the fields that appeal to you. Do the jobs still sound interesting? Enthusiasm is a definite step to success! Whatever the job, will you still enjoy doing it ten years from now?

Talk to friends and neighbors. Make a people resource list and use it. Join a network. Check the Yellow Pages. Read trade magazines. Are there already similar established businesses in your area? Does your business fulfill a community need? If there are competitors, what are they doing? How are they failing to serve the public? Where do **you** fit in? Is extra schooling needed? An apprenticeship?

"...I can make my own hours. Since I sometimes have surges of energy at 5 AM, I can take advantage of this situation. I can put on my robe, walk across the hall, and spend a few hours expending energy in a creative and profitable manner."

Public Relations Consultant

14

We already mentioned the importance of enthusiasm. With that goes a sense of purpose and commitment. Are you willing to take risks and make sacrifices? You'll be giving up a certain amount of free time and personal time. There will be changing priorities and a changing lifestyle and, because of them, perhaps unexpected conflicts with the family. (On the other hand, family members could surprise you with large amounts of help, patience, and support.) Only you can decide if what you may be losing is worth what you may achieve.

Of course, don't overlook the amount of available capital. This may influence a business decision more than any other factor. Determine how much is needed to pay for stock, equipment, supplies, and advertising. Then figure out how much you can invest and (just in case) how much you can lose.

Anybody can start a business. The trick is to stay in it. Choosing a business—whether at home or an outside location—calls for good judgment, honest advice, and common sense. When the decision is made, jump into the new venture wholeheartedly. Give it everything you can. We all make mistakes, and we learn from every one of them. As the business grows, so you will grow.

Judith Hendershot
Stencil Artist
Photographer:
© Terri P. Tepper 1978

Getting Started Right

by Elizabeth T. Lyons,
Management Consultant

Getting started right applies to the original start-up of a business and to those times when a change in ownership, expansion, new products or services, financial viability, or other factors provide an opportunity for review and reevaluation of the business plan. A woman whose business grew out of a hobby or personal skill often skips the design of the business plan because it (the business) just grew like Topsy. Without realizing it, an entrepreneur might be ignoring tax or labor laws, licensing regulations, or employer's responsibilities.

If you are thinking of starting a business you will probably find yourself explaining your idea, product, service, goals, objectives, fees, prices, etc., to a great number of people. From some you'll have unenthusiastic or negative feedback or tough questions. A well-thought-out business plan will fortify you for inquiries from potential customers, lenders, and the professionals whose services you'll need. The time you invest in business research and the development of your plan will save you money in professional fees and will improve your ability to sell yourself as a business owner.

A business consultant might be helpful to you in suggesting some of the questions you should ask your accountant, lawyer, insurance consultant, or banker. I suggest you begin your research by writing the answers to the following questions—if you don't have the answers, you'll know where to begin to gather data:

■ Why are you starting a business? Is this to be temporary or long-term?

■ What type of business, product, or service do you own or want to own?

■ What are the objectives of the business? Your personal objectives?

■ What are the financial objectives? Are you profit oriented?

■ Do you have the experience or expertise required for this business?

■ What disciplines, skills, experience, personality, and other qualifications are required?

■ What licensing laws or regulations govern the production and sale of your product or service? Must you be licensed or bonded?

■ Is your product or service season- or fad-related (pet rock, hula hoop, etc.)? If so, do you have secondary products or services?

■ What is your philosophy regarding customer service, quality, public relations?

■ Have you set objectives for the first five years?

- How have others fared in this type of business? Percent of failures and successes?
- How might a recession or poor cash flow affect the firm's viability?
- What are the first year's goals for: sales, gross income, net profit, name recognition, clients/customers?
- What will your costs be to produce and market your product or services?
- Have you established contacts with potential customers? How?
- Should your product be protected by patent, copyright, or trademark?

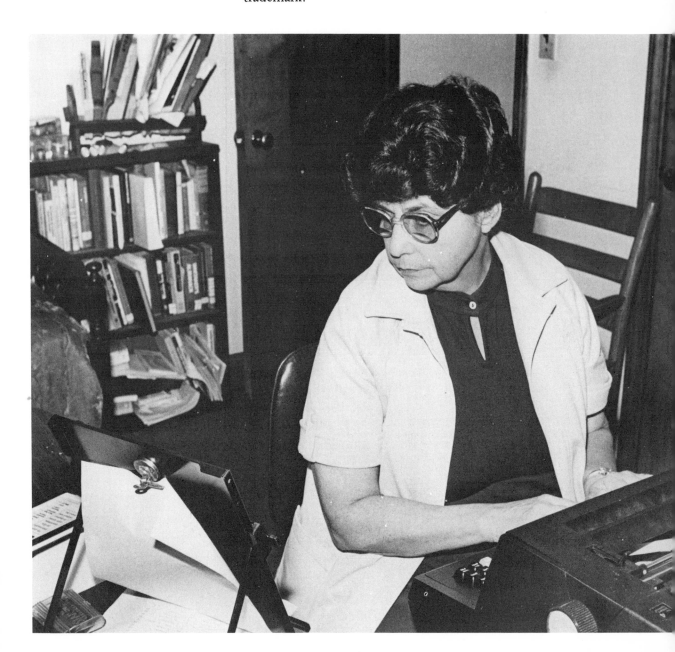

Dora Back
Secretarial Services Director
Photographer: The News Tribune

- Do you understand accounting terms and customs enough to keep simple books, collect and pay taxes, take discounts, build and maintain good credit?
- What business structure would best suit your needs? Sole proprietorship? Partnership? Corporation?

- If you have a partnership, does your contract specify the term of the agreement and how the partnership might be dissolved without endangering the business?
- Which partner holds the greater number of shares? Why? What are the rights and responsibilities of the partners (draw, expenses, etc.)?
- How will budgets be established?
- How will prices and fees be set to insure a reasonable profit?
- How much space will be required for production, inventory, supplies, offices, records maintenance, etc.?
- If your business is in the home, how will business telephones, mail, checkbooks, files, and other business paraphernalia be isolated from the family activities?
- Have you identified which of your purchases and expenses should be paid from the business checkbook and charged as business expenses, so you are not spending taxed income from another source on expenditures which should be charged to the business?
- Have you applied for separate credit cards for billings of business-related expenses?
- How much cash will you need to operate your business for the first 12 months?
- What is the span of time from purchase of raw materials through production, distribution, sales, billing, and payment? Can you continue to purchase materials, pay staff, taxes, overhead, during that period?
- Is visibility important in your business? How will you plan to create or enhance a public image?
- Have you budgeted membership dues for business and professional organizations?
- What kind of equipment or vehicle will you require? Have you considered whether it should be purchased, leased, new, second-hand?
- What telephone service will you require? Should you have an answering service or an answering machine? Will you require a post office box?
- If you are operating from your home, are you violating any local ordinances?
- What have you done to improve relationships in your neighborhood?
- Do you have people working for you? How are they paid?
- Are you considered (by them) to be an employer or contractor?
- In either case do you know how to report earnings or fees paid?
- Have you considered whether you are responsible for payment of employer contributions for social security taxes, unemployment, and disability taxes? Ask your accountant to explain all this in detail.
- Are you aware of the Equal Pay Act, O.S.H.A. (Occupational Safety and Health Act), the minimum wage, age discrimination, and employment of minors laws?

■ Have you consulted your insurance agent about liability, key person, and other insurances?
■ Have you considered attending selected courses or workshops on business to gain information about entrepreneurship?
■ Do you know of the booklets and reference materials available through the Small Business Administration and Offices of Economic Development and Small Business Development Centers (of universities)?

Please do not become discouraged, just apply the same determination to this project as you've used in getting to where you are now, and you'll begin to ask the right questions of the experts.

Bibliography
Lane, Marc J. *Legal Handbook for Small Business.* New York: AMACOM, a division of the American Management Association, 1977.
Lasser, J.K. *How to Run a Small Business.* 4th ed. New York: McGraw-Hill, 1974.
White, Richard M., Jr. *The Entrepreneur's Manual.* Pennsylvania: Chilton Book Co. 1977.
Dible, Donald M. *Up Your Own Organization.* California: Entrepreneur Press, 1971.

"It all started 12 years ago...I decided to sell my handcrafts in my home. My husband thought I was mad—Who ever would come to the house and buy all those 'non-essentials'?...This fall I will have my 12th Christmas Boutique where I sell handcrafts from 15 states—the work of 220 crafts-people. The Boutique is well known with customers willing to wait 45 minutes to give my husband money for all the 'non-essentials' they bought. (My husband now takes two weeks vacation to 'man' the cash register at each Boutique.) And of course I remind him of his words of 12 years ago—it'll never work."

Craftsperson

Sally R. Campbell
Writer/Consultant
Photographer:
© *Terri P. Tepper 1979*

Personal Indicators of Success

by Kay Andres,
Psychotherapist

There are some personal qualities which are good indicators of business success. First: enormous physical and emotional vitality, attached to an achievement drive centered within yourself, and for yourself. No matter what your business, you are "alone at the top" and must be your own feedback, your own dependable support, your own supervisor and giver of rewards. A certain comfortable "loner" quality is probably a part of your very energetic personality.

Second: staying power and bounce-back—the ability to live with nonsuccess, to experience failures, and to keep on going. For if you can't survive failures along the way, you can't survive.

Third: creativity—the learned knack of finding alternatives, of seeing things in new ways, of diversifying your products or services, of hearing the different drummer and testing out whether anyone else will march to it.

Fourth: curiosity—as in the wry dictum, "Keep moving, sooner or later you'll stumble over something." People who take things apart with their minds tend to be able to put things together in new ways. (If necessity is the mother of invention, curiosity is its fairy godmother.)

As your dreams of becoming a successful small businesswoman begin to come true, you will probably discover some gradual changes in yourself and in your living style. You will probably accommodate a tightened schedule by developing an ever-increasing efficiency in performance of tasks. New interests may crowd out some old ones as values and satisfactions evolve. Social life may change, perhaps becoming more limited. Recreation may be less random and more selectively chosen, for such specific needs as mental and physical health maintenance.

Even your dreams are likely to change. In fact, change, involving your personal and professional development, seems, paradoxically, to be the only constant. And in this exciting and absorbing growth trajectory of yours there is little taste for coquetry, for the kind of pretend humility that denies capabilities or accomplishment, or for automatic deference to any other human being. You're developing the habit of looking yourself, and the world, in the eye. You're developing a sturdy courage.

The woman who has dreamed her dream and who is living it into reality, even as she dreams new dreams, is a hard woman to stop, once she has started well.

LaVerne Hunt Gallob
Music Teacher
Photographer: Doranne Jacobson

Turning Volunteer Skills into Marketable Skills

by Marie MacBride, Author
of *Step by Step*

The hours you have spent as a volunteer were of great benefit to someone or to some organization. Now is the time to make them count for yo

The traditional 25- to 50-year-old housewife/volunteer more often than not is finding it necessary to seek financial reward for her efforts. She has earned the right to have her volunteer accomplishments recognized by business. One businessman said that any woman who can work successfully with a PTA board has management skills. The trick is to examine the volunteer experience to discover how it can be used to help women who have or are planning to have homebased businesses.

We tend to think in boxes or categories. Perhaps you equate skills with something learned in the classroom or only of real value when it is paid for. The classroom provides theory, but a skill is the proven ability to do something. It doesn't matter whether it was learned in the home, in a volunteer position, or in a paying job. The bottom line is the ability you have.

For whatever reason, if you have decided that you need —or just want—to work from your home and you have no special product or service in mind, take heart. Don't ever say, "I can't do anything." You do have a marketable skill. More than one woman, after taking inventory, has identified her own skill and used it as the heart of a thriving business. For example, one woman had a flair for taking bits and pieces of her last year's (and previous years') wardrobe and changing and combining them to express this year's styles. Now she does this for a handsome fee for people lacking the flair or time to do it for themselves. All she knew was how to dress stylishly. Other businesses have been developed from what women learned to do at home: planning/managing weddings, dog sitting or grooming, window trimming, shopping for shut-ins or out-of-towners, sandwich supplier, wake-up service; the list goes on and on. One woman who is especially good at organization, organizes other people's closets and cupboards, offices, or homes for a fee.

If you already know what business to operate from your home, but are convinced one aspect of that business is impossible for you because **you can't do that,** take another look. Bookkeeping, for example, is not a great mystery. Did you ever keep accounts for an event for a volunteer organization or pay the bills for your family? You can do it for your business; at least you can do it until your business grows so that it makes sense to hire someone to keep books for you. But, to start with, you can keep accurate records, with bills, receipts, and cancelled checks, of what comes in and what goes out.

Dot Hofmann and Marna Gold
Party Planners
Photographer: Doranne Jacobson

"I am a homemaker who enjoys the free-

dom of this job! However,

today's economy seems to de-

mand additional income above

that which my husband can earn.

I began my job at home sewing

custom-made items of clothing

for my friends and neighbors. I

do this during school hours and

weekends when I have spare time.

To accomplish this I find budget-

ing time of utmost importance."

Dressmaker

Your volunteer habit of giving service is a valuable skill that will show through in your business dealings; service is the heart of good business practices.

If you have successfully managed a large event for a church or a community organization, you have more management skills than you realize. You had to set goals, develop a strategy (or means) for reaching the goals. Then you had to put the strategy into operation and you had measurable results. You probably selected workers, coordinated their activities, controlled the finances, promoted the event, and kept to a production schedule. All of these activities are management skills. You have them.

If you fear you do not have the ability to provide your product or service and then also manage the business end of your endeavor, remember that you have proven you can take care of a number of things at the same time. While you volunteered many hours and days, you continued to keep your home running and your family fed, well, and happy. In order to do that, you had to use your time and resources wisely. Businessmen devote much time and pay large fees for workshops on time management and the husbandry of resources. You have those skills!

Suppose you have taken inventory of your skills and feel you need to add or update communication techniques, or typing on modern machines, or setting up displays with the latest equipment. Take a volunteer job and make it work for you. Seek a well-organized nonprofit or cultural organization that will ac-commodate your need to learn while you supply volunteer work hours. Increasingly, these organizations are learning that the volunteers have the right to fill their own needs while giving ser-vice valuable to the organizations. Shop around until you find a volunteer job that will help you learn the skill you need. Start with a Volunteer Bureau or Voluntary Action Center nearest you. They know what community groups will be able to provide the volunteer job to help you sharpen your proficiencies, and they understand that you have the right to learn while volunteering.

There's no need to hesitate using a record of your vol-unteer work to document your ability in a given area. Such work is accepted as job experience for civil service employment, and business is beginning to look more carefully at the correlation between volunteer work and the same work defined in business terminology.

And finally, use some volunteer help, yourself! Mem-bers of the National Alliance of Homebased Businesswomen can give you voluntary guidance. SCORE, the Service Corps of Retired Executives, is a volunteer adjunct to the Small Business Administration that gives free advice to people with business problems. The Small Business Administration is listed in the tele-phone directory under "United States Government."

Volunteering has value for you. Use it!

How to Market Yourself

by Sylvia Allen,
Marketing Consultant

"I've seen many businesses start locally, with beautiful decor and large advertising expenditures. Some succeed. Most fail. I am glad that I did it the cheap, slow way. Now that I know better what services are wanted and needed and what fees are reasonable for what I provide, I can begin to market my services intelligently."

Researcher

Marketing is simply finding out what goods and services are needed, where to sell them, to whom, and at what price. In order to effectively market your product/service, you need to answer the following questions:

1. What am I selling? What is my product?

Define it in writing, whether it is making dried flower arrangements, plant sitting, or providing public relations services. Writing it out clarifies it in your mind and crystallizes your thinking. Do not expect this phase to be easy. In fact, it will be one of the more difficult steps in the marketing process.

2. Who will buy it? What is my market?

Draw up a list of people/businesses who need your product/service. Look through the Yellow Pages, call friends, check with local clubs and associations. Don't be afraid to ask people for their help and suggestions.

3. What is my product/service worth? What do I charge?

Check your competitor's prices. Do some local market research. Find out who else offers something similar. If so, how is it sold/marketed? What do they charge? Of course, included in this is an evaluation of your own time and what it is worth, as well as the cost of the raw materials that are used to make your product.

4. Who, or what, is my competition?

Again, a simple resource is the Yellow Pages. Another good source is your local library. Check with local business people who comprise your marketplace. They will know your competition.

Santa Pandolfo and Daria Finn
Home Contractors
Photographer: Norma Holt

"I run a small marketing-services firm

from home, as I have a young

child and local day care is nonexis-

tent for the middle class and in-

adequate for the poor. I love what

I do, and spent many years in this

field before deciding to add a

daughter to my client list. Until

there are better solutions for day

care, or until equal parenting

responsibility-division is a reality,

more and more women will choose

to work from home. It was the

only sensible choice for me."

Public Relations Consultant

Although very basic, taking time to answer these questions can help you formulate a good, definitive marketing plan. Don't expect to answer any of these questions quickly or easily. Take time and be patient with yourself. Be prepared to drop an idea or alter it.

If you need additional help or answers to specific questions pertinent to your particular product or service, there are two services that provide free consultation: AWED— American Woman's Economic Development Corporation; SCORE—Service Corps of Retired Executives.

Check your local telephone directory or regional employment office for the address nearest you.

One final word of advice—go through this same procedure every year. This marketing review is important to assess your status in the marketplace and to review changing conditions. Be prepared to change your goals and objectives if the situation warrants it. If you discipline yourself in this way, you will be assured of success in your business venture, whatever it may be!

How to Set Fair Prices

"In all honesty, I don't know if there is a set fee for the work of piano accompanists. I usually let the artist (or soloist) suggest a certain amount they have in mind (or can afford) and, in most cases, I find that acceptable."

Music Teacher

Congratulations! You've decided to go into business! You know what you're going to do and how you'll go about it. You know whether you will be selling goods or providing services. Now comes the most difficult part for many business people. What prices? How does one set fair market value?

There certainly is no easy answer. It is a problem all of us have to deal with at some time. Some of us may have even reached the wrong conclusions, then we have had to do some fancy footwork to keep pace with reality.

Let's talk of specific items for sale, products which others may be selling as well, such as clothing, wallpaper, or hosiery. You could set prices comparable to those in area stores, but since you have low overhead and possibly no employees, you can still make a profit by charging less than the store price. A dress that wholesales at $50 is sold in stores at $100. If stores have such a mark-up, then you can discount. Determine how much profit you want. You can sell a few items and earn a decent amount or sell a great many items with a little profit on each. That same $50 dress can be sold from your home for as little as $60 and up, and you still make a profit! This is true for any product not manufactured by you and purchased from another source. Comparison shop! Know your competition!

If the product is an item you have handcrafted, then the rules are very different—and more complex. The cost of materials and the time required to complete a handcraft must be considered. That time includes not only the actual hours of creativity, but the minutes it takes to drive to the supply house or prepare your working area.

Polly Reilly of Westfield, New Jersey, is the designer and creator of more than 33 different whimsical wooden Christmas ornaments. One of her best sellers is the "Executive Housewife." To her credit, Polly sells thousands of ornaments each year —mostly at spring and fall craft boutiques which she herself organizes and promotes. She does the preparatory work on each figure, then distributes them among three other women who work at home—"painters" who block in the large areas of color. The ornaments are then returned to Polly who finishes them off with the detail work—putting on faces, making mops, adding clothing, etc. She usually works on 50 or 60 items at a time, assembly-line style, so it is difficult for her to be specific about the amount of time it takes to complete each ornament, but she "guesstimated" at between 20 and 30 minutes.

26

Polly Reilly

handpainted wooden ornaments/boutiques

Polly Reilly

520 Sherwood Parkway,
Westfield, New Jersey, 07090

520 Sherwood Parkway, Westfield, New Jersey, 07090/(201)233-2510

William E. Garrison in his book *Selling Your Hand-craft* has a formula that can be used to determine the retail price of a handcrafted item. We need to know costs of labor, material, and overhead. Taking the ''Executive Housewife'' as an example, here's how the formula works.

According to Mr. Garrison, Labor (L) equals Minimum Wage times the amount of Time it takes to complete the item. In this case, we took about 24 minutes as a median, because it's a nice round 40% of an hour, and a Minimum Wage of $3.25 an hour. Then our formula reads: Labor = $3.25 × .40, or $1.30.

For each ornament Polly estimates that wood is $.08; paint, $.10; and decorations, $.20. While she thinks that $.20 for decorations is a generous guess, she did not include costs for tags, stationery, brushes, or bags that are used when she sells at shows. For our purposes, let's assume it balances out and that her total price for Materials (M) is just $.38.

"Our business is growing, but we are still operating out of our house. We prefer this as it keeps our overhead low enough so that we can offer high quality goods at a very reasonable price."

Craftsperson

Next, Overhead. As defined by Garrison, it is the "total of all costs other than direct labor and materials." He breaks it down by stating that "overhead covers tools, bulk supplies, paper, pencils, electricity, heat, water, telephone, and the work area in which the craftsman produces the things he sells. Everything not directly part of the production process is properly called overhead. Training, the time spent in ordering supplies, time spent on designing, time spent in talking to customers or potential buyers—all of this is hidden cost and in total is O for overhead." If work is done at home and there are no employees on the payroll, the rule of thumb is that Overhead is one-third of either Labor or Materials, whichever is higher. In that case, Polly's Overhead would equal one-third of Labor, $O = 1/3L$, or \$.433. (Garrison suggests never rounding off numbers when figuring costs.) If the home business has even one employee, as does Polly's, then Overhead equals one-third of Labor plus Materials, $O = 1/3 (L + M)$, or \$.56. Close enough! Polly pays \$.60 to a painter for each ornament!

Andy Fiddleman
Clothing Designer
Photographer:
© *Terri P. Tepper 1978*

Add $L + M + O$ to figure Wholesale Price (WP). For the ornament, WP = \$(1.30 + .38 + .56), or \$2.24. Double the \$2.24 Wholesale Price to get the Retail Price, which is \$4.48. In fact, Polly sells each handcrafted ornament for \$4.50. Comparable items sell in stores for \$5 and \$6, so she could be charging more! But it is probably the balanced combination of quality design and reasonable price that has her selling so many thousands every year. Polly did not figure her Retail Price with the Garrison formula, yet how very close she came! Remember that any change, no matter how small, in labor, materials, or overhead will also change the wholesale and retail prices. Therefore, keep updating your own figures for your specific handcraft. There may be changes from year to year, or even season to season.

If your figures seem too high, rethink your process. Perhaps you are traveling too far and too often to pick up supplies that are too expensive. Do you really need to pay someone to do a job you could better afford to do yourself? While you may be able to underprice competitors because of a homebased business, if an item is too cheap, it is often looked upon as having little value!

The same is true of services, whether it be design consulting, landscaping, library research, or product testing. Time is money! Know where goodwill ends and good business begins. Don't sell yourself short. You have skills that others may not have and you deserve to be paid for them. Do doctors and attorneys ever question their fee scales? Service-oriented businesses must also know what the competition (if there is any) is charging. Hopefully, the service is unique in your area and so absolutely fantastic that the phone never stops ringing! Yet, even fees for services must have fair market value or the phone will stop ringing. There will be advertising costs, office supplies and expenses, and new shoes to replace the old ones that wear out while pounding pavements making personal contacts. Labor estimates are still based on minimum wage times the amount of time it takes to complete the service. Add to that material costs and overhead. Be fair. Don't set a price so high that your service is unaffordable by the people you are trying to reach. On the other hand, business is not charity. You want to show profit or else you probably wouldn't be working. Your personality, competence, responsibility, and judgment combined with the convenience and comfort of your office will make your business successful.

In all cases, whether selling products or providing services, it is important to make your customers feel they are getting some, or all, of the following when dealing with you as an individual in a homebased business: lower prices, top quality, personalized service, and fast service. Word will spread that you are the type of person with whom it's a pleasure to do business. The best advertising is word of mouth references from satisfied customers.

Bibliography
Garrison, William E. *Selling Your Handcraft*. Pennsylvania: Chilton Book Co., 1974.

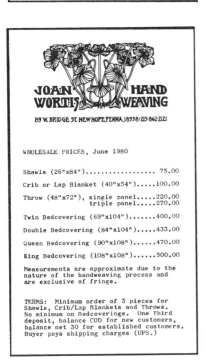

Advertising Strategy from the Home Office

by Adrienne Zoble,
Advertising Consultant

My business, an advertising agency that is heavy in marketing consultation, operates from my home with one full-timer and several free lancers. My business cards show both a post office box number and a street address. So does my letterhead. The envelopes have the same typeface but show only the post office box number. I'm beginning to think that, on the next reorder, I should revise the envelopes to look exactly like the letterhead.

SOMETHING CREATIVE
237 SPRUCE DRIVE/BRICKTOWN, NEW JERSEY 08723/(201) 920-1314

INVOICE

SOMETHING CREATIVE
237 SPRUCE DRIVE/BRICKTOWN, NEW JERSEY 08723/(201) 920-1314

INVOICE NO.

DATE

DATE	DESCRIPTION	RATE	COST

PURCHASE ORDER

SOMETHING CREATIVE
237 SPRUCE DRIVE/BRICKTOWN, NEW JERSEY 08723/(201) 920-1314

To expedite prompt payment please include job number on your invoice.
☐ DO NOT CHARGE SALES TAX. RESALE CERTIFICATE NO. 162385414

JOB #_____

DATE_____

QUOTED_____

CLIENT_____

DESCRIPTION_____

CHARGE_____

INVOICE #_____

DELIVER TO:_____

NO LATER THAN: _____

NT

When I run newspaper ads, they are basically a reproduction of my letterhead or business cards, but the street address is never in the ad, only the post office box. It is a matter of security. For homebased businesses, aside from the crucial matter of security, I fail to see too many other real differences in advertising.

Are you a consultant or a tutor? Do you go to clients, or see them at your home? Whichever the case, you then have a different perspective of how far away from your home you should advertise.

Traveling out (as I do, mostly), you might set no limit on distance, provided you can be reimbursed for at least some fair share of portal-to-portal. Asking people to come to you means you have to assume that they will simply not travel more than three to five miles. If they travel beyond that distance, chalk it up as a bonus. Especially with frantic lifestyles and high gasoline costs, think near.

If your ads say, "Call for appointment," the address is irrelevant. Just don't forget the phone number and area code. You might state "Trenton Metro area" or "Serving Mercer County for 10 years" to give a clue beyond the telephone exchange. You might list a post office box number and "since 1960" to overcome whatever negatives there might be about post-office-box holders moving away in the middle of the night. Perhaps you can regionalize the part of the state you're in, so that you provide locational tips. In services, clients feel safer dealing locally, because they feel they'll be better served. But there will inevitably be someone to contradict that with the in-

"*. . . I must build up my own business and contacts. One way of doing this has been teaching adult education classes in home landscaping for several years. It is a slide presentation of examples of both good and poor designs, horticulture, and general info on how to plan and why to lay it all out before you dig a hole! I usually get one or two customers from these classes. The other 95% of my work is by referral from satisfied customers. I have gotten almost nothing from the Yellow Pages—the only place I advertise.*"

Landscape Architect

Stephanie Urso Spina
Advertising Agent
Photographer:
© *Terri P. Tepper 1978*

"After completing New York School of Interior Design, I went looking for a job. Again the hours were too confining for my family needs. I then struck on my gimmick. Wallpapering! I had done my entire home and helped several friends. I placed an ad in a local paper and began spreading the word that I was in business— wallpapering. Once I got into the home, I told the client I was also a decorator. The first year I had 18 clients and 16 chose to have some kind of decorating done."

Interior Decorator

verse statement: you must go to some huge metropolitan area to obtain the best expertise. You'll never please everyone!

What are your advantages and disadvantages, compared to competition, exclusive of the fact that your business is homebased? The only time I mention that my business is in my home is when I'm explaining our fee schedule. For those cynics who think I'm too expensive, I drop the little golden nugget that my business is in my home with significantly lower overhead than most other agencies. It works like a charm.

Another way that I advertise, besides the newspapers and public relations, is by being extremely active in three organizations. Yes, they take up a lot of time; there's no question about that. But it's also obvious what I have derived from such involvement: many clients and consultations and a marvelous list of far-reaching contacts. I have learned to live networking among men and women, and I promote my business to a great degree in this manner.

I give speeches; I write articles; I conduct workshops at colleges. Essentially in a service business, I work at positioning myself as an expert. Few newspaper ads can accomplish that with good payout. In retailing geared to a mass audience, newspapers and radio work well. In service, radio works extremely effectively, but is too costly for small businesses like mine. The same goes for magazines. I can't use transit; I can't afford billboards; and direct mail would be super, if I were so inclined. Mine is not a mail-order business.

How does your product or service reach your target consumer? Mail order, retail one-on-one, sales staff, sales reps, distributors, consulting one-on-one, telephone solicitation? Lastly, think about promotion in terms of the following: how does your competition promote? If they don't, you must. If they do, don't copy them. Be creative and unique in your copy and strategy. Advertise when you're certain they won't. Always keep your name out in front of your marketplaces. Give your business continual exposure and promote your unique attributes. How? By direct mail, teaching, speechmaking, networking, telephone, cable TV? Think it through.

Calling in a marketing consultant can help in crystallizing your thinking. It will remove the subjective tendencies in media selection. Too many people place advertising on radio stations with their favored formats, or in newspapers they enjoy, while ignoring the media that are really reaching their target markets. You're not advertising your company to you, but to your customers! You may not like the formats or editorial positions, but they do!

Learn what the marketplace perception of your product or service is all about. Most companies won't admit to negative perceptions regarding their own industries and would love to sweep these negatives under the rug. Wrong! Bring them out in the open and address them head-on. You know what the rental car company claimed a few years back! Admitting they were only Number Two put them on the map!

Do you use an answering service? Does anyone work with you? Do you have a phone system that takes messages when you're not there? If you're thinking homebased, you may not be thinking professional; few companies or individuals enjoy dealing with others who are inaccessible, have irregular hours, or whose children answer the phone. Don't throw away business to your competitors. Be superior in staff, service, and follow-through.

Advertising is an integral part of marketing and, as such, should be considered part of a total picture. Dwelling on your home location will prove wasteful. You have a business. You're an entrepreneur. Convey to others that you have a product or service they need.

"Here's My Business Card..."

The first thing that establishes your authenticity and serious intent, as a business person in the world beyond your home, is a business card. This rectangular piece of paper is used for introductions and identification. It is, in many ways, a passport to the business world.

A business card reflects your personality and projects an image of your enterprise. One of quality and good taste suggests distinction and gives the person who sees it a feeling of confidence in your abilities. Cards should be clear and simple, yet professional and eye-catching. Include name, address, or post office box (if relevant), phone number, and perhaps a logo (symbol) or line of copy to explain what you do. If you operate under a special business name, this should also be included.

Business cards differ. Be creative in your use of materials: a fashion illustrator or textile designer might use a card with cloth veneer; an individual or corporation working with plastics might prefer to have the information printed on a plastic surface; an artist or craftsperson might relate to her medium, as does the woman who etches on slate and whose business card is printed on dark paper with the appearance of slate. Your photograph on your card can emphasize who you are and what you do.

Before deciding on the card that will best represent you, study as many as possible pertaining to your field. Look through a catalog showing varieties in type and style. Go to several printers and look at their samples. Note those that are memorable. Why do they stand out? Placement of words? Type? Catchy copy? Striking logo? Since a business card is a form of advertising, a certain amount of originality can be beneficial. There are choices in the use of color, texture, type styles, unusual papers, logos, photographs, or other special effects. The proper use of special features can make some cards stand out from competing ones, thus creating a lasting impression on a potential client. Draw a small sketch to see what layout seems best. Do a mock-up, if it helps. When satisfied with the end result, contact the printer of your choice and discuss the final presentation. Remember that the cost difference between good and cheap paper is minimal, but the effect can be considerable. Incidentally, it might be advantageous to tie in your business card with your business stationery and advertisements.

MEDIEVAL
BRASS
RUBBING
CENTRE
Marjorie E. Fox
On the Green
Windham Center,
CT. 06280
(203) 423-2785

SIR ROBERT de BURES

"For the most part I sell through Art and Craft shows, and the resultant follow-up business. I have had business cards printed, which are a definite help in obtaining orders following a show."

Artist

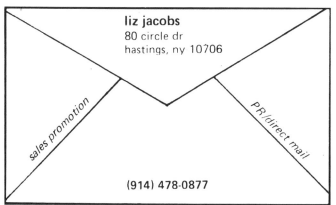

If you can afford it, engraved cards with raised letters and visible impressions of the lettering on the reverse side are excellent. The clarity of such type is most attractive. If cost is an important factor, there is a cheaper process called thermography, or "imitation engraving," which produces raised letters on the front side but leaves the reverse side flat. Other optional features, some of which are shown elsewhere in this book, include: embossed cards, which have lettering or a logo that is raised without being inked; fold-over cards, which open to accommodate extra copy or to allow space for writing a message; hot-foil-stamped cards, which have gold or silver metallic lettering; round-corner cards; textured cards, which simulate linen or other materials; translucent cards, which are made of a durable, high-oil-content stock you can read through; vertical cards.

While they should never be a substitute for real advertising, business cards are like miniature billboards that can be tacked on bulletin boards, stuck on refrigerators, or inserted in desk blotters or mirror frames and are usually small enough to be carried in wallet pockets. Carry them with you at all times. You never know when one might be needed, or when a contact might ask for several to pass around. This is a networking opportunity not to be missed!

Business cards are one of the least expensive, most important items in your budget. They are a simple, yet powerful entry into the world of business.

The Importance of Being Organized

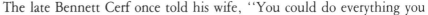

by Sonia Schlenger,
Management Consultant

The late Bennett Cerf once told his wife, "You could do everything you wanted to in life if you were organized." This is especially true for the woman working at home, who really needs to be an organizational expert at keeping track of all the balls she's juggling. However, there is no value in being organized simply to be organized. You need a framework, an approach that will help you accomplish what you want to do and need to do in the time available to do it. As such, being organized does not mean the same thing as being neat. Neat-looking surroundings can be very nice, but being neat is not the same thing as having a system. Being organized means having a system—one that enables you to find what you want when you need it. For example, an appropriately labeled sloppy-looking file folder is better than a miscellaneous neat pile which has to be gone through to determine if what is wanted is actually in there.

Organization should make life simple. Systems should work for you helping you to achieve your goals and objectives. A certain amount of self-discipline is called for, but the payoffs are worth it.

So where should you start? Much as you might wish otherwise, you only have 24 hours in a day, and the success of your organizational systems will depend, to a large extent, on how well you utilize that time. Effective time management does not come about by accident. It comes about through careful planning, which takes into account your own priorities and the needs of your family. Being aware of your own priorities is important, because as time demands increase, it is usually a woman's own needs that are sacrificed first. It's essential to strike a balance between what activities you consider to be important to your individual growth and development, and those which contribute to the well-being of your family. Careful planning will allow you to devote time to both.

Try to schedule your activities to take into account your personal energy level (i.e., how energetic you feel at various times during the day) and external demands on your time. Utilize your changing level to the greatest extent possible, reserving tasks demanding the utmost in concentration for those times when you're willing and able to devote your full attention to them. Likewise, group less-demanding activities for those hours of the day when your energy level is lower, or interruptions tend to be more frequent.

Behr

A separate or reserved place to work is also very important. Not only will it enable you to organize your environment more effectively to accomplish the task at hand, but it will also put you in the appropriate frame of mind as a businesswoman. One of the major pitfalls for women working at home is the tendency not to separate business tasks from personal/household tasks. When you enter your office, studio, or even the corner of your dining room which you've reserved for working, you should be prepared to devote yourself exclusively to your current project without jumping up to dust the shutters or vacuum the rug.

Working at home makes it difficult to ignore the demands of housekeeping, because the results of your inattention will surround you. Unfortunately, housework is a part of our lives with no real beginning and no real ending. It will take up as much of your time as you allow. Housekeeping has to be attended to, by someone, in order that it doesn't interfere with your work. Options include setting aside a limited amount of your time to clean—either in a large chunk or smaller periods, enlisting the aid of your family, or hiring someone to do the cleaning for you. Just remember that if having a perfectly clean and orderly house seven days a week is one of your priorities, then the time or money needed to accomplish that has to come from somewhere. That is, it needs to be planned for in your organizational scheme.

You will find it much easier to get right down to work if everything you own has a place to "live," from your paper clips on up to important documents which will be needed for reference. However, in deciding where something should "live," you want to ask the correct question. You **don't** want to ask, "Where should I put this?" You **do** want to ask, "How do I plan to use this?" In answering the question of how you plan to use it, you will very often find out where you should put it. For example: a post card comes in the mail, telling you of an upcoming sale at your favorite clothing store. If you plan to take advantage of the sale, the card should be posted in a place where it will remind you when to go (e.g., in your calendar book, on your bulletin board, on your refrigerator door). Putting it in a pile on your desk will most likely result in your being reminded of the sale after it is over.

It is not easy to change old habits. To be successful, you need to be flexible and maintain your sense of humor, keeping in mind that the appropriateness of solutions will change as your needs change. What is right for you this year may not be right for you next year. What works for your best friend might not work for you. You have to assess your own current situation, determine your objectives, and implement the organizational systems that will get you where you want to go.

'I have one large room set up as a studio with two drawing boards, file cabinets, desks, and 'tools of the trade.' I also find an answering device for my telephone is essential. I only take calls during normal business hours, because otherwise my home life would be completely disrupted and I have found some division must be maintained between business and private life."

Advertising Consultant

Home is Where the Kids Are

Kids! If you've got 'em, you can't live with 'em and you can't live without 'em! Home is where the kids are! If you still have children at home and are also conducting a homebased business, then you can, you must, and you will deal with this reality! There are no choices.

It should come as no surprise that a majority of the women listed in this directory began businesses at home specifically because they had children living there. Some could not afford child care; some liked the convenience, comfort, and flexibility of working at home and being with their children; others felt it was important to be around when the youngsters were in their developing years. A theater director and drama coach works at home to be available for her children's needs because she has never met a baby sitter that could match "the mother's touch." A lawyer wrote that being home in case a child needs her, gives each one a sense of security and self-esteem.

A divorced jewelry manufacturer now works at home to be with her teenagers. When growing up, she felt that she never saw her mother who worked away from home, and she doesn't want her own children to have similar feelings.

For the single parent, two reasons for working at home take on special meaning. One is convenience. Home is where a woman can have a maximum amount of time to be both mother and father to her children, yet also be in surroundings that are safe and secure. Security is particularly important for some. Although one of our respondents had legal custody of her son, her ex-husband disappeared with him for six months. To be on the scene in the hope that this child-snatching would never recur, this woman was determined to work from home and now has a successful business.

These examples give a brief summary of why women work at home because the children are there, but it doesn't explain how to work and mother at the same time. The realities are—you're in the middle of dyeing a fabric when the baby wakes up from her nap crying! You have an important business phone call and your two children enter the room fighting loudly! Just when you've hit on that one brilliant creative idea to tie together a client's advertising campaign, you realize it's time to pick up your son at school and take him to the dentist! Recognize these examples? There are many, many others that are all too familiar. There's no getting away from it! The children are at home at some time during the day. What to do?

"I have time to work because I have established priorities for each part of my day or week. My children know when it is 'their' time or my 'work time.' I average 15-20 hours of work each week. I work at home because I believe my children need my guidance and presence in their early years."

Calligrapher

Sandra Tannenbaum
Teacher
Photographer:
© Terri P. Tepper 1978

"I enjoy the diversity and challenge of

working out of my home on

many different phases of art

history. The biggest bonus to me

as a single parent is I usually can

work around my son's vacation

and at times even strep throat,

virus, chicken pox!"

Art Historian

"Working conditions often depend on

whether I have good child care

for my 2-year-old son or whether

I'm trying to work with him com-

ing over to show me a drawing or

ask for water, milk, hair brush,

crayon, or whatever."

Writer

If the children are young, have a babysitter come to the house to play with them while you're working. During the summer if possible, hire a mother's helper. From September through June have a teenager come to your home several days a week directly after school to play with your children and free some of your working hours. If and when possible, enlist the help of a child's grandparent, aunt, uncle, or father. Try to work out a cooperative arrangement for preschoolers a few half days each week. One woman reports that where possible she takes her infant son with her on client calls. In many areas there are women who prefer to stay in their own homes to babysit for children. Perhaps you can bring your child to a babysitter's house to give yourself a few hours a day, or a few days a week of absolute concentration!

When children are young, you must be flexible and inventive. At home encourage quiet games for preschoolers, and quiet hobbies, like drawing and reading, for the school-age set. Enlist the help of your older children! They can stuff envelopes, staple materials, move boxes, and use scissors. A dog breeder with four children all involved in the family's paying hobby has the kids do their share of the work after school. Each has his own dog and full responsibility for it.

Request cooperation. "Please give me thirty minutes to finish this painting. I'd really appreciate the extra consideration today." Negotiate, if necessary! "If you give me thirty minutes, I'll take you bowling later!" When the children are older, work during school hours. A great deal can be accomplished between 9:00 and 3:00. An editor who needs quiet for concentration puts a red cardboard stop sign on her front door as a signal to neighborhood kids, who like to drop by, so they don't disturb her when the sign is up. Be creative!

Actually women working at home have a unique situation. Most children never see where their parents work or how they do it. But in the home setting, they can see not only where we work, but how we function within that framework. If the combination of mother and businesswoman succeeds, we may also be passing on a meaningful lesson to future generations. There is often an involvement in the work at home that stays with the child into maturity. We've heard of several successful parent-child teams. For example, a young adult son of a husband-wife photography team is now a partner in the business—so is the son of a woman who operates a maid and party service—and so are the two daughters of a woman with her own advertising agency.

Home is a participatory work setting. Just as you must not violate the children's work area, they will learn to leave yours alone. You can draw analogies between homework and home work, explaining why each is important in its own way. Showing respect for their work and their place of business will hopefully teach them respect for yours. Having your own room, closet, or basement area for the sole purpose of business helps define your territory for other family members, and you will be able to separate yourself from your work area or from your home environment when necessary. One editor bought a circular expanding wooden gate, set it up in her living room, put her desk and chair in the middle of it, and gave her young son the rest of the house!

There are times when you can play with your children and times when you have to say, "No, this is my time." You have a right to insist that certain hours belong to you alone. It's okay to say that just as you are learning to be independent and creative, the child can also learn to be independent and creative. Obviously, this being on his or her own some of the time, must also be balanced with large amounts of love at other times. Children of all ages need a little TA, and we don't mean transactional analysis, the phrase in current vogue, but Time and Affection. One writer we know stops whatever she's doing when her girls return from school so they can share the events of their day or discuss any problems. Each also knows that if at any time it's really important that she talk to Mom, she can suggest a hot chocolate break. Her mother will "break" as soon as possible and the two will sit down to discuss whatever is troubling the child.

"My husband is also involved...and is supportive.... He is most helpful by equally sharing in the responsibility of raising and guiding the children."

Dog Breeder

BEHR

Successful mothering for the working mother means letting your children know that while you love and enjoy them, there are also things you need as a person that come only through your work. A beauty consultant described it this way: "I believe that operating my business from home, although it may sometimes be inconvenient, has won me admiration from my husband and family because they are directly involved on a day-to-day basis with my successes and frustrations and seem to be more appreciative of my efforts to contribute to the support of the family and at the same time enrich my own life."

A proofreader expressed it in this manner: "I chose to work at home because of my children. Although they are both in school all day, I still feel it is important to be close by. I tried to work in an office...but sick days, snow days, and early closings complicated things too much. I find working at home simplifies

"When the children were small, I had a babysitter come and play with them during the hours when I was teaching. That worked fairly well, but I think it was harder for the children knowing I was here but unavailable to them than it would have been if I had been out of sight. My working hours were unfortunate, too, as, once they started school, I started working right after they got home. . . . I hope it was some compensation to them that the money I made went to pay for their nursery schools, music school, ballet lessons, summer camp and vacations, college tuition, etc."

Music Teacher

Naomi Kolstein
Lecturer

my life quite a bit." A writer resigned from her college teaching position to work at home after the birth of her son. "I wanted the best of both worlds," she wrote. "I wanted to enjoy the companionship of my baby and the satisfaction of earning an income." "Where else could I design my batiks while being a full-time mother and wife?" asked one artist. A homebased lab technician with five children had this to say: "I am for equality in women, but I still feel family and all it encompasses is the most important thing in the makeup of a woman, and how the woman handles it is what makes it or breaks it. Certainly [mothering] is the most difficult full-time profession of all—and by far the most satisfying. The dashes in a painting make the highlights brighter—so the problems in a life make the joys more meaningful." A psychologist summed it up when she stated that "...having my office at home, sharing my home, my family, and my life with my patients is consistent with the personal style of therapy that I practice. There is integration of my work, my family, and my life. This is my choice and how I want it to be."

Finding creative ways to deal with kids at home while you're working is indeed a problem, but it is also a price of motherhood. Working—anywhere—requires a juggling of schedules. Far better to do the juggling at home. You will benefit from the convenience, comfort, and flexibility of the work setting; your children will know how important home and family are to you.

What we're suggesting is revolutionary! Fifty years ago mothers had large families, and 99% of their efforts went into raising the children. There was no time to have outside work. Now families are smaller and motherhood is still important, but the quality of mothering remains at 99% only 35% of the time. There is time for other pursuits. If working is what you want to do, what's so terrific about leaving home to do it? You have a home and children and can enjoy both!

Women working at home will help daughters feel free to see home as a place where a person can have ambition and a career if she chooses, and it will help her sons see women as people with varied needs and talents. It's okay to want to be a mother and a working woman at the same time. It can be interesting, stimulating, fulfilling.

First Impressions

by Katherine F. Bailey,
Senior Sales Director,
Mary Kay Cosmetics

*Nadine Weiss
Travel Agent/Guide*

"You never get a second chance to make a good first impression." This expression is often repeated throughout the Mary Kay organization to promote an understanding of the supreme importance of how closely our personal appearance is equated with our initial success in business. The simple fact is that the prospective client or employer is "sold" on us and indirectly on our product or service as a direct result of the physical impressions made within the first five minutes of contact. Be that fair or not, it is the unequivocal truth.

Psychologist Dr. Joyce Brothers, a successful businesswoman if ever there was one, confirms this theory in detail in her latest book, *How to Get Whatever You Want Out of Life*. This syndrome is known as the Halo effect. "The Halo effect can be negative or positive. Whichever it is, it radiates out in all directions from the initial effect or impression. At its best, it helps make people think we are even better than we are." Indeed, people are very likely to rate us highly in all positive personal traits if we create a positive first impression. Harvard psychologist Zick Rubin says, "Given the power of first impressions to shape lasting opinions, it is wise for a person who wishes to make a particular impression to present herself in that way from the outset."

Recently, a researcher from Fairleigh Dickinson University disclosed that a study involving identical resumes with different names, etc., submitted with before and after cosmetic makeover photos, resulted in up to 35% higher starting salary offers for the applicant whose "after" picture reflected the more "acceptable" image.

42

It is very important to place serious emphasis on the first impressions women are creating in their businesses. When I train our sales personnel, who, by the way, are all independent contractors running their own small businesses from home offices, one of the first points we discuss is what I call "voiceprints." We all tend to visualize our callers. The voice that is projected over the phone wires will clearly indicate the frame of mind of the caller and evoke either a positive or negative response. I ask our consultants never to pick up the phone in the morning until they have dressed and applied their cosmetics. When you know you look well, you will present a positive, confident, successful image. Placing a mirror directly in front of your phone area will help you to "smile" into the conversation. Take a few minutes to prepare your exterior, and you will also be psychologically prepared to begin a constructive workday.

Positive image consultants to the business world have unanimously concurred that the woman who hopes to be successful would be well advised to build her wardrobe around suits and tailored dresses. Perhaps you would be more comfortable in slacks or jeans, but you definitely will not exude that all important aura of success. A "put-together" appearance is another essential phase in your business development. John Molloy in his *Dress for Success* book remarks, "The way we dress has a remarkable impact on the people we meet professionally or socially, and crucially affects how they treat us." You will not be taken seriously unless you look the part. [Editor's note: Wearing slacks or jeans may be part of such professions as painter, writer, road tester, animal breeder, etc. One advantage of working at home in a relaxed atmosphere is that one can dress casually and comfortably when working alone.] In my own business I would usually not approach a prospect for the purpose of discussing our business opportunity unless I was stimulated to action by the positive "vibes" she projected by caring about her personal appearance.

Finally, the most marvelous opportunity we have to make a positive first impression is to pay particular attention to the first thing that anyone sees and that, of course, is one's face. One of the fastest, most economical and most obviously dramatic changes which will immediately reinforce your self-confidence and increase your success quotient from the first day is to critique your facial appearance and update the effect with a cosmetic makeover. A pleasing appearance definitely stimulates a positive response on the part of your prospective clients. "If you are dissatisfied with your looks, just re-invent yourself," says Joyce Brothers. "We think good-looking people are more sensitive, more intelligent, more interesting, and more successful than those people who are mediocre." People openly prefer to do business with other people who appear more pleasing to the eye. Fortunately, this is relatively easy to achieve.

"...another reason for choosing a line of work that keeps me on the other end of a telephone rather than out there more visibly is that I look much younger than I am and love to wear jeans and comfortable clothes. I was avoiding the IBM uniform, or so I thought. More recently, I've realized that I was also avoiding having to sell myself and my services. ... I realize now that in order to grow, I have to take the risks and stick my neck out, make calls, try bigger and harder assignments. ... Choosing invisibility was somehow related to fear of rejection and failure."

Researcher

Bibliography
Brothers, Dr. Joyce. *How to Get Whatever You Want Out of Life*. New York: Simon & Schuster, 1978.
Molloy, John. *Dress for Success*. New York: Warner Books, 1975.

Borrowing Time

One of the greatest advantages that comes from working at home is the ease with which one can ''sneak'' into the home office or studio at all hours of the day or night. One of the most difficult tasks faced by any woman with a homebased business is **not** sneaking into the home office or studio.

In a recent nationwide study for the National Institute of Mental Health, researchers found that most women in middle-income households who have part-time jobs devote seven hours daily to household duties! These were broadly defined by the women themselves, who listed 80 different activities from child care and car repair to buying clothes and attendance at school meetings. Women with full-time jobs spend five hours daily running their households! These already overburdened women, with ingenuity and determination, can and must plan free time for themselves.

Just as organization and discipline are essential when beginning your at-home business, they become even more important as time goes on. At first you may say: ''Don't mop the kitchen floor now, better to spend this time working!'' But it is likely that as your business grows and **grows,** the hours for housework and, more important, time for relaxation will diminish. You will then say: ''How can I mop the kitchen floor now — I'm working all the time!'' If you don't enjoy housework or can't manage doing everything alone, hire help as soon as you can afford to do so. If you have a young family, write job lists for the children. Stick with these lists. If children help with the chores, it furthers their spirit of cooperation! Don't let chores rule you, either. You're the boss, remember? Skip anything that's not important. Simplify what has to be done—and do it faster!

There comes a point when a business of any nature, if it's going to succeed, **takes off**! Suddenly you find yourself a workaholic. Your business has grown this far because of your dedication, ambition, enthusiasm, and a lot of hard work. Now you see bigger and better things ahead. As your business grows, invest in adequate household equipment and quality assistance, so you will have more time to do the work that makes your business unique. Twenty-four hours in a day aren't nearly enough for the homemaker/businesswoman. If you can't borrow time, steal it anywhere you can! Wake up half an hour early for your morning exercises. If possible, shop during the dinner hour or at night when stores are empty. Do all your errands at one time. Shop by mail. Learn to say no to nonbusiness demands on your time. Be a two-timer! While talking on the phone, write your grocery list.

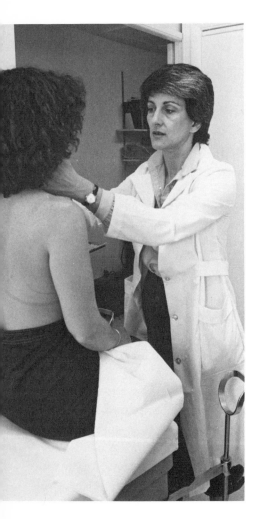

Toni Gloria Novick, M.D.
Photographer: Helaine Messer

44

Watch TV and catch up on your magazine reading. Set fake deadlines! If you have an appointment at 2 PM, put 1:45 on your calendar and spend those extra minutes reading the papers or preparing notes.

If time pressures are overwhelming, you might consider a partnership with someone you trust who has similar interests and varied abilities, so that stresses and strains can be divided. In an expanding business, never forget that its prime purpose is to enable you to enjoy life to its fullest.

Write a list for yourself filled with specific objectives for private pleasures:
1. Get six hours sleep tonight!
2. Do exercises!
3. See an exhibition or show!
4. Call a close friend!
5. Read a good book!
6. Lie in the sun!

A museum, a racquetball game, a picnic, a day of pure joy **not** work related can give you a fresh head to think with, a heart that will endure competition, and the nerves needed to survive in this complicated, hectic, slightly crazy, very exciting time we live in today!

You can borrow time, steal time, and even buy time! Your business is growing. Still you need help. This can come in two forms: people and machines.

Although the capital costs of machines may seem high, they can usually be rented or leased in a very tax-advantageous manner. The rental of a machine is fully deductible as a business expense, but you do not own anything after a long period of rental payments. If, instead, you purchase a machine, you can take deductions for its depreciation plus get an additional first-year investment tax credit. The choice of rental versus ownership depends very much on the expected life of the equipment and the rate at which modernization is expected to occur. A sewing machine could be bought since enormous strides in improvements are not expected. Renting or leasing a computer might be wiser since more efficient models come on the market about twice a year. Clearly, these choices involve quite different cash requirements. This is an area in which it would be wise to receive advice and guidance from other people in your line of work, as well as from your accountant.

The type of people help required will greatly depend on the type of business. A lawyer can increase her output enormously by hiring another secretary or perhaps a paralegal. A weaver might have to bring in another craftsperson of equal ability. A caterer may need an assistant to take over some of the culinary duties while she frees up her time to see customers. The important factors here are compatibility and trust between the newcomer and the original business owner, since dissolving any type of relationship within a small business is a traumatic event which can be fatal.

As you grow, constantly be aware of how your growth can be supported by personnel and/or machines.

The Form of the Firm

When going into business, there are three main forms of business organization: proprietorship, partnership, and corporation.

Individual Proprietorship

This is the oldest and most common form. One owns and operates the business and hires all other help for pay. The business stops when the individual chooses to stop it. There are no special legal requirements to be met, beyond obtaining any necessary license to operate and a resale tax number (not required by a service). Business profits are taxed as personal income and the owner files a Schedule C on the 1040 tax return indicating all expenses and revenues. Losses (heaven forbid) may be deductible. The proprietor is fully liable (that is, responsible) for all business debts and actions, and in case of a lawsuit, one's personal assets (car and home, for example) are not protected.

If the business is not in your own name but is conducted under another name, that business name must be filed with the clerk in the county in which the business is transacted, to enable creditors and others to determine the actual ownership of the business. This "Certificate of Doing Business Under an Assumed Name," available at most business stationers, must be filled out in triplicate. The county clerk will file the original and certify the other two copies, if requested. Take one to the bank and open a commercial checking account in your business name. The bank requires this copy by law. Keep the other for your own files; or, depending on the type of business, you may prefer to frame and display it.

The name you choose, incidentally, should be unique. To be assured of that — if your business is local, do a name search in the office of the county clerk to see if the identical name is already being used; if statewide, check with the secretary of state. If yours is an interstate business, such as mail order, the name would have to be checked in each of the fifty states. This can be done quickly by a trademark attorney.

Partnership

It's like a marriage between two people, that formally results from a contract or agreement in which two or more persons agree to combine property and/or labor for a common purpose and common profit.

Friends are not necessarily the best business partners. Many a friendship has dissolved over heated discussions of money and business policy. It would seem to be the ideal arrangement but may not always be that way.

As with the proprietorship, in a **general partnership** there are no special legal requirements to be met beyond licens-

"We started with T-shirts and now have a line of handpainted and embroidered totes and skirts, dresses, and caftans. The totes are made for us by a manufacturer and the gowns, etc. are designed by us and handmade, one at a time, by craftswomen before we embroider and create a colorful design. We have sold to many retail stores and presently are showing in a gallery. My partner and I get together several times a week to work. All designs are done together. She does most of the painting and drawing. I do the embroidery."

Quest NEWS

Feb. 1978 specialists in funding OmniQuest inc

OQ Finds the Missing Elements, Saves Project

It was office party time--2pm Friday, Dec. 23, not a time for doing business--when a desperate client called OQ. With five typists coming in on Tuesday (the first working day after Christmas) to work against a tight production deadline, he had only two of the five special optically readable typing heads they needed. IBM-Manhattan was out of stock, as were most office equipment outlets. The rest either didn't answer their telephones at all or said "Sorry, no one can help you until Tuesday morning."

Could OmniQuest find three elements?

Within two hours, our client had his elements, thanks to OmniQuest and to the two Harrison IBMers OQ managed to convince of the mission's urgency --Jim Ryan, who located the elements his office doesn't ordinarily stock, and Randy Graeff, who waited in the lobby till the elements were picked up, long after everyone else went home.

Contents

ing and sales tax number. Debts incurred by one partner must be assumed by all partners; if the business fails, creditors can take, by legal authority, each partner's personal income and assets, as in an individual proprietorship. A general partnership can be formed very simply. The agreement is not filed with the state, but it's good to have it written down with provisions for organizational, operational, and dissolution phases of the business. It is also advisable to consult an attorney to explain the rights, duties, and obligations of each partner and to interpret the laws of the state in which the partnership is organized. (Insurance to cover the death of a partner is discussed in *The Basics of Insurance.*)

More protective for some individuals is a **limited partnership** which relieves the limited partners from liability (obligation) beyond the amount of money invested in the business, but it is more difficult to set up. This form, in addition to at least one general partner who assumes responsibility, includes one or more other partners who contribute money or property to the venture but need not be involved in the management of it. If you wish to form a limited partnership, it is absolutely necessary to consult an attorney to be certain you are in compliance with the laws. The "Certificate of Limited Partnership," in states where it is permitted, must be notarized and the original filed with the clerk of the county in which the principal office is located. A certified copy of the certificate should be filed with the bank at which the firm's account will be kept. After filing, another certified copy must be published once a week for six successive weeks in two of the county's newspapers. The county clerk will tell you which ones qualify. Check regulations for your state.

Corporation

Why bother? The simple answer is that it limits the financial liability of the individual who forms a corporation, by protecting that individual from personal liability if the corporation does not meet its obligations. A new corporation generally cannot borrow money on its name alone. Lenders usually require the business lender behind the corporation to personally guarantee the loan until the corporation has enough assets of its own.

Unlike proprietorships and partnerships, the corporation is wholly a creation of the state. If you think of it as a privilege rather than a right, then perhaps you can understand why each state can and does subject the corporation to certain special conditions and regulations. Also, unlike proprietorships and partnerships, it can have rights of its own, and thus does not die with the retirement or death of its officers. Furthermore, the number of owners can increase or decrease without changing the nature of the corporation.

An individual who owns a business can form a corporation. She transforms her individual proprietorship by transferring the assets of the business to the corporation—personal property, real property, and/or goodwill—in exchange for shares. The stockholder is an owner who has invested in the business but does not necessarily have the responsibility of management, while the managers are employees on salary who do not necessarily own

*Pat and Fred Sagarin
Chimney Sweeps
Photographer:*
© *Terri P. Tepper 1978*

"In addition to the decision to work at

home because of the family, there

was also the consideration of

being my own boss, the hours I

worked were of my own choosing,

so that the doctors' appoint-

ments, etc. could be worked more

easily into one's day. If at mid-

night I suddenly got some inspi-

rational idea, all I had to do was

pop into the studio and work on

it, which, I might add, I've done

many times."

Fiberist

controlling financial interest. Though they are classified differently by law, there is no reason why manager, stockholder, and a member of the board of directors cannot be one and the same.

The corporation, which is treated as a separate taxpayer, pays a corporate income tax on its taxable income. Income not used up in deductible expenses is subject to a corporate tax. Income distributed as dividends is again subject to personal income tax payable by the recipient. You, as a stockholder, pay tax on your receipts of salary, dividends, and interest from loans made to the corporation. The corporate tax year does not necessarily correspond with the calendar year, so there is an opportunity to move income around to its best advantage.

Under a Subchapter S election, which is available on a year-to-year basis, the possible double tax is avoided by allowing you, as the stockholder, to pay a tax on corporate income directly. Under Subchapter S, the corporation reports its taxable income or loss. On your personal tax return, you report this taxable income whether or not you withdraw money (salary or interest) from the corporation. If the corporation has losses, you deduct the losses in your tax return. In other words, it permits the business to have its income taxed to the shareholders as if the corporation were a partnership, yet it retains certain advantages of the corporate form. When there are no more than ten shareholders, this Subchapter S election is possible for new or low-income businesses. (This number may soon be changed by an Act of Congress.) There are other qualifying requirements, as well. Check all this out with an attorney.

You can create a corporation only by following the legal procedures in the state in which the corporation will be established. A "Certificate of Incorporation" must be filed with the state, along with an organization tax, or license fee, and the filing fees.

Although it is possible to file a Certificate of Incorporation on your own, it is not advisable. Because of the complexities of corporate structure, it is wiser to have an attorney prepare the incorporation papers due to the type of information required, such as purposes of the corporation; length of time for which it is being formed; names and addresses of incorporators; location of registered office of corporation; maximum amount and type of capital stock to be issued; proposed capital structure; capital required at time of incorporation; provision for preemptive rights, if any, to be granted to the stockholders and restrictions, if any, on the transfer of shares; provision for regulation of internal affairs; names and addresses of directors; the right to amend, alter, or repeal any provision contained in the Certificate of Incorporation. The Certificate should be signed by the incorporators and notarized before being sent to the secretary of state.

Under corporate laws, the name of the corporation must not be identical to the name of any other corporation authorized to do business in the state in which the papers will be filed. To avoid problems in commercial use and confusion in the marketplace, names should not even be similar. The name must not confuse or mislead the public, either. Check with the Department of State, Division of Corporations. If the state official deter-mines that the name of the proposed corporation is satisfactory, that the Certificate contains the necessary information and has been properly executed, and that there is nothing in the Certificate or in the corporation's proposed activities that violates state law or public policy, the charter will be issued.

The stockholders must then meet to complete the incorporation process. This meeting is extremely important. It is usually conducted by an attorney or someone familiar with corporate organizational procedure. In this meeting, the corporation bylaws are adopted, and the stockholders elect their board of directors, who have primary legal responsibility for the corporation. The board then elects the officers—president, secretary, and treasurer, for example—who actually have charge of the operations. In small corporations, members of the board of directors frequently are chosen as officers of the corporation.

The bylaws of the corporation may repeat some provisions in the charter (the Certificate of Incorporation), but often cover such items as the following:

1. Location of the principal office of the corporation.
2. Time, place, required notice of annual and special meetings, quorum requirements and voting privileges of the stockholders.
3. Number of directors, salaries, terms of office, method of election and of creating or filling vacancies in the board of directors.
4. Time, place, and required notice of regular and special directors' meetings, as well as quorum requirements.
5. Method of selecting officers, their titles, duties, terms of office, and salaries. (Some states allow one person corporations, and that individual can be named for all positions.)
6. Issuance and form of stock certificates, their transfers and control in the company books.
7. Dividends—when and by whom they may be declared.
8. Fiscal year, corporate seal, authority to sign checks, and preparation of annual statement.
9. Procedure for amending bylaws.

Which legal structure is best for your business? Get the advice and guidance of an attorney and tax accountant. In no way should the information written here be any substitute for competent legal advice. Several factors determine the choice: your personal financial situation, your marital status (and, if married, your husband's tax bracket), the type of business and its possibilities for growth. While the tax laws and other aspects of regulation are not designed to influence your choice of the form in which you do business, the fact remains that the structure of such laws do influence choice.

The business and everything that relates to it is your business. Only you can decide what is best for you and what form will best protect both you and your business. Legal guidance in these matters will insure that you understand the various aspects of tax obligations involved, that you will be in compliance with local, state, and federal laws, and that the articles of incorporation and the bylaws (if you choose to go that route) will be tailored to the needs of your particular business enterprise.

The Basics of Insurance

by Isabel Bogorad Fleiss,
Executive Director,
WomanSurance Advisory
Services

Homebased businesses are becoming more and more popular. With proper planning and advice, you can have a sound and profitable venture. Insurance can help you safeguard your business against crippling financial losses and promote its continuation, growth, and profitability.

Your insurance needs as a homebased business owner are much the same as if you were an individual with a separate place of business. You do not want to inadvertently void your present homeowner's insurance policy by running a home business. Therefore, be sure to notify your insurance carrier as to the type of business and where it is to be conducted—in the main residence or in a separate structure on the premises. If the anticipated use is not compatible with your Homeowner's policy, then you will have to replace the coverage on the dwelling. If you are planning an office, a school, or a studio, you may be able to have this type of "pursuit" or "occupancy" endorsed onto your Homeowner's. So that you are fully protected at all times, discuss this situation with your insurance agent.

If, as it turns out, the primary use of your home is for business, and you still maintain your residence there, you may need a renter's policy to cover your personal belongings—even though you own the building.

Check the personal liability clause in your Homeowner's policy, which protects you as an individual, and increase it to its limit. If you want to go beyond the top limit of your policy, you can buy an umbrella policy that takes over where your regular liability coverage stops. Usually the first $1 million of protection costs about $100 a year, with each additional $1 million costing about $10. However, you must have a certain amount of primary liability coverage on your regular policies before the umbrella coverage takes over.

Why would you need that much? There may be an unusual or unforeseen claim against you, and injury to another may result in a lawsuit and a large jury award. A Homeowner's policy is a personal plan. Now that you have a business, you must purchase a commercial liability policy for full protection.

Liability insurance includes auto liability and liability other than auto that, for the most part, pertains to claims arising out of your responsibility for injuries or damage caused by ownership of property, manufacturing operations, and sale or distribution of products. It is also possible to get product liability coverage, which protects you in the event one of your products—a toy or baby item, for instance—causes injury to the user.

"We purchased a beautiful barn and have converted it into a house, gallery, printshop, and two studios."

Artist

"My husband takes care of all my books and has designed a scaffold for wallpapering foyers. He has occasionally helped me on foyers and installing shutters."

Wallpaper Hanger

50

Other coverage available that may fill your needs are host liquor liability, malpractice insurance, and medical payments insurance payable if someone is injured in your place whether it was your fault or not.

In order to be properly protected, the individual owners, as well as the business trade name, corporate or operating name, should be insured under these policies. If you incorporate your business, separate fire and liability policies must be written.

Do you have any employees working for you—even part-time, temporary, or seasonal help? Then be smart—get Workmen's Compensation. All 50 states, Puerto Rico, the Virgin Islands, American Samoa, and Guam have workers' compensation laws. This coverage provides benefits to employees for injuries sustained as a result of their employment regardless of blame. It pays the cost of medical care and weekly payments to the worker, or if he dies, to his dependents. If it seems that your employees may ever have to travel out of state, ask for an "all states endorsement."

Also, be sure you obtain "non-owned auto liability" to cover your business if your employees ever use their own cars for business use. Your family auto policy would not even cover defense costs in case of an accident.

What would happen if your business is damaged by fire or some other cause, and you must totally or partially suspend operations? You know that your earnings will cease or diminish. Meanwhile, your need for money continues in the form of operating costs, mortgage, taxes, payroll, payments on equipment, and other expenses. Where's the money going to come from?

This is a very unfortunate situation to be in. In order to make sure that doesn't happen to you, you should buy (as soon as you are eligible) "business interruption insurance," also sometimes called earnings insurance. If, during this black period, you would move to temporary quarters in order to stay in business and not lose customers, you might want "extra expense insurance" that would cover just that—the extra expenses. It is usually bought by business owners whose customers depend on them for uninterrupted service. A "restoration period" would give you some extra time to get back to full resumption of business.

Just as your business interruption insurance would protect you if your business breaks down due to physical damage, "disability income protection" (a form of health insurance) would protect your income if you became disabled. Don't count on Workmen's Compensation, because if you are self-employed, you are not entitled to these benefits. Meanwhile, bills continue —mortgage payments, dentist, gas and electric, food, and other personal expenses. Disability income insurance can help you meet these expenses. If you think that you can't afford to pay these premiums now when you're healthy and working, think again. You certainly won't be able to afford to pay for much if you're laid up. If you're disabled for years, your savings are bound to run out. This valuable protection isn't always easy to get, especially if your income record is irregular or below a certain minimum, your health is not perfect, or you are in certain job categories. Try to obtain this while you are buying your other medical coverage, such as hospitalization or major medical.

Remember: it's important to keep complete records. Keep them in a safe place with duplicates in your safe deposit box or with your accountant. You may keep your policies at home where you can refer to them as often as necessary, but record the policy numbers and insurance company's name for each policy and store these in your bank vault, also.

Margo Brown
Potter
Photographer:
© *Terri P. Tepper 1977*

Prudent insurance planning also permits you to shelter tax dollars. Anyone who is working and is not covered by a company pension plan may establish an Individual Retirement Account (IRA). With an IRA, you are allowed to deduct up to $1500 per year from your taxable income by putting it in a specially set up IRA account, where it grows and grows. You pay no taxes at all until you retire (minimum age for withdrawing funds is 59½) on either the amount you invest or the interest and earnings generated. The Keogh Plan works the same way, but is available only to those who are self-employed. In a Keogh, you can put up to $7500 a year away and take it off your taxable income. A government authorized Defined Benefit Keogh Plan allows you to put even more than that away. If your business is incorporated, you can shelter even more dollars in corporate pension and profit-sharing plans. You can tailor these plans in sophisticated ways to suit your needs and build up a sizable nest egg for your retirement. Why give that money away to the Internal Revenue Service? Best of all, you can be assured of an income that can never be outlived, even if you live to be 100. Retirement plans can be established with banks, stockbrokers, insurance companies, and other financial institutions.

Tax-deferred annuities in your investment portfolio give you tax-deferred appreciation. You will have to pay taxes eventually as you withdraw the interest that has accrued, but, presumably, these taxable dollars will be withdrawn when you are in a lower tax bracket. You are guaranteed safety of principal—not only do you get a good return **on** your money, you are guaranteed the return **of** your money. If set up properly, this plan avoids the publicity and costs of probate (validating a will in court), and it is possible to pass it to a beneficiary without her having to pay any income tax on it.

If you ever need to borrow a sizable amount of money, the lender may be more favorably disposed to grant your loan if he knows that repayment is guaranteed even if you die before the loan is paid off. This is accomplished very simply by assigning a portion of your life insurance policy to the lender. Of course, you can only do this if you already own life insurance, and in sufficient amounts to apportion some of it to this vital business purpose. You may think that you can always get it, but, for some of us, the clock or our health runs out more quickly than we had planned.

If you have a partner, be aware that the partnership dissolves upon her death. If her heirs insist on liquidation so they can receive their share in cash, how will you be able to come up with all that money? The best solution is a Buy-and-Sell Agreement with your partners. This agreement requires the surviving partner(s) to buy, and the heirs to sell, the deceased partner's interest. The heirs receive cash for their share of the business, and the surviving partner becomes the sole owner.

All you need to carry out the terms of the arrangement is money. It is guaranteed to be there when you need it—at death—if you purchase insurance on the lives of each of the partners. Of course, you have to do this while you're all alive and well.

Other business reasons you, the business owner, need life insurance, include the need of your heirs or estate for cash to pay outstanding debts, costs of probate, administrative and legal fees, your final medical bills and expenses, and estate, inheritance, and income taxes.

With you gone, without a leader, your business will come to a halt. Can your family or key employee step in and keep profits up as you could? Your family (or other beneficiaries) may still require the income you used to make for them. Proceeds from your life insurance will provide them with the money to continue as before.

Don't expect that they'll be able to make much money if they have to sell the business, equipment, or inventory to pay off debts or taxes. The dollars earned at such a "forced sale" are very disappointing. Insurance buys time — the time required to train new management or replace the services you used to render.

You are your most important asset, the key employee, and your drive, energy, vision, and intellect are irreplaceable. Without you, your business will certainly suffer, but with the money you had the foresight to provide in life insurance, your heirs can try to keep your work and your business together.

Tax Information
for the Homebased
Businesswoman

A taxpayer may be able to take sizable business deductions if she uses part of her home exclusively and regularly either:

1. as her principal place of business, or
2. as a place of business that is used by patients, clients, or customers in meeting and dealing with the taxpayer in the normal course of her trade or business.

An employee may claim a deduction for business use of the home only if all exclusive and regular use requirements are met and if such use is for an employer's convenience. If the business use of the home is only appropriate and helpful in the employee's work, the deduction can not be taken.

Exclusive use of a part of the home means that one must use a specific part of the home only to carry on a trade or business. If a writer's bedroom has a corner set apart for work with a desk, typewriter and phone, she cannot claim a deduction under present law because the room is also used for personal purposes, in this case, sleeping. A seamstress who does alterations on the sewing machine in her den cannot take the deduction. An artist who paints in her sunny kitchen cannot take the deduction. An exercise teacher who conducts classes in her family room cannot take a deduction.

The one exception to this exclusive use rule that applies to women working at home is that of storage of inventory. The inventory must be held for use in the business; the home must be the only fixed location of the trade or business; and the trade or business must be the selling of products at wholesale or retail. The storage space must be used regularly and must be a separately identifiable space suitable for storage. An example of this is the storage of clothing in boxes and on racks that a woman who sells clothing from home would require. Half of the basement is used for inventory storage and occasionally for personal purposes when she does the laundry. The expenses for the storage space are deductible even though this part of the basement is not used exclusively for business.

Regular use means that the taxpayer uses the exclusive part of her home on a continuing basis, though she may have more than one business location. For her to deduct expenses for the business use of the home, she must determine whether it is the principal place of business according to:

1. the total time ordinarily spent in performing duties there;
2. the degree of business activity there; and
3. the relative amount of income received from doing business at home.

"As my husband is self-employed, running my own business enables me to meld our schedules neatly. A homebased operation is also a tremendous tax saving, via deductions. So, reasons for working at home: convenience, family responsibility, suitability of work area, flexibility, tax advantages, diminished expenses for operating, artistic freedom."

Artist

Marian Rubin and Ann Jacobson
Furniture Designers
Photographer: Helaine Messer

An example of this is a secretary-typist who works part-time in an office two days each week for a total of $3500 per year. Three days each week she works in a home studio, used exclusively for her art work, and earns about $5000 per year. Her home thus qualifies as her principal place of business.

The Tax Court recently had a chance to interpret the business-use-of-a-home rule in a case involving a doctor who worked a 40-hour week in a hospital and who also owned and managed six rental properties. He intended that the rental properties would provide a source of income when he retired from medical practice. The liberal position the Tax Court adopted should be quite encouraging to taxpayers. In essence it was stated that a principal place of business need not be an exclusive principal place of business. A taxpayer may have more than one business, and the home office may qualify as the principal place for conducting a particular business.

Let's take that same secretary-typist again and the Tax Court ruling. If she worked five days a week in a company office, earning $13,000 annually, and evenings and weekends in her home office as an artist, earning $5000—her home office qualifies for deductions because it is the principal place for conducting a particular business (assuming it meets the other requirements). However, this concept of recognizing a secondary business is in a

55

state of uncertainty, since the Treasury Department has proposed issuing regulations which do not allow the Tax Court case described above.

If, in the normal course of business, you meet or deal with patients, clients, or customers in your home, your expenses for that part of your home used exclusively for business are deductible. Individuals with occupations that generally meet this requirement are doctors, attorneys, therapists, and other professionals who maintain offices in their homes, as well as those who operate businesses such as beauty shops or clothing outlets.

The expenses for a separate, freestanding building next to one's home, such as a studio, garage, or barn, are deductible if the building is used exclusively and regularly for business. It does not have to be the principal place of business or the place where one meets patients, clients, or customers. Examples of this would be an artist's studio, a florist's greenhouse, or a riding instructor's stable.

What's deductible?

The part of your home that is used for your business is treated, for tax purposes, as property separate from the personal part of your home. You must divide the expenses of operating your entire home between the personal and business uses of your home. Some expenses are divided on an area basis, others on a usage basis. Certain items are totally deductible; others, totally nondeductible. You must have proof to show:
1. the part of your home used exclusively and regularly for business;
2. that the part of your home used exclusively and regularly for business is either your principal place of business or the place where you meet with patients, clients, or customers in the normal course of business;
3. the amount of depreciation and expenses for keeping up that part of your home which is used for business.
To substantiate deductions claimed, keep cancelled checks, receipts, and other evidences of paid expenses for at least six years.

To figure the percentage of your home that is used for business, divide the square footage utilized for business by the total square foot area of your home. Or, if the rooms in your home are all about the same size, simply divide the number of rooms used for business by the number of rooms in the house. Translated into actual figures, that means that if you use one room in your home that is 10′x12′, or 120 square feet, for business, and your home has 1200 square feet, you are using 10% of the total area for business. If the rooms are about the same size and you use one room in a five-room house, you are using one-fifth, or 20%, for business.

There are always certain expenses required to maintain and operate a home. Some of these expenses are directly related to the business use of your home—painting or repairs to the specific area or room used for business, for instance. Others are indirectly related—painting the outside of the house, repairing the roof, lighting, and air conditioning, for example. These must be allocated to the part of the home used for business. Others are not related at all—a swimming pool is an example.

A capital expenditure is an investment of money either to get property that will be useful for more than one year, or to improve property already owned. Examples of capital improvements are replacement of electric wiring or plumbing, a new roof, a new addition to your home, or remodeling existing space. The cost of such property may not be deducted entirely in one year, but must be depreciated and allocated to the part of the home used for business. Homeowners must distinguish between repairs and improvements and keep accurate records of all expenditures.

If it sounds confusing, that it is! And that is why a homebased businesswoman would be wise to seek professional advice. We are dealing with strict rules and regulations set up by the Internal Revenue Service. Tax laws and tax return forms can be a maze of confusion to the uninitiated. Besides, tax laws are constantly changing and unless you intend to keep fully informed on all these matters, you had best get the help of a competent tax adviser. That individual can often save you far more in taxes than the amount charged for services, and the fee itself is tax-deductible. The adviser will help you prepare returns, tell you whether you must file quarterly tax returns, and calculate the amount of money due each quarter—payable January 15, April 15, June 15, and September 15. Use his/her services fully—but wisely. To save time and money, be well prepared with facts, figures, and orderly files pertaining to your home business. Have a receipt for everything, even if it's only $.30 for an eraser. Save bills and cancelled checks. Maintain simplified, accurate records that balance costs against sales, money out and money in. Standard account books for small business can be purchased at any business stationery store. You may even be able to find one especially designed for your particular business. The IRS is not specific in the type of records it requires. That is up to you! But you must include whatever is needed to determine tax liability and to support statements made in tax returns. You don't want to lose valid tax deductions and credits, or pay taxes if they could be deferred to another year.

"I continued to get calls to do editing from my old company and from other companies that needed the same kind of service. They were willing to have me do their work from my home. I found that I could keep my hand in my field, make a small amount of money, and, more importantly, have the time I felt I needed for my family. From time to time I've had very attractive job offers for full-time work. I've always considered them, but felt that none of the advantages was worth trading off for the flexibility I have at home."

Licensing, Sales Tax, and Social Security

Marion E. Carden
Dog Groomer
Photographer:
© Terri P. Tepper 1977

Licensing

Many different types of businesses—whether small or large, at home or away from home—are subject to government regulation by licensing.

A license is formal permission granted by governmental authority to a person, firm, or corporation to carry on some business, occupation, or activity that would otherwise be unlawful. A license usually requires a fee and may also involve some form of examination to see if the recipient can qualify under certain standards. The license is a tool of regulation to control a course of conduct relating to public health or safety—for example, plumbers, chauffeurs, physicians, and hairdressers.

A permit is similar to a license but is granted by local authorities. It is often required for businesses involving food, door-to-door selling, and home shops.

Prospective businesswomen should be sure to consult local, county, and state ordinances to see if their particular business is included, so that they are in full compliance with the laws. Check with your town administrator or City Hall.

Sales Tax

Most states require a sales tax and, in some places, there are city and county taxes, as well. If you make anything for sale or buy goods for resale, you must apply for a sales authorization certificate. This document has a resale tax number that will enable you to buy, without paying sales taxes, any materials at wholesale prices for resale.

Once you have that important sales tax number, you will be responsible for collecting sales taxes on everything you sell directly to consumers, and then remitting these monies to the appropriate state, county, or city offices.

Sales tax information and forms to apply for the tax number and for making returns may be obtained from your State Department of Taxation and Finance, Sales Tax Bureau.

Social Security

Social Security taxes enter into the obligations of a small business, also. After the end of any year in which you have net earnings of $400 or more from a home business, you must file a Self-Employment form along with your regular income tax form and pay into your Social Security account. Forms are available from the IRS and at many banks and post offices.

If you do not already have a Social Security number, you may apply for one at any Social Security office.

"Why work at home instead of in a commercial kitchen? Because home is where I am. I avoid the feelings of guilt of sending my two children into a day-care situation. I'm free to put in my working hours when it's most convenient for all of us, and my overhead is practically nil. Yes, it's very difficult to manage on the day of a big job, but for now working at home is the best compromise I can reach."

Caterer

Budgeting, Record Keeping, and Accounting

by Arnold L. Glickman,
Certified Public Accountant

"Sometimes I wonder if it wouldn't be easier to get a 'real' job—and then the idea for a sculpture about women and their lives curls itself into my mind, and I get back to work."

Artist

"My life style would be impossible without the financial support of my husband, who is also the good friend who lugs pots to shows and puts in time to help me in the dozens of ways necessary in this field. I rarely go to a show either as a participant or a viewer where I don't see a family member somewhere in the background as a part of a support system for the craftsperson exhibiting."

Craftsperson

Planning is a necessary part of small business management, and budgeting is an integral part of planning. Financial planning and budgeting is as critical to the small business as it is to the large ones. Accordingly, the businessperson just starting out should sit down and prepare a budget, not only of those expenditures which will be required to start up the business, but also an estimate of the monthly working capital needs of the business. Start-up costs include such items as equipment, supplies, utilities and/or telephone deposits, and other items of a nonrecurring nature. Working capital needs generally include those items which recur on a regular monthly basis such as telephone bills, postage, and similar types of expenses. The budget should be carefully planned and subsequently reviewed by the accountant who has been retained to handle the financial affairs of the business. The initial startup budget indicates whether or not the business will require additional capital in the form of loans or investments, while the operating budget provides a guideline by which the small businessperson can measure the progress of the business to be certain that she is proceeding toward the goals she has established.

If, from a financial standpoint, budgeting is the most critical aspect of a business, then certainly record keeping has to be considerd the second most critical aspect. However, since record keeping is not very exciting, it is often assigned a very low priority by the small businessperson. This approach to record keeping can be a costly one. The records created are generally used to prepare tax returns for the entity. Failure to properly record expenditures leads to lost deductions on tax returns which, in turn, leads to taxes paid unnecessarily. Since record keeping provides the basis for preparation of the financial information needed in making decisions, sloppy record keeping will lead to sloppy decision making, and possibly, costly errors in judgment.

While no magic exists to make record keeping as exciting as closing a substantial sale or expanding into a new market, there are systems available which can make record keeping less of a chore. These small business systems generally are based on what are called One-Write Systems, which capture information at the time the transaction takes place, eliminating the need for recopying data. These One-Write Systems can be very efficient and, subsequently, as the business grows, easily lend themselves to the introduction of electronic data processing.

Starting a small business for the first time is like embarking upon a journey to a land you've never been to before.

As you proceed, you will encounter not only new experiences but you will face obstacles in the form of government-imposed laws and regulations, and decisions relating to such things as geographical location, finance, business law, marketing, insurance, credit practices and procedures, record keeping, risk evaluation, customer relations, and very possibly, depending upon the nature of the business, purchasing and inventory management. As with any journey through unfamiliar territory, it's nice to have a trustworthy guide. If chosen correctly, a certified public accountant can be that guide.

The accountant's role, with respect to the small business, is similar to the general practitioner's role as the family physician. By nature of the service rendered, the accountant becomes the one professional with whom the businessperson maintains a continuing relationship. Accordingly, it is important that the chemistry be right between them.

Many people select an accountant based upon their family or social contacts. While this can make for a satisfactory match, often it does not. As with any service business, referrals from satisfied clients are the best recommendations one could follow. Accordingly, if you know of someone who has been successfully operating a small business, ask whom they use. If you don't know anyone in that category, you can ask a local banker or the local office of the State Society of Certified Public Accountants for a listing of three or four Certified Public Accountants (CPAs) in the area whom you can meet and evaluate.

Most accounting firms today bill for their service on an hourly basis. The rates depend upon the level of the work being performed, and the skill level of the individual performing the service. Fees should be discussed in advance, and most accountants are willing to provide estimates as to what they expect the annual fees will amount to. Also find out if there is a fee for the first meeting.

All accounting firms offer a number of services for the small businessperson. These include: bookkeeping services which include the maintenance of books of original entry, preparation of bank reconciliation statements, and posting of the general ledger; accounting services such as the preparation of balance sheets and income statements, and other forms of financial statements; management services which include the design and implementation of various accounting and record keeping systems; tax services which include preparation of tax returns and tax planning and advice.

Individuals in small business should make every effort to plan ahead and make full use of professional resources available. It is wise for each person to consult with her attorney and CPA prior to forming the business to determine which form— sole proprietorship, partnership, or corporation—is best. She should discuss tax advantages and disadvantages of the various forms of doing business and should be fully aware of the benefits available before making any decisions. With these matters firmly in place, the individual can build a successful business secure in the knowledge that it is based on a firm foundation.

Credit: How to Get It and How to Keep It

Credit is permission to pay in the future for money, goods, or services received now. It is used by businesses to facilitate trade, solve temporary cash flow problems, and to increase sales. It allows an individual of limited means to engage in a business of her own, and it encourages the growth and development of all business.

The ability to secure credit affects your life more than you realize. Credit is a convenience, a budget-stretcher, and sometimes a necessity. Establishing a good credit record is an important step to creating an independent financial identity.

While women constitute almost half of our nation's work force, comparatively few have established credit histories. Although in some cases women have no financial identity simply because they have not needed credit, in many other cases it is because until recently they have been refused credit.

"The business has grown and continues to do so. We have money to buy the clothes we want and to go to the ballet and the theater and time to belong to a tennis league, take exercise classes . . . and chauffeur our children to their lessons."

Stationer

In October 1975, Congress passed the Equal Credit Opportunity Act to put an end to unfair discriminatory credit practices. Specifically, a creditor may not deny credit on the basis of sex or marital status nor disallow income received regularly from alimony, separate maintenance, or child support, or because the woman is of child-bearing age. Under this same law a woman may: have credit in her own name, based on her own income, if she is creditworthy; keep her own accounts and credit history if her marital status changes; build up her own credit record while married, because new accounts must be carried in the names of both husband and wife if both use the accounts or are liable for them; apply for her own credit without providing information about her spouse or having him co-sign (unless property rights are involved); get a copy of her credit record. (The lender is not required to disclose certain information on a credit report, so don't be upset when you are referred to the Credit Bureau. There will be no charge if you tell the Credit Bureau you've been turned down on a credit application; a slight fee if you are merely checking your report.)

When building your credit history, be consistent in using your own name—that is, your first and middle names and either your maiden or married last name. The use of ''Mrs.'' before your husband's first name, while legal, is only a social title and should not be used for building a separate credit history.

According to Maureen Gopel of United Jersey Banks, there are five transactions that will help you build a credit history.

1. **Open a checking and savings account.** Your local bank can play an important role in your credit future. Although opening a checking or savings account does not give you a credit background, it does help you establish an independent identity at a bank and demonstrate your ability to manage your own finances. Opening an account will also give you an opportunity to get acquainted with bank personnel who may be able to help you with future transactions.

2. **Apply for a department store charge account.** When using your checking account at a local department store, ask for a charge account application. You will probably be approved if you have your own verifiable income and if your application meets the store's other credit requirements. If you have previously had a joint account, point that out, stating that you now want to establish your own separate credit account. It is a good idea to apply for charge cards first at larger department stores. Such stores are likely to subscribe to a Credit Bureau which will record your transactions for future credit reference. Once you receive your charge cards, use them to build your credit rating and repay each obligation promptly. (Usually, if your bill is paid by a certain date, you pay no interest.)

3. **Apply for a bank charge card.** Since the credit standards of a bank are more stringent than those of a retail store, and since bank credit transactions are always listed with a Credit Bureau, the value of a bank charge card such as Master Charge or VISA in building a credit identity is greater. In order to secure a bank charge card, you may be required to have held your current job for 12 months or more, but applying at the bank where you have your checking and savings accounts increases your chances of obtaining the card. Again, once you are approved, build your credit history by using your card and paying your bills promptly.

4. **Secure an installment loan.** A successful record of installment (monthly payment) borrowing can be an impressive part of your credit history. Just as with a bank charge card, your chances of obtaining this type of loan are greatest at the bank where you have your checking and savings accounts. You probably wouldn't consider applying for a loan if you didn't need the money. Yet it is often easier to secure a loan when you don't need the money than when you do, and it's a good way to improve your chances of gaining future credit. You will lose money in interest charges, but by placing the loan in your interest-bearing savings account, making prompt payments for about 12 months, then paying off the obligation early, you will have earned a good payment record at the Credit Bureau and at the bank. While this may not be a wise method for everyone, it is another way to approach credit.

5. **Apply for an overdraft checking account.** Overdraft checking accounts provide a relatively new form of credit for banks' more established customers. Such an account protects you when you overdraw your checking account by advancing you money from your approved "line of credit." This type of loan requires fixed monthly reductions from your checking account unless you pay it back in one lump sum. Overdraft checking accounts have many advantages—your good name is protected from returned checks, you have the convenience of merely writing a check when you want to borrow funds, and you can repay the money you borrowed in a day or two if you like, therefore eliminating extensive interest charges.

Ms. Gopel, in her pamphlet titled *Women and Credit* that is distributed by United Jersey Banks, stated that the way a bank loan officer reviews credit applications serves as a good example of the evaluation procedures used by most lenders. You should approach the lender with two predetermined facts— the amount of money you wish to borrow and the purpose for which you want to borrow it. You will also be asked for other pertinent information, such as your date of birth, social security number, credit references, bills outstanding, number of dependents, telephone number, employment history, salary, and prior residences. When you have provided the basic information, don't underestimate the importance of the personal interview. Lenders are looking closely for extras. Their impression of your character and honesty makes a difference in the lending decision. Be sure to disclose all borrowings. Lenders receive a Credit Bureau report of your credit history, and an undisclosed loan can weigh heavily against you.

Banks are not the only source for loans. There are other types of lending institutions: finance companies that make high risk loans at higher rates of interest; credit unions for smaller amounts; and the Small Business Administration.

r me, it's the fact that people are

happy to spend their money on

something that I work hard on

and make with my hands. I feel

that my Boutiques are successful

because customers come from

Connecticut, New York, and

Pennsylvania, as well as all over

New Jersey, and do all their

Christmas shopping there, and

also their Easter shopping. Success

also means for me the fact that

each year my two separate

businesses grow."

Craftsperson

Among the ways to build a financial identity, there is one common denominator—installment or monthly payment obligations. Most lenders consider the regular repayment of installment debt as one of the more important factors in establishing a credit rating. Regular monthly reductions in accordance with a pre-established agreement are a good indicator of your financial stability. Most people run into occasional financial difficulties and your response to these "ups and downs" becomes a vital part of your relationship with a prospective or current lender. This doesn't mean that you will always be able to meet your monthly payment obligations, but merely that you react in a responsible manner.

It is not our intent to be the bearers of bad tidings, but it is unfortunately true that in many areas credit is exceedingly difficult to get these days. Because of the double whammy of a usury ceiling (the maximum interest rate a bank can charge) combined with present economic conditions, banks are not as willing to loan money out for high risk situations or to those who are first-time borrowers. It is wise to shop around, be cautious, and know your lender. An imaginative individual should be able to suggest various kinds of loans appropriate to your needs, as well as various kinds of repayment plans. It is your business, however. You alone will know if what you are planning is workable.

[We wish to thank Maureen Gopel and United Jersey Banks, Princeton, N.J., for permission to borrow freely from their brochure, *Women & Credit.*]

Get Credit Where Credit is Due

by Beth Preiss, Economist

Access to credit is directly related to access to entrepreneurship, home ownership, education, and consumer goods. Women using time at home to produce income have the same credit needs as other businesses: to manage cash flow, to meet emergency situations, and to take advantage of increased flexibility and a higher standard of living. You may have to purchase inputs (from materials to machinery) and develop an inventory before receiving income from sales of goods or services to cover their costs. Other advantages are deducting interest payments for tax purposes and borrowing when rates of inflation are higher than expected.

Many writers stress the fact that credit is a privilege, not a right. Others have noted that credit has become a way of life and that it is vital to the upgrading of women's economic status. Even viewing credit as a privilege, women do have the right to be considered for it without regard to sex or marital status. This is guaranteed by the Equal Credit Opportunity Act (ECOA), which also prohibits discrimination with respect to any aspect of a credit transaction on the basis of race, color, religion, national origin, age, receipt of public assistance, and exercise of any consumer credit protection or rights.

Specific provisions of the regulation implementing the ECOA include the following:

1. If you are denied credit, specific reasons for the adverse action or whom to contact to obtain the reasons must be given in writing. In addition, the Fair Credit Reporting Act gives you the right to obtain a summary of your credit history and to correct inaccurate information. If you are denied credit based on information in a credit report, the name and address of the reporting agency must also be given. You then have 30 days to obtain a copy of the report free of charge.

2. Creditors may not ask about your childbearing intentions.

3. If you will not rely on alimony, child support, or maintenance payments to repay the debt being incurred, you do not have to disclose the payments. If you choose to rely on alimony or part-time earnings, a creditor may not discount the income unless it is unlikely to continue.

4. A creditor who fails to comply with the ECOA is liable to an individual applicant for actual damages and punitive damages up to $10,000. In the case of a class action, punitive damages may total $500,000 or one percent of the creditor's net worth, whichever is less. In a successful suit, attorneys' fees may also be awarded.

In addition to the ECOA, state and local governments have their own equal credit statutes. You can only seek financial redress from one of these sources. Because of this and the complexity of equal credit opportunity laws in general, it is important that you seek legal advice if you feel that you have been discriminated against on a prohibited basis in a credit transaction and you intend to file a complaint or a law suit. Because a lawsuit is time consuming and expensive, you might first try discussing a denial of credit with the lender—and correcting any inaccurate or incomplete information on which the decision was based. (Note that discrimination can take place even before a formal loan application is made—if you are discouraged from applying.) Discussing your application with a person at a higher level of management in the lending institution might also help. The Women's Legal Defense Fund in Washington, D.C. maintains a credit counseling committee to assist women in these matters. It is recommended that you read their handbook before calling for information. Alternatively, you can consult your attorney.

Understanding and exercising your right to equal credit is very important. In fact, consumer complaints aid enforcement agencies in their efforts to ensure compliance with the law. The appropriate Federal enforcement agency with which to file a complaint depends on the type of institution involved.

National Banks: Comptroller of the Currency, Consumer Affairs Division, Washington, DC 20219;

State Member Banks: Federal Reserve Bank serving the district in which the bank is located;

Nonmember Insured Banks: Federal Deposit Insurance Corporation (FDIC) Regional Director for the region in which the bank is located;

Savings Institutions Insured by the Federal Savings and Loan Insurance Corporation (FSLIC) and Members of the Federal Home Loan Bank (FHLB) System (not insured by FDIC): The Federal Home Loan Bank Board Supervisory Agent in the district in which the institution is located;

Federal Credit Unions: Regional Office of the National Credit Union Administration serving the area in which the credit union is located;

Small Business Investment Companies: U.S. Small Business Administration, 1441 L Street, NW, Washington, DC 20416;

Retail, Department Stores, Consumer Finance Companies, Nonbank Credit Card Issuers and Other Creditors: Federal Trade Commission (FTC) Regional Office or FTC, Equal Credit Opportunity, Washington, DC 20580.

ne of the major reasons I needed/ wanted the house was because it was difficult to maintain an apartment with room for both my son and the office. So I bought a small Cape Cod (I got my own mortgage) and the entire second floor is office now."

Editor

At the present time, economic conditions are such that it is very difficult for both women and men to get credit. This will change—but in the meantime do not underestimate your creditworthiness. Lenders base their decisions on several factors, including the amount and stability of your income (and the debt it must cover), the length of time at your job, the length of time at your residence, and past credit experience. There are several things that you can do to establish a credit history, such as applying for and using a department store charge account. (Be sure it is issued in your own name—in the case of individual, unsecured credit, you cannot be asked questions about your spouse.) If your credit application concerns your business at home, show the creditor that you mean business. Be prepared with your financial statements and estimates of future prospects.

Women can expect increasing acceptance in the credit market over time. Consumers and lenders will better understand equal credit legislation, especially as it is tested more and more. As more women receive credit, realistic views will replace stereotyped views of the risks of lending to women. It is in the interests of both borrowers and lenders to put an end to discrimination in credit.

For more information, the following publications may be useful. Single copies are free of charge unless a price is indicated.

Borrowing Basics for Women (1978)
Citibank
Public Affairs Department
399 Park Avenue   18th floor
New York, NY 10043

Consumer Handbook to Credit Protection Laws (1979) and
The Equal Credit Opportunity Act and...Women
Publication Services
Division of Support Services
Board of Governors of the Federal Reserve System
Washington, DC 20551

The Credit Game—How Women Can Win It (1980)
Women's Legal Defense Fund, Inc.
2000 P Street, NW
Washington, DC 20036
This comprehensive manual includes details on District of Columbia, Virginia, Maryland, and Federal law. The self-help section has sample letters to creditors and reporting agencies. $3.00.

Give Yourself Credit (Guide to Consumer Credit Laws) (1977)
Superintendent of Documents
U.S. Government Printing Office
Washington, DC 20402
Request stock number 052-071-00524-2. Includes copies of the
laws. $2.10.

How Women Can Get Credit (1978)
National Organization for Women
425 13 Street, NW, Suite 1048
Washington, DC 20004

How to Establish and Use Credit
Department of Consumer Affairs
Federal Reserve Bank of Philadelphia
P.O. Box 66
Philadelphia, PA 19105

think I want to do well for so many

personal reasons, but the bottom

line is that I want to show my

ten-year-old that a woman can do

anything she damn well wants to

if she's prepared, qualified, and

not afraid to work."

Salesperson

As for my definition of success, I never

have thought about it! I know

that I want to perform useful

services and be recognized for

it. I'd like the company to grow.

But I've never put a dollar figure

on success nor any time limits on

growth."

Researcher

The NYCLU Guide to Women's Rights in New York State (1978)
Eve Carey, Author
New York Civil Liberties Union
84 Fifth Avenue
New York, NY 10011
Includes a section on how to file a discrimination complaint in
N.Y. and one on credit. $1.65 plus $.85 postage and handling.

Pocket Credit Guide
Consumer Assistance Division
Massachusetts Banking Commission
100 Cambridge Street
Boston, MA 02202

The Women's Financial Survival Handbook (1980)
Gail Perkins and Judith Rhoades, Authors
P.O. Box 999
Bergenfield, NJ 07621
A Plume book, published by the New American Library—it con-
tains a chapter on establishing credit and one on banking institu-
tions. $5.95 plus $.75 postage and handling.

Idea Insurance:
Patents, Copyrights,
and Trademarks

by Dr. Omri M. Behr,
Patent Attorney

You protect your business, your life, and your health with insurance policies, but do you know that the United States government will help you insure the most valuable property of all—the products of your mind? Depending on the type of idea, these insurance policies are called patents, trademarks, or copyrights.

One of the first needs of a business, after working capital, is the need to make a lasting and recallable impression upon customers and clients. Even the smallest business should have a word, phrase, or picture to remind people of that one business and no other. It should be unique and should suggest the business activity but not describe it. For example, Women's Insurance is unregistrable for insurance for women but Woman-Surance is a mark which suggests insurance and women. As a fanciful phrase, it would be considered registrable by the Patent and Trademark Office.

Registrable—what's that? Most states and the Federal government have laws which define registrability, or the conditions under which it will protect a trademark and prevent others from using it. The widest protection is granted by the Federal Lanham Act which will protect a mark used for goods or services passing across state lines. If your business, services, or products remain solely within one state, then you need only apply for state protection.

Choose your mark carefully. Have an attorney search it for you and then use it as widely and prominently as you can. Always emphasize the mark in print. Most marks should be capitalized (either totally or just initial letters). If your mark has been chosen deliberately in lower case, then it is preferable to print it in a bolder face type than the rest of the text or advertising material. Use the mark as an adjective but NEVER as a verb. The people in Rochester will never ask you to xerox a letter but always make a Xerox® copy. The ® tells everyone that the United States insurance policy—the Federal Registration—has been granted. If interstate use of your mark is required, an attorney will prepare the papers for you. The grant takes about two years (most of it just waiting), but you can and should use the mark in the meantime. The ® cannot be used until registration has been granted, but you may use the letters TM next to the mark to emphasize trademark use—though these letters have no legal effect.

Between the fifth and sixth year after registration you can confirm continued use of the mark. This is done by filing a Declaration in the United States Patent and Trademark Office under Sections 8 and 15 of the Lanham Act. The mark is then clear for a total of twenty years from registration at which time it must be renewed.

No matter how small your business, choose a good mark for it, and as the business expands, use that mark alone or in conjunction with new marks for each new, important line of goods. Over eighty years ago, Coca-Cola was a small, Georgia brand. The product is still going strong and so is the mark.

Your trademark identifies the quality and origin of goods and services to your business. But what if the products are unique? If the uniqueness is artistic, then copyright may be appropriate; if it is technical, then perhaps a patent.

A copyright will protect any artistic or literary work from the moment it is "fixed." Fixing supposes a form in which the work can be detected by others such as writing, printing, painting, a sculpture, phonograph records, electronic tapes, and the like. The time of protection is long—expiration is generally fifty years after date of author's death. To be able to enforce this right, the copyright must be registered with the Copyright Office of the Library of Congress as soon as possible. Copyrights are not examined for novelty or originality—only a court can determine that. Registration identifies the work and its date of fixing by you. Where artistic or literary works are published or offered for sale, national and international protection is available by additionally affixing the copyright notice, usually ©, your name, and the date of first publication. The exact requirements vary with the type of work.

This type of protection covers the right of reproduction. It does not protect the thoughts, ideas, or intellectual approaches contained in the work. It is, however, very inexpensive. For certain works, compliance with the notice provision is enough, and registration is not actually required unless litigation is to begin. The great advantages of copyright should be carefully considered by those whose business is in the literary or artistic world.

If you have developed a product or a process (but not a method of doing business) whose nature cannot be kept as a trade secret, a patent may provide appropriate protection.

For copyright registration, the services of an attorney, while helpful, are not really necessary; for trademark protection they are advisable. Where patents are concerned, a registered patent attorney must be consulted as patent rights are very strictly defined by the law and can be easily lost.

A patent can be granted for an invention which is "new, useful, and unobvious" and which has neither been sold in the United States nor described in a printed publication anywhere in the world more than twelve months prior to the time an application for patent is filed. The invention must have been made by the person or persons who apply—joint inventorship is quite proper. While in the United States a twelve month grace period for application is available, it is better to proceed as if this grace period did not exist. Merely use it as a fall-back safety measure if needed, since it does not exist in most other countries, and sometimes you may wish to obtain foreign patent rights, as well.

A patent can be granted for a thing (product) or a way of doing something (process) provided this involves a physical activity. A method of heating ceramics in a kiln to achieve a particular glaze effect is patentable, but a system of sales promotion is not. Computer programs are in a never-never land right now, but generally are not considered patentable. Asexually produced plants, i.e. roses, apple trees, tulips, etc., may be the subject of plant patents. Design patents are granted for the **appearance** of a **useful** object. The line between copyright and design patent is often very close—it required a decision of the United States Supreme Court to define it. A sculpture by itself may be copyrighted, but where the sculpture is incorporated with a lamp fixture, the entire lamp may be the subject of a design patent. On the other hand, if you have created a new type of switch for the lamp, then a regular patent would be appropriate.

When you have an idea which you think may develop into an invention **write it down**, preferably in a bound notebook with numbered pages. Avoid scraps of paper. Sign and date the idea and have it witnessed by a friend you trust who can countersign and date with the words "read and understood by..." Write down everything in the same way—ideas, experiments, results, both positive and negative, until you have something you **think** will work. It is not actually necessary to have built the device or practiced the process to get a valid patent.

At this stage, consult a patent attorney. He will advise you if you have enough information for him to conduct a search. A search is an unavoidable expense and will vary with the complexity of the invention, $300 to $600 should be considered proper for most ordinary inventions.

If the invention is deemed patentable by your attorney, he will prepare the application papers and negotiate with the United States Patent and Trademark Office. Costs over the two or three years of the process will run about $2,000 to $3,000, of which at least $1,000 to $1,500 will be for the initial application.

Moon 9½″   Narcissus 10″   Sunflower 9½″

Gail Reclining 10″   Two Figures in a Landscape 8½″   Back View with Hands 12½″ x 12½″

Day Lillies 11½″ x 10″   Nude in Chair 11½″ x 10″   Lesley on the Couch 11½″ x 11″

Cynthia Winika
Craftsperson

Joyce Richards
Fiberist
Photographer:
© *Terri P. Tepper 1979*

Properly handled, a patent is a valuable means of enabling creative individuals to protect a special share of a market for themselves. It has formed the bedrock of successful enterprises, both large and small, but it must be handled strictly according to the rules, so let the professionals advise you.

When you have made an intellectual creation, please remember some of the **Do's** and **Don'ts.**

Trademarks

Do pick a mark which you think is unique.

Don't use a mark which is descriptive.

Do emphasize your mark in print.

Don't use the mark widely, i.e. in a large advertising campaign before having a search done.

Do use the mark as an adjective; **don't** use it as a verb.

Copyrights

Don't publish without the copyright notice.

Patents

Do write down your ideas in a notebook.

Do keep good records.

Do be fairly certain the idea will work.

Before you see an attorney—

Don't disclose your invention, orally or in writing, to anyone (except in your notebook as mentioned above and to a trusted friend who witnesses it, and of course eventually to your attorney).

Don't give newspaper interviews about the invention.

Don't sell the invention.

Don't offer the invention to any company or sales organization.

Don't think you can protect yourself with a description mailed to yourself in a registered envelope.

Grants

by Jan Anderson, Assistant
Director for Research and
Project Support,
Princeton University

Financial assistance is available from a number of sources to support individual projects of women who work in their homes. Both the federal government and the private sector offer grants for which an institutional or organizational affiliation is not required. There are many types of funding—from professional and project fellowships and grants, to awards, prizes, and in-kind services. Eligibility criteria and other restrictions regarding nationality or academic or professional credentials vary from source to source. One should, therefore, inquire about these criteria when requesting information on application procedures and deadlines.

The following are some important sources of funding:

National Endowment for the Arts (NEA)
2401 E Street, NW
Washington, DC 20506
202-634-6369

The NEA, an independent agency of the federal government, was established in 1965 to encourage and support the American arts by offering financial assistance, through its fellowship program, to artists of exceptional talent. The NEA fellowships, designed to enable artists to advance their careers, are usually restricted to citizens or permanent residents of the U.S., and the stipend rates range from $2,000 to $10,000. Recipients include architects, artists, art critics, choreographers, composers, craftsmen, designers, jazz and folk musicians, film-makers, museum professionals, opera singers, photographers, and writers. The selection process is carried out by a review panel composed of experts in various branches of the arts, who read and evaluate all the applications. The Endowment encourages the submission of a second or third application if a first is declined. It is recommended that prospective candidates initially review the NEA ''Guide' to Programs,'' to select programs most relevant to their projects. Application forms and guidelines can then be requested by letter or phone from the appropriate program offices at the Endowment.

National Endowment for the Humanities (NEH)
Division of Fellowship
NEH 806 15th Street, NW
Washington, DC 20506
202-724-0238

The NEH was created to support projects of research, education, and public activity in the humanities. The NEH funds projects in the fields of history, philosophy, languages, literature, linguistics, archaeology, jurisprudence, sciences employing historical or philosophical approaches—such as, anthropology, sociology, political

74

theory, and international relations. Although the NEH does not award as many individual grants as its sister agency, the NEA, it does provide some funding in this area.

The Fellowship Division offers fellowships for independent study and research, and the competition is open to both scholars and nonacademic candidates. This program has one annual deadline and provides a maximum stipend of about $10,000 for six months and $20,000 for twelve months. The Division also offers fellowships and stipends to individuals in professions outside teaching, such as law, journalism, and medicine, in order that they may study the various historical, cultural, social, and philosophical dimensions of their professions. In addition, the NEH Youthgrant Program provides support to persons under the age of 25 for the pursuit of individual projects.

Like the NEA, the NEH employs a panel review system to select projects to be supported. It is suggested that prospective candidates obtain the NEH ''Program Announcement'' in order to select an appropriate program. Basic information on specific grants programs, as well as addresses and phone numbers of the program offices, are included in the announcement. Applications should be requested from the specific program office.

In addition to these federal agencies, most states have State Humanities Committees and State Arts Councils, which may also provide funds to individuals for various projects. For further information about the funding programs available in local areas, one should contact the State Cultural Affairs Department.

Some independent federal government agencies, such as the Smithsonian Institution, the Hirschorn Museum, and the National Gallery of Art, have limited funds to award to individuals each year. For further information on the specific programs currently funded, write to: The Smithsonian Institution, North Building, 955 L'Enfant Plaza, SW, Washington, DC 20560.

In the private sector, foundations also award grants to individuals, although traditionally, the primary emphasis is on educational programs, and the majority of foundation grants to individuals are scholarship awards. However, there are independent projects or research, including grants to support doctoral dissertation research. Some of these grants require academic credentials or make stipulations about nationality or residency. Some of the more widely known foundations providing individual fellowship support are the Ford, Guggenheim, and Rockefeller Foundations.

There are a number of books available providing detailed information on the types of foundation support. These publications offer information on the appropriate people to contact at the various foundations, as well as application procedures and deadline submission dates. Three of the most comprehensive books are: *The Annual Register of Grants Support, Foundation Grants to Individuals,* and *The National Directory of Grants and Aids to Individuals in the Arts.*

The competition for grant support is keen, both in government agencies and in the private sector. Nevertheless, there is money available for those who are well qualified and aggressive enough to seek and apply for it.

Reaching Out

Edith Martinez
Moccasin Maker
Photographer:
© *Terri P. Tepper 1978*

A homebased business can be stimulating and rewarding and may help to improve and protect your present or future, both financially and emotionally.

To prepare yourself for new challenges in business, reach out systematically in all directions to acquire as much information as possible about your fields of interest.

Research the library. Some have a great deal of reference material about a variety of occupations. Learn as much as you can about jobs that appeal to you.

Organize your thoughts and questions before reaching out. If you write down your questions, answers, and ideas in general, you will develop a written record of what you wished to know and what you learned.

S—Sense of direction—do something for people, they can't, or won't do for themselves and charge what it is worth to you.

—Understanding and communication with people.

—Courage—do something, act, take a risk.

—Charity—deal with people because you care about them, enjoy doing for people what you do best.

—Esteem—appreciate your own worth, forget your failures.

—Salvation—self-confidence, know you can do what you want to with God's help.

—Self-acceptance."

terior Designer

Contact individuals working in your fields of interest. Discuss your ideas with them. Listen to their suggestions, experiences, present and future concerns. Most people enjoy discussing what they do well. Listen for ideas on management, advertising, pricing, and marketing. Listen for general statements, as well as small details.

Narrow your field and focus your interest. Work for someone active in your chosen field, or a closely related one. Familiarize yourself with price lists, materials, marketing methods, machines available (if any are required), and other pertinent information.

Don't reject outright a field of interest in which you haven't had the necessary education. Consider an apprenticeship or take a course in that subject. Adult education classes can be very useful, as well as special classes for entrepreneurs.

Seek information from available agencies, organizations, and associations, such as the following:

Small Business Administration (SBA)
1441 L Street, NW
Washington, DC 20416
Refer to phone directory for local district office.
The SBA provides free counselling and training to help individuals plan, start, or manage a business. It also helps secure loans through local banks by guaranteeing up to 90% of a loan to $500,000. One can apply for a direct loan, providing funds are available. Direct funds are limited to $150,000. Mini-loans for women also exist for amounts up to $20,000 at an interest rate of 9¼%, subject to change.

Division of Economic Development
NJ Department of Labor & Industry
CN 380
Trenton, NJ 08625
609-292-9587
The Division of Economic Development provides technical, management, and financial assistance. It helps women to get started or to expand by putting them together with appropriate agencies or individuals. Check with the local SBA office for information about a small business assistance program in your area sponsored by the Department of Commerce or of Labor.

Service Corps of Retired Executives (SCORE)
1441 L Street, NW—Room 100
Washington, DC 20416
202-653-6279 or refer to your local phone directory
SCORE now has more than 7,800 counselors at work across the nation—volunteers, who are seasoned business executives, providing management assistance to small business owners. (SCORE is a service of the U.S. Small Business Administration.)

American Woman's Economic Development Corporation (AWED)
1270 Avenue of the Americas
New York, NY 10020
212-397-0880
AWED provides technical training, assistance, and free counseling to women business owners and those planning to go into business. (AWED is partially funded by the U.S. Small Business Administration.)

Department of Agriculture
Agricultural Co-Op Service
500 12th Street, SW—Room 550 GHI
Washington, DC 20250
This is an excellent place for rural area craftswomen to get information about cooperative craft programs and technical assistance.

U.S. Department of Commerce
Office of Assistant Secretary of Commerce
Washington, DC 20230
The Department of Commerce offers business development loans and loan guarantees to individuals, partners, and profit-making organizations.

"Also, my customers, who are generally referred by word of mouth (no advertising) come to me, talk over their wishes over tea, and I personally tailor their writing paper or party announcement to their preference without sacrificing mine. It is a rewarding emotional experience as well."

Stationer

U.S. Department of Labor
Office of the Secretary
Women's Bureau—Room S3005
Washington, DC 20210
The Handbook on Women Workers for 1980 should be available in Spring '81. Single copies are free of charge and can be obtained by writing to the above address.

National Economic Development Law Center
2150 Shattuck Avenue
Berkeley, CA 94700
415-548-2600
The Center will answer simple legal questions free of charge and indicate when a lawyer is necessary.

began this service from home in the

mid-70's on a very limited scale.

Put an ad in the local paper, but

receive most assignments through

word of mouth and people who

knew of me through extensive

civic and political involvements

and years as a journalist.''

Writer

was invited . . . to show my larger

work in a bank. While the bank

exhibit did not please me a lot, it

certified my intent among my

friends, and identified me pub-

licly with what I do. It ceased

being a basement hobby and I

and others both related to it more

seriously.''

Artist

National Alliance of Homebased Businesswomen (NAHB)
P.O. Box 95
Norwood, NJ 07648
NAHB is a network of women who work from home dedicated to encouraging, educating, and promoting all women who work, or wish to work, from their homes.

Seek professional advice. You may wish to speak to an attorney, accountant, management consultant, or advertising agent. When you have questions requiring expert answers, be prepared to pay for a professional's time. Write down your questions in order of importance. If you can only afford one hour's service, then make that hour count! It is definitely a sound investment to obtain advice from individuals who spend most of their working hours finding solutions to problems similar to those which concern you. Money spent to increase your dollar sense is good business. An experienced person may also help you anticipate problem situations and thereby save you time, money, and aggravation in the future.

When you are reaching out, a name—your name—is what people remember! If all goes well, you may live with that name for the rest of your life. The name can introduce and advertise your business simultaneously. Something Creative represents a homebased advertising agency. Witty Ditty is the name two women selected for their singing telegram service. Woman-Surance speaks for itself. A puzzle creator and designer calls her business Personally Puzzled. There are other examples throughout the directory.

After you decide what to do and how to do it legally, be aware of day-to-day activities that can help your business grow. Word of mouth can bring a substantial number of customers. If you've been active in organizations, let the members know what you're doing. Get a second telephone number with an answering machine or answering service and, as the commercial says, ''reach out and touch someone.'' Newspaper, television, and radio interviews provide marvelous opportunities to reach thousands of people at the same time.

To sum it up, here's the list again:
- Do library research.
- Organize your own thoughts and questions before reaching out.
- Contact individuals working in your field of interest.
- Focus your interest.
- If necessary, work for someone active in your chosen field.
- Where required, take additional courses.
- Seek information from available agencies, organizations, and associations.
- Choose a good name.
- Talk to the experts.
- Talk to friends and reporters.
- Finally—reach out—so that others might reach you!

Networking

For years, women have had an informal, unofficial, home-related network. It was made active when the need arose: when a relative needed a job, when a good price was needed on an appliance, when impartial advice was called for, when a friend needed a date, when a specialist was required.

It is the men who have had the official, formalized networks in business that develop and grow through office contacts, in professional associations, at the golf course, and around town. The network is a referral service and an effective system of communication. It stimulates socialization—in all those business lunches and agreements made at the 18th hole—and it's just plain good for business.

But times are changing. It's no longer the exclusive privilege of businessmen. Women are developing and enlarging their own networks in all directions. There are vertical networks that cover the range of one skill, type of job, or field of work—caterers, secretaries, women in the arts, or for our purposes, all women who have homebased businesses. Their common bond is their gender and the societal conditions that may handicap women in the working world. There are horizontal networks made up of women who work in the same or different occupations but who hold jobs at similar levels—determined by salary, title, and/or professional credentials. These are women with comparable responsibilities and experience.

Till now, new networks have emphasized women working outside the home. But they can be just as valuable for the homebased businesswoman. There is always a need for open lines of communication.

To illustrate the way it can and should work, we'll give a brief rundown about the way this book was put together. The idea was there. We needed names. We approached certain individuals we thought might be helpful. They were. Very often they directed us to other sources. All names, addresses, phone numbers, and other pertinent information were filed on index cards. Suggestions were made to contact specific organizations. We did. They, too, were helpful. Our card file began to grow. Questionnaires were sent out to women working at home. Those returned were filed alphabetically by state. All information was indexed alphabetically by county and occupation. Advice was needed, as well as layout artist, typesetter, printer. We got recommendations. People who had heard of us through radio, television, newspaper, or magazine publicity contacted us with more names and offers of help. Every piece of promotional material, every let-

"I do miss the opportunities for discussion and brain-picking you have when you work with others in an office. I feel that is the only negative. You sometimes feel you're reinventing the wheel, or there is no-one who understands the problem you're trying to solve. To hire someone to work with me would not be feasible at this time, so I must depend on A.S.L.A. meetings and research for current info and contacts."

Landscape Architect

When the system disintegrates, I hire

teenage help or subcontract with

other cooks. Luckily, I have my

own 'Good Old Boy' system on

which to rely for support. Most of

my friends share my views, and

each of us is willing to help in

whatever way is necessary."

Caterer

am still studying pottery and sculp-

ture in graduate school, but as I

improve the lighting and facilities

in my own studio, I will take

fewer courses outside. Workshops,

however, lasting from one day to

several weeks are necessary to

keep growing from outside feed-

back and learning of new and dif-

ferent techniques."

Craftsperson

ter, every name, number, offer of help, or request for more information was (and continues to be) systematically acted upon, indexed, and filed. The name list grew. So did our contacts.

Our own developing network of women with home-based businesses gave us help when we needed information, advice, leads, referrals, and ideas which enabled us to be more effective; introduced us to stimulating, knowledgeable allies; and boosted our spirits with moral support.

In *Networking,* an excellent book by Mary Scott Welch, there is a list of suggestions for those who are members of a network. Some bear repeating, even in abbreviated form. First and foremost, accept offers of help from others and give generously in return. You'll recognize that maxim as an updated version of the Golden Rule! If someone gives you a name to call, follow up on the lead and report back on the results. It prevents possible embarrassing situations. Be businesslike. Ms. Welch recalls that old etiquette books suggest avoiding the subjects of "Death, Disease, and Domestics." The newly evolving etiquette for women in business warns against "Criticism, Children, and Confidences." Don't overlook anyone. There are local, regional, and national networks: church fellowships; community groups, such as the League of Women Voters; educational groups, such as the American Association of University Women; alumnae groups; professional associations, such as National Association for Female Executives or National Association of Women Business Owners; and trade associations, such as Women's Caucus for Art or American Women in Radio and Television. Know your subject and choose carefully whom you ask, as well as what you ask for. Request only one thing at a time. Include women of all ages. Keep in touch just to "keep in touch." It's pleasanter that way and socially more acceptable. Don't always need something—you may find others start avoiding you. Networks are not specifically designed for personnel placement, though having contacts in the right place at the right time can certainly be beneficial. Finally, network support is based on performance, but only you can determine how best to use the resources.

It is true that most times, women seek out other women for information, advice, and moral support because it so often seems that only other women can understand the problems in business that men just don't have—especially when that business is operating from home. There are not only general business problems, but additional ones pertaining to children, family schedules, and kitchen duty. It may, however, be a mistake to depend solely on a network of women. Some men are ahead of us in business experience, and we stand to gain from their expertise. In business they, too, can be our teachers, mentors, and allies.

Still, it's the phenomenon of women networking with other women that generates the most excitement today and, perhaps, the most promise for the future.

Bibliography
Welch, Mary Scott. *Networking.* New York: Harcourt, Brace, Jovanovich, 1980.

Women's Caucus
for Art

Pat Morris, President WCA/NJ

All women working at home share one thing, no matter what kind of work they do. Their workplace imposes an isolation on them and makes their working conditions quite different from those of others who go each day to an office, factory, or other place of business. For the artist and craftswoman, that isolation is often deepened by the nature of their work. Even when a work of art is commissioned or made with a specific audience in mind, its execution demands long hours working alone and a kind of concentration that shuts out other people. The work of art is accomplished using ideas and skills different from those of the marketplace, and artists often experience a conflict between their role as workers producing art for exhibition and sale and their desire to make something that satisfies their own creative desire.

Successful artists resolve this conflict in a number of ways. By looking at and reading about art and by talking with other artists, gallery owners, and the public at large, they learn what kind of work is of interest and weigh the merit of their own work. They exhibit their work, subjecting it to criticism, and find understanding among some who come to see it. By working hard, being true to and refining their own visions, they eventually produce a body of work that is intelligible and commands attention in its own right. Although it is produced in isolation, the work takes on a life of its own and becomes part of the community of men and women. In the past, however, it has been particularly difficult for women artists to resolve the conflict between the private meaning and the public value of their art. Their isolation within the home and family, and often their geographical isolation from art centers necessitated by the role of wife and mother, added to the almost complete lack of interest in women's art on the part of galleries, museums, and critics. Art made by women had very little public value, and women were denied that public life in art which breaks down the isolation of the studio, and turns a hobby or consuming interest into a career.

This situation has changed considerably during the last ten years. The works of more women artists are being shown, written about, and talked about than ever before. This has come about in large part because women began to work together, forming groups and networks to bring about change. It was necessary for women to break the barriers of their isolation from each other and to work collectively before their contribution as individuals could be recognized by society.

In 1969, women artists and critics began to meet in small groups in New York City, forming organizations like

"It pleasures me to work at home. My husband and I live . . . in the woods in a farm house that once was an old ice house; a place of beauty, peacefulness, and sharing. I am quieted here where most of my creativity comes to life."

Artist

With all the madness my work creates,

I still wouldn't trade one crazy

moment of it for the sedate

homemaker's life of some of my

friends. Being active and creative

is the fuel that keeps me alive!"

Artist

Martha Otis Wright
Potter
Photographer: Nina Alexander

Women Artists in Revolution, Redstocking Artists, and the Ad Hoc Committee of Women Artists, to discuss issues and organize protest action, like that against the Whitney Museum for exclusion of women artists from its annual exhibitions of American art. On the west coast in the early 1970s, Miriam Shapiro and Judy Chicago pioneered new techniques in the education of women artists at Womanhouse; and in Chicago, Washington, and New York, women's cooperative galleries were organized as alternate spaces to show women's art. A national network of women artists and art historians was born in 1972, when the Women's Caucus for Art (WCA) was formed by women members of the College Art Association (CAA), the professional organization of teachers in college and university art and art history departments throughout the country. Papers given at the national meetings of the Women's Caucus for Art, books on women artists by women critics and historians, many of whom are WCA members, and publications like the *Feminist Art Journal, Woman Art,* and *Women Artists News,* have focused attention on important issues and artists, providing a means of communication for the movement, which by the mid-seventies had burgeoned into a national phenomenon. Eventually the Women's Caucus for Art split from the CAA, opened its membership to all professional women in

the visual arts, and collaborated with other women's art groups to found another separate organization—the Coalition of Women's Art Organizations, which has been working in the political arena for women's and artists' rights.

In 1976, local and regional chapters of the WCA began to form to meet the particular needs of their communities. The New Jersey Chapter of the WCA (WCA/NJ) began in 1977, and as its first project, worked with Caucus members from New York and Connecticut to organize a tri-state exhibition of women's art at the City University of New York. During this time, New Jersey artists who had previously been unknown to each other began building a network to mount nine more exhibitions in two years in various places throughout their state, including exhibitions at the corporate galleries of Nabisco World Headquarters, college galleries at Newark, New Brunswick, and Brookdale Community College, and the offices of the NJ State Architects Association. Members of WCA/NJ have worked for passage of the New Jersey Arts Inclusion Act, which allows a portion of the funds spent for public buildings to be spent on art for those buildings. The WCA/NJ newsletter has kept members informed of issues and events of importance to NJ artists and provided information on members' work and exhibitions. During 1980, a grant from the NJ State Council on the Arts provided support for an ambitious project, a rotating gallery of color photographs of members' work, to be circulated to corporations, decorators, and others who may be interested in buying or exhibiting that work. In December, 1979, a statewide conference was held in cooperation with the Art Department at Rutgers-Newark. Various ways of showing and selling art in New Jersey were explored, and Lucy Lippard, an important feminist critic, spoke about current directions in women's art.

The brief history of WCA/NJ has given those of us involved in it ample instruction in the value, as well as the difficulties, of establishing a women's network in a particular profession on a statewide basis. An organization is a sort of "official network" and as such shares the problems of structure and funding common to all organizations. The advantages of institutionalizing a network are that it becomes possible, by working together in an organized way, to undertake projects that would be difficult to manage on a more informal basis. A degree of continuity is maintained, so that one accomplishment can be used as a steppingstone to another. A large membership makes a wide range of skill and talent available for programs and exhibitions. Nevertheless, much of the valuable interaction that takes place in an organization like WCA/NJ is in the less formalized network of friendship and communication that springs up when women of similar interests meet to work and talk together.

The real rewards of networking come to those who take an active part in planning and carrying out projects, who communicate their own ideas and search out the ideas of others. The rewards of this kind of participation are many and range from the inspiration of knowing other women whose commitment to their

"I built an addition onto the house last summer, and here I keep all the work in process. I find that by shutting the door, I can and do let go of that. However, the desk is in my bedroom and it always seems to be piled high. Have developed a way of entering the room and not looking in that corner as a way of locking out that work. However, since, like most artists, I love what I do in terms of the actual process, I consider myself to be in a most fortunate position.

Artist

work equals your own to the kind of knowledge to be gained by observing women whose ability to organize and administer a project far exceeds your own. Someone with whom you work on a newsletter may turn out to have skills you need to know more about to develop your own work. Someone you work with on an exhibition may know of a cooperative gallery you might join. The kinds of information to be gained by talking with other artists are equally hard to classify. An artist talking about her work reveals her vision and tells about the way she handles materials, but she often has other valuable information, such as where to get certain kinds of paper, how she builds her canvas stretchers, what solvent dissolves color Xerox, or how she builds her sculpture so that she can take it apart and fit it into her station wagon, sure that, disassembled and packed, it will be no larger than the size allowed for mailing by U.S. postal regulations. Sometimes, the most important knowledge to be gained is just an idea of the way in which another's ideas conform to or differ from your own.

Anyone who wants the benefits of networking, in the visual arts or elsewhere, should not wait for the network to come to her. If you have an idea, reach out with it, test it against the ideas of others who are involved in the same area, and, most of all, come prepared to help carry it out. You will be surprised to find skills you never knew you had. And you will learn from the ideas and skills of others as you work with them to make your ideas and theirs a reality.

For membership information in Women's Caucus for Art, write to the WCA Operations Manager, 731 44th Ave., San Francisco, California 94121.

Bibliography
Lippard, Lucy. *From the Center, Feminist Essays on Womens' Art*. New York: Dutton, 1976.
Wilding, Faith. *By Our Own Hands, A History of the Women Artists' Movement in Southern California*. California: Double X, 1977.
Feminist Collage: Educating Women in the Visual Arts. Edited by Judith Loeb. New York: Teachers College Press, 1979.
Women Artists News. Vol. 6, Nos 2-3, Summer 1980. Contains the following articles on the history of the women artists' movement: *Looking Back, The Past Ten Years*, by Jacqueline Skiles; *Feminist Art in California*, by Faith Wilding; *Toward a Feminist Art Education*, by Holly Hughes; *Chicana Art in California*, by Lorraine Garcia and Gail M. Crippen; *The Politics of Culture: Black, White, Male, Female*, by Faith Ringgold.

bought an old house two years ago

and converted the separate

double garage into my work area.

Its sole heat comes from a wood

stove, so in the winter I have to

get up early and start the fire so

the place will be comfortable to

work in."

Potter

need to feel that my work is

immediately available to work on

at any time."

Artist

National Alliance of Homebased Businesswomen

It's an American tradition. Since the days of convivial quilting bees, women have met in groups to achieve a common goal. The difference is that today women are relating to each other in a whole new way. Whereas they once discussed the best ways to piece together fabrics, they are now making executive decisions about methods of simplifying the operation for efficient and profitable operations, and for handling sales and distribution.

It was with great excitement and anticipation that in 1980 a determined and diligent group of businesswomen met to form the charter and bylaws of the National Alliance of Homebased Businesswomen—the first step toward building a community of women working from home which would cut across professional and occupational lines. We are, indeed, a community of women who are, in many respects, altogether different from each other. Yet, because we are all women with a common purpose, it is that thread that runs through our fabric of affiliation—just as that common thread ran through the patchwork quilt of long ago.

"Almost two years ago I started this venture. I have seen it grow from nothing to something rewarding and exciting. Besides the pleasure of making something lovely, I have met many fine people who have become my friends."

Interior Decorator

86

"It would be helpful to me if there were more of a writer's community, especially of women, where one could go for succor and intellectual criticism."

Writer

"Working at home I am able to regulate my own time and energy. It is always a challenge to do this well. Being self-employed in a creative venture, the responsibility for my personal and financial success is, to a large extent, dependent on my own initiatives. I have to create my own supportive environment if that is what I need, my own inspiration, and working conditions."

Artist

There is great hope for the Alliance, as it is affectionately called, for we envision a vast network of women spreading across the United States united in mutual understanding and support. Specifically, our purposes are:

■ to emphasize, encourage, and stimulate personal, professional, and economic growth among women who work from, or wish to work from, their homes;

■ to project a positive image of women with homebased businesses as equal partners in the work force;

■ to provide a forum for the discussion and exchange of information and experiences related to homebased businesses;

■ to provide publications to disseminate current information and to exchange views on mutual concerns;

■ to provide a network of professional contacts, education, and encouragement to serve as a support system for women with homebased businesses and to enhance one another's professional advancement;

■ to showcase members' goods and services.

If you are interested in becoming a member of the Alliance because you are a woman with a homebased business or because you support our goals, use the membership form at the back of the book. We would be glad to include you in our growing list of members.

A Changing Lifestyle

by Martin Lazar, Psychotherapist

Women are at the forefront of many revolutions in this Twentieth Century. With the changes taking place in the woman's family role, one of the more subtle types of change is the development of new areas for work which some women have quietly and creatively found. Women have for centuries been the chief executives in their home with slight acknowledgement. Some women these days are obviously capitalizing on that experience and becoming chief executives in the home in more ways than one.

The woman working at home has had the rare opportunity in our sophisticated times of carrying on the traditions of the individual entrepreneur. With this role has gone the ego benefits of individuality, autonomy, decision-making, creativity, and self-worth. It is interesting that these are the very factors so often cited by experts as necessary for ego development. The ego is that part of the psyche which helps us strike a balance between ourselves and our environment. When the balance is comfortable, we are considered "well-adjusted." For the balance to take place, there must be ongoing stimulation of a positive nature from ourselves and those we value around us. We feel important when our ego synthesizes this input, and we conclude that we are on par with our goals, expectations, and background pressures.

The woman working at home must realize her special opportunities and nourish her ego with the knowledge that she carries on the real American tradition—that of the individual entrepreneur. To do this she must develop a cadre of peers, with whom she can easily communicate, who are equally individualistic, independent, and resourceful. The ultimate goal of a consciousness-raising group—that technique so germane to the women's movement—is to achieve those very freedoms that the woman working at home already has. While resisting the seductive corporate advertising which suggests glamour for women in the corporate cubbyhole, she must continue to explore her own individuality with more self-confidence and security than she has shown in the past. Beginning, more often than not, as a problem-solving device because of family responsibilities or limited capital and hours, she has built a career, but not a mental attitude of the rugged individualist. She has been given this opportunity, however, and must begin to realize how ego-appropriate her functions are.

"I catered birthday parties while in high school but allowed myself to be persuaded to attend college in Elementary Education. After teaching, then supervising, and finally administrating, . . . I was secretly glad when I quit to have children. These last five years have been a welcome respite which has given me the chance to switch careers. The libber in me is embarrassed to admit that this 'non-working' period has its benefits, but I might never have mustered the courage to abandon a steady though paltry salary in an uncertain economic market."

Women are stereotypically not used to this responsibility and technique. Professional women often refer to the "women's syndrome" while chatting with their colleagues over coffee. By this term they refer to the way little girls are not trained to make decisions or develop their own sense of identity. They are trained instead to cater to the dictates of others, to be someone else's commodity. The woman working home has independence as part of her job and needs—to make a bad pun—to capitalize on it in building identity, to seek out others in similar careers, and to feel good about herself.

Marjorie Bowman
Craftsperson
Photographer:
© *Terri P. Tepper 1977*

Not only does the woman working at home stay at home with all of the usual problems; she plays the role of her own supervisor as well. While we have been a nation truly strengthened by our individual entrepreneurs, most of us have been raised to work in groups—especially women, trained to handle large families. With modern changes in family roles, some women have now looked elsewhere for their life tasks, supervision, and groups. One of the subtle and somewhat seductive expectations of the past has been the suggested sense of freedom that has always been associated with the marketplace. In mythology, men were leaving home to partake of this marketing delight while the women drudged at home. Reality, however, has now placed the greater number of women, often leaving spacious and comfortable daily home surroundings with relative freedom of choice in their time schedules, into cramped, often uncomfort-

WOMAN IS A SANTA! HAS SECRET PRAYER TO MAKE TOYS "LIVE"

MRS. WENIGER, THE WOMAN SANTA, IN HER WORKSHOP; BELOW, THE KIND OF ODD TOYS SHE MAKES.

"It feels right. A lot may have had to do with self-acceptance. I think I know who I am now—I'm a wife, mother, writer, with needs, ideas, drives, appetites that need to be answered in all these roles. Sometimes it's still terribly hectic. But I am happy with the combination and feel I'm not cheating my kids of attention, nor depriving myself of the chance to grow and develop during the most energetic period of my life."

Writer

"I consider it torture to be chained to a desk for eight hours a day with a supervisor breathing down my neck."

Copywriter

BOSTON, Mass., Dec. 22. — There's a woman Santa Claus in Boston. Mrs. Maria Weniger has imported from her native home in the Black forest district of Germany ideas for making children happy and has her own workshop where she carves out weird creatures of wood and paints them to look more quaint and humorous.

Since the earliest days she could remember, this woman Santa Claus had knack for making toys. When a she whittled playthings for hers and friends. Later she took a course in manual training to become more expert.

When she came to Boston she opened shop. She created grotesque and ludicrous wood creatures. Dachshunds with their tongues hanging out; open-jawed crocodiles, clowns, rocking horses, sea lions and other animals in queer forms come from her shop.

Here is where Mrs. Weniger is really a Santa Claus: before she lets a single toy out of her shop she repeats a prayer over it!

And that makes the toy a real live animal, not just a piece of wood, says Mrs. Santa Claus.

"Little blue-eyed Gretchen taught me the secret, the incantation, you must say over the dolls and other toys before they are real live things," says Mrs. Weniger. "Before this they are just pieces of wood."

But the prayer is Mrs. Weniger's secret. If that were known by others, she would not be a woman Santa Claus, she contends.

able spaces; with continual psychic stresses; with increasingly rigid time capsules; and at the beck and call of bosses they don't like and who have made all kinds of servitudinal demands upon them. They have, therefore, traded a role in life, perhaps imperfect but of obvious worth and importance, for one most often lacking in individuality, cog-like, and of passing value at best. Health problems have increased; happiness has not. Working away from home has been a mixed blessing at best, and there has been no indication that "getting away" has produced mental health. Often it has been just the opposite. Margaret Mead talked about the schizophrenic nature of modern man, commuting from nowhere to nowhere and spending the day performing meaningless tasks in between. Women do that now, too.

In psychotherapy our job is often to help troubled clients learn how to sustain a fragile ego balance with some continuity. For the woman working at home, the job becomes one of isolating those factors which can lead to ongoing ego satisfaction. It is ironic that women working at home do not generally feel the kind of importance and excitement that their chosen careers offer them. One of the principal reasons for this problem may be the isolated position that the woman working home has had vis-a-vis her peer group (other women working at their homes). Isolation is an immediate red flag for the therapist. One must presume that the current efforts for setting up a network providing for information, communication, recognition, and possible social opportunity—as represented by this book and the developing National Alliance of Homebased Businesswomen—will go a long way toward helping to solve this problem across the nation.

Women at home should use this tool extensively. They should plan to make contacts with other women listed in the book and build them into their business schedules. They should develop business referrals through it to other women listed here, expecting the same in return. Women in local areas should visit each other and meet with each other regularly. They should spend much time sharing their feelings—their joys in business, their successes, their fears, and frustrations. The ephemeral social contact that corporate women have can be developed by women at home. Together with the independence and achievement of their own businesses, this activity should provide women working at home with opportunities for mental health and ego balance second to none.

Accenting Abilities:
The Handicapped
at Home

"When what you do coincides with who you are, you have it all!"

Publisher

"How can I manage to do all that I do? Everyone asks me that question. I suppose because I have a good sense of priorities."

Craftsperson

During the past few decades the employment history of the handicapped population has changed. With application, struggle, and hard work, the number of opportunities for purposeful and creative industry has increased for sizable segments of the handicapped population, making employment the rule rather than the exception. The same considerations have not been present for women working at home.

While on one hand the concept of working out of the home would seem to solve many otherwise intractable problems for some handicapped people, it has unfortunately been equally true that other problems, apart from their handicaps, have surfaced. The agencies for the handicapped, as well as the federal Office of Vocational Rehabilitation, have therefore been cautious in responding to questions about the concept of handicapped women working at home. One of their main concerns has been that such women have, at times, been taken advantage of in one way or another.

It is unclear why handicapped persons at home have faced additional disadvantages at the hands of their creditors or competitors—but as in other situations, this consideration must be dealt with. In some respects, the homebased business would seem to be made to order in dealing with the problems of the handicapped. The generally accepted therapeutic approach to learning to deal with one's handicap has been predicated on developing a positive approach to problem solving and developing skills in order to fashion flexible and balanced adjustment to one's life situation. These are the very assets that make for a businesswoman, as well.

There is great psychological satisfaction and stimulation from starting a business and then operating it successfully. Success comes from many sources: skill, determination, a mental attitude that accents abilities and minimizes disabilities, a willingness to participate in training programs, and an eagerness to be in touch with other people in the community.

There are many possibilities for home employment. The choice, as with any individual, is based on an analysis of one's skills, interests, values, and the assessment of problems, perhaps including one's handicap. Often important for the handicapped individual are access to public transportation and a system for pick-up and delivery, where applicable.

One possibility for home employment is offered by Isabel Fleiss, Executive Director of WomanSurance Advisory Services, a woman who also works from home. She operates the Phone Power School of Insurance for the purpose of training, licensing, and employing individuals to work from their homes as commissioned sales representatives. According to Ms. Fleiss, these professional representatives will be capable of earning an income from home, utilizing insurance knowledge and telemarketing techniques.

Additional business suggestions and help may be had from the local 4-H office which specializes in people-development programs. Look for it in the phone book under your county listings. The 4-H pledge dedicates the head to clearer thinking, the heart to greater loyalty, the hands to larger service, and one's health for better living. Many 4-H groups have special programs for the handicapped and information on a variety of subject matter—animals, clothing, gardening, and foods, to name just a few.

This concept—the handicapped woman working at home—just doesn't seem to have been developed to its full potential. The network of women working at home has ample room to help develop it to more sophistication. With the additional contact of this growing network, there is every possibility that it will so develop.

My definition of success is being fortunate enough to work at something I love, in an area in which I have expertise, and knowing that I am a professional at what I do. I share the feeling of others you've interviewed who are weary of being thought of as housewife hobbyists merely because they work out of their homes. I'm serious and work very hard at my job—do I have to pay a high rent in a commercial environment to be accepted! I say NO, but it is a struggle."

Salesperson

"Success...an inner sense of revelation through creativity...and an outer sense of effective accomplishment...along with a monetary reward to confirm one's success."

Inventor

93

The Home Studio and the New Jersey Woman Artist

by Lynn F. Miller

"I have done a lot to try to raise the awareness of people, especially here in this area, about the Arts and most especially fiber work as an art form. This I feel I have done to some extent and am thought of as a professional and not as someone who does macramé in their spare time."

Fiberist

"Success, at this stage of the game, would be to earn equal (first) then much more than I did teaching. Also to be known as an artist."

Artist

Many New Jersey women artists who work at home have taken steps toward greater visibility. In 1973, a route to improved exposure was developed through the registration of slides of their work and all pertinent information about themselves in the Slide Registry and *Directory of New Jersey Women Artists,* now housed in the Multimedia Services Department of the Rutgers University Library.

The Registry and *Directory* represents the beginning of a clearinghouse of information about women artists creating in any artistic medium, who live or work primarily in New Jersey. All arts are included as long as the work is original: needlepoint or crewel executed from an original design, photographic works, stained glass, ceramics, paintings, drawings, graphics, sculpture, fabric, fiber work, and other non-paint media.

The *Directory* records and disseminates the names and media of the women artists of New Jersey and serves as a means for them to contact one another and develop a network.

The Registry is used by students and faculty for courses on women in the arts, by dealers, arts and cultural organizations, arts councils, women's groups, interior designers, and curators who select artists for their shows. Since 1973, the Mabel Smith Douglass Library at Douglass College has sponsored an annual group show of New Jersey women artists selected from slides in the Registry.

Anyone may be included in the Slide Registry. Send three slides of representative current work, each labeled with name, address, and phone number of the artist, together with the date, dimensions, medium, and title of the work to: Lynn Miller, Multimedia Services Librarian, Rutgers University, College Avenue, New Brunswick, New Jersey 08903.

For a copy of the *Directory,* send your request with an 8½"x11" envelope, self-addressed and stamped ($.80 postage), to the above address. The Slide Registry changes weekly with new entries and updated information, whereas the *Directory* includes only that information available at the time of publication. Constant revision of any published listing is needed to keep materials current.

An updated version, to be retitled *Guide to NJ Women Artists,* will be issued in 1981. The revision will offer geographic and media indexes as well as the names, addresses, and phone numbers of the artists.

Potter
Photographer: Nina Alexander

can see myself growing all the time, but being an artist is such a lonely job! It takes so much discipline! My definition of success changes all the time, but my standard reply when people ask me is that I would like to be rich and famous. When I first started painting again, success was just to be able to paint a decent painting. Then success was selling my paintings. Soon success also meant winning awards and getting into juried shows....In the future I would like to be a very good painter and command high prices for my paintings."

Artist

95

Witty Ditty

by Emily Rosen

We were into our mid-years, cowriting and producing shows for our country club, when Madelene placed her elbows squarely on the bar one gala evening and said, "What are we going to be when we grow up?" Her background as a champion amateur golfer, tennis player, and physical education teacher seemed to offer no quick answer to her question. My background as an editor, copywriter, reading specialist, counselor, and closet poet, indicated a clear lack of direction. We both knew unequivocally what we didn't want.

We wanted nothing that required the standard nine-to-five commitment; nothing that required an investment of over $2,000 each; nothing that would require great amounts of travel time to an office; nothing that would interfere with our families, vacations, or lifestyles. That was indeed a big order!

We were able to enumerate the positives. We wanted something creative; something where we would have personal contact with people; something which would allow us to work alone, independent of each other, and at the hours that suited our individual convenience; a kind of something where none of the above would interfere with the success of our venture, or pose any hardships on each other or any of the people we were to be servicing.

A week after the elbow-on-the-bar discussion, I noticed a small item in the newspaper. Sammy Cahn, the song writer, the article had said, would no longer write parodies for parties for his friends for free. Henceforth, he would charge $20,000 per party for his services. I cut out the article and dispatched it to Madelene with the comment: "We could certainly undercut him by a couple of thou." Her response was a typical no-nonsense Madelene, "That's for us! Let's go into business." And so we did, in January 1979.

We assessed our combined talents. We were both imaginative and talented verse writers, and both had a familiarity with the kind of music that makes for good parodies. We had a sense of showmanship and theatrics and could both finger-pick at the piano. We knew what looked and sounded right in front of an audience; we each had a reputation for being good at writing, directing, and producing amateur shows; we had a tremendous area of social contacts from which we could potentially draw business. Our husbands were very supportive. Our only problem was that neither of us could sing, which liability we have turned into a running gag.

Madelene had seen a singing telegram delivered in California, and we were both aware of the growing market in the east. It seemed to be the kind of business which met all of our qualifications, so we shook hands and considered our partnership to be in operation.

We were convinced that a name was our first priority, and we each made a list of dozens of possibilities. (In those early days, we were propelled by lists.) We met over coffee in my kitchen, and after rejecting them all as being mundane or re-hashed, we agreed to meet again the next day with a new list. As Madelene walked toward the door, she sighed, ''I don't know why we're having such a hard time with a name. We want to write witty ditties, but nothing seems appropriate.'' She had her hand on the door knob about to exit when I screamed, ''That's it!! That's it!!'' And thus was Witty Ditty born. Now the name is used synonymously with ''singing telegram.''

We attended a conference on ''Small Businesses'' and proceeded to pick brains, calling and visiting other singing tele-gram companies. We toyed with the idea of franchising, but by then had a clear idea of how our singing telegrams would be dif-ferent from the others. We eschewed the concept of volume, and decided that low overhead, highly personalized service, and custom-written original lyrics would be our guiding goals. We expected it would take from three to five years to see any profit, but we were comforted by the knowledge that we would be building a solid reputation in that time.

Madelene's house was a perfect base, since it had an area apart from the rest of the house which was originally de-signed to be an office. Conveniently, it is less than five minutes from my home.

We filed our partnership agreement with the county clerk, and then we began to get to know each other on a level we never had before, in terms of personality and abilities. I could set up books, organize procedures, and manage the office. Madelene could do a mean soft shoe. I made public relations contacts and arranged for advertising and publicity. Madelene could whip up a costume and teach a song and dance. We were a good balance for each other. If we needed pencils, I would tend to buy a hundred dozen. Madelene would get an estimate on the cost of one before she would spend the dime. We each learned to give in a little.

A local artist and printer collaborated with us on a logo. We invested in high quality parchment-like, two-color sta-tionery on which we reproduce the original words of each song we write. This is then rolled into a scroll and tied with a red ribbon and presented to the recipient. People have had these framed, and in some cases taken to an engraver to be preserved as mementos. Our business cards are high quality gloss with two color ink and also give the impression of class.

The next important item was a telephone. We gave Ma Bell a choice of numbers we preferred and lucked out with GR 2-GRAM. Madelene purchased the telephone answering machine at the best discount price in town.

We mailed flyers to members of local country clubs, florists, musicians, caterers, and virtually anyone we ever said "hello" to, and then marched ourselves to our local costumer and conjured up an appropriate eye-catching uniform: a red and white striped vest, a straw hat with a red and white band, a red bow tie, and a red arm band. The singers would supply white shirts and black pants. Eventually we made short black skirts for the girls. It was a minimum budget, and we chose large sizes so that they could be taken in as necessary (Madelene's specialty). We made a grand purchase of four sets and immediately hand-lettered Witty Ditty onto the hat bands. We then purchased four kazoos from our local music shop, and we were ready to go.

It was February when we planned our first promotion. We wrote a group of songs for Mother's Day, which seemed a century away at the time, and arranged for space to present these songs in a local department store, beginning several week-ends prior to Mother's Day. We printed a call for singers and mailed these flyers to the music departments of local colleges and high schools, to drama coaches, to local private music teachers, and to music stores. Our first applicants came en masse and auditioned in the playroom of my house where we could use my piano when necessary. They were senior music majors from the State University of New York at Purchase, who had been involved in shows and production for many years. The sight of these three husky young men translating their talents to some sloppy sentiment regarding "mom," while the two "old ladies" tried to give them tips about projecting to a department store audience, still makes us giggle in retrospect.

(914) GR 2-GRAM

PERSONALIZED SINGING TELEGRAMS

Madelene Fink   Emily Rosen

29 CORNELL STREET, SCARSDALE, NEW YORK 10583

We established a per-delivery payment for our singers at a rate currently higher than that paid by any company we had researched. We could make no promises regarding total earnings since at that time we had yet to get our first order. We finally found an Iona College singer willing to hang in with us, and with great trepidation sent him on our first delivery, ordered, as you may have guessed, by a very loyal friend for a fortieth surprise birthday party. From that one party we received several calls for more orders, and through our flyers and each succeeding delivery our business has grown beyond our hopes. We had just missed an insertion in the Yellow Pages and were in business almost a year before our small ad finally appeared. This accounts for a high percentage of our new business.

At the beginning, we sent many complimentary telegrams to strategic people and places. One of them was to the sports editor of our local newspaper chain. It was delivered to the office for the purpose of thanking him for his interest and fine coverage of amateur golf in our county. I had prepared a feature story concerning our business and Madelene accompanied our singer to this particular delivery. The sports editor, as we had hoped, was so pleased that he introduced Madelene to the Lifestyles Editor, to whom our "copy" was presented. Pictures were subsequently taken and an article appeared about us just prior to Mother's Day. Witty Ditty was off and running. Since then, we've received excellent publicity in all of our local print media as well as a feature in the Westchester Section of *The New York Times*. We've been called upon to write a skit for a local political luncheon, for a Town Club meeting, and for private parties. We've done telegrams for movie stars, TV personalities, rock groups, bank presidents, executives of every description, and love-lorn teenagers. We get calls from Canada, Puerto Rico, Mexico, and all over the United States. We delivered to a one-year-old baby and to a ninety-five-year-old great-grandma. We deliver to people who are alone in their homes and to parties of over 1,000 guests. Our singers have been lost in Westchester, New Jersey, Connecticut, and Long Island, but have always managed to deliver on time. We have reams of "It was the hit of the party" letters, and every Monday our phone rings with customers who thank us for the success of their party or the joy of some recipient.

We now have a roster of approximately twenty singers. They represent much of the joy of our work. High school seniors, college students, aspiring theatre people, some in their late twenties and early thirties. They all come to us with enthusiasm and eagerness. One gal traveled with a six-month-old infant in her car and always managed to have someone watch him during the time it took for her Witty Ditty delivery. We meet as a group every few months to rap and exchange stories, and we have enough material for volumes, just from these exchanges.

We arranged with all the major credit card companies to use their services, but discovered that by indicating that we have a prepayment policy, 90% of our telegrams are actually paid for before delivery. Our accounts receivable are rarely more than two or three weeks old. In the time we've been in business, we've had only one tough collection, and Madelene hung on to that one doggedly through small claims court, to the sheriff's office, to a lien on a house, all for $40. We finally collected $120, reimbursing us for court fees and time.

Working at home has its advantages and disadvantages. On the plus side, of course, is economics. We have been able to eliminate the cost of rent. There is an informality to working at home which we both love. We are able to run our personal lives and business together, without either interfering with the other. We are always covered. We can check the answering machine at odd hours, enroute to any chores we might have. We have the use of a piano, and stereo equipment, and an inventory of records and sheet music without having to make a tremendous investment. Our singers meet with us in a home atmosphere, where we serve refreshments and put them at ease. We have plenty of room for storage, and we look out on trees and gardens, a peaceful setting for inspiration.

On the other hand, we do not present the most sophisticated look to media sellers, nor to potential sources for publicity. That, however, is compensated for by our homey warmth and personal attention. Dinners are often interrupted, and we have received calls as late as midnight for emergency deliveries.

We can pretty much control our volume by the amount of advertising we do. At the beginning we never said "no" to an order. Each one was a challenge, regardless of where it was to be sent or when, and we struggled to get out many last minute requests. Now we can be more discriminating, although it is still rare that we refuse an order.

Emily Rosen and Madelene Fink
Creative Consultants

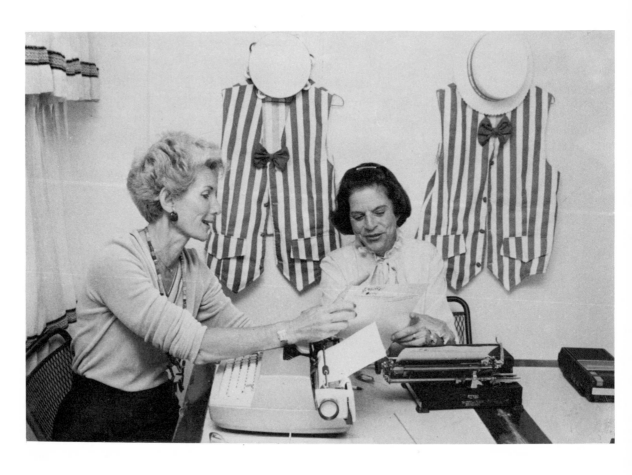

We find ourselves writing Witty Dittys wherever we go, and at all hours of the day—in the doctor's office, on the train, in the beauty shop. We were most productive on the now nostalgic gasoline lines. We whip them up before or after golf or tennis, sometimes during a day in the city, or during a break when I am attending a class.

But the Witty Ditty story is really in our logs, in the reports we get from our singers, in our telephone conversations with our contractors, in the experiences we encounter every day dealing with the joys of other people's lives. It is the man who asked us to tell his wife that he appreciated what a drag it was for her to be couped up with a measled two-year old, and to ask her to get a baby sitter so that they might have dinner alone that night—"and tell her I love her," he reminded us. It is the many who ask us to patch up fights they've had with loved ones; or the pre-nuptial telegram delivered in a blackout; or the songs we wrote pretending to be the recipient's psychiatrists; the ex-spouses communicating with ex-spouses; the couple we awakened at 7 A.M. with $100 worth of lox, bagels, and wine on a silver platter; telegrams delivered on a boat, in an airport, on a tennis court, at the first tee of a golf tournament, at a supermarket checkout counter; the overflow of loving sentiments we are asked to convey on Valentine's Day, Mother's Day, and Father's Day. And the list goes on.

Our business is a source of creative fulfillment, inspiration, and just plain laughs. Our customers are our friends, and we are their confidantes.

Our total investments were returned to us in one year. Every month our volume increases. Word of mouth and repeat customers are the staple of our business. Something exciting happens every day and mostly it is unpredictable. Madelene still plays championship golf. I play tennis and take courses, and I get to my Florida condominium at decent intervals. We still make holiday meals and get our kids off to college, arrange for the painter and the plumber and the TV repair man. We take days off to do our things, but we work crazy hours, pressured hours, concentrated hours, and we love it that way. We think we have it made because we've figured out how to have our cake and eat it too!

Newspaper in Education

by Peg Carey, Newspaper in
Education Consultant

What's a Newspaper in Education Consultant? The question is simple; the answer, a bit more complex. It is someone who has the zeal of a missionary, creative energy that won't quit, a confidence in self that makes tilting with windmills a pleasurable experience, and an unfaltering belief that the newspaper is one of the most dynamic teaching resources available to teachers today.

A few years ago with a newly acquired masters degree under my arm, I was hired as a reading resource teacher in a high school. There were 1600 students and 88 teachers in the school. I was given the mighty sum of $200 to set up a reading program. A pencil and paper isn't needed to figure out that my budget was somewhat limited.

Fortunately, one of the teachers was interested in doing a unit on communications and was incorporating the newspaper into this course of study. The newspaper was an unbelievable success. The students were reading without being told.

Many of these students had reading problems. I am not going to tell you that students who lacked basic reading skills picked up the paper and read, but students who had modest reading ability, 5th and 6th grade reading level, did read. They read because there were articles in the newspaper that interested them.

The local newspaper was willing to sell the papers at one-half the newsstand price. For a small amount of money, there was a new textbook for each student every day the papers arrived. During the second year of the program, the newspaper money was near depletion. Students were told there was a possibility that the newspapers would no longer be used due to lack of funds. They then gave whatever they could afford, sometimes a few pennies to keep the program going. Why? They were reading about the real world and about history that would not be in a textbook for a year or two. They were being shown how to be efficient readers and learned that news stories, editorials, and feature stories have different organizational patterns. They laughed at the political cartoons and found that learning the concepts of symbolism and satire did not have to be cut-and-dried. They learned to recognize fact from opinion and that propaganda is neither right nor wrong. Their vocabularies were expanded in a meaningful way. Words had more significance when read within the context of a real live situation. They wrote their own headlines to news stories for reinforcement in learning the main idea of the story. To put into practice all that had been learned, they printed their own newspaper.

They were being prepared to take their place in the adult world by becoming more aware of the role of a free press in a democratic society. They were using adult materials to learn reading skills. It made them feel good about themselves, and their grades improved.

The newspaper program that started at our school spread to other schools in the county, but our local paper still did not have a Newspaper in Education program. That was soon remedied. I went to the publisher and talked myself into a job as a Newspaper in Education Consultant.

I have my office at home where I keep track of the "administrivia." I tend to let it pile up and occasionally will hire someone to straighten out the piles of paper. I also develop workshop materials and keep up with other Newspaper in Education programs. There are close to 500 newspapers in the United States and Canada providing this educational service to their communities. Most of my time is spent in the field—I am now doing consulting work for the *Trenton Times,* have just finished teacher training sessions, have done consulting work for *The New York Times,* and have developed "Getting Ready to Read with *The New York Times,*" a tabloid showing parents how to use special sections of the paper to teach children beginning reading and math skills.

After 6 Secretarial Service

by Dora Back

I decided to go into the home typing business because of my experience in all phases of secretarial work. I had studied court reporting for many years but never became a court reporter because of the length of time necessary to acquire shorthand speed. Also, I had just read a book, titled *How to Make $25,000 a Year in a Home Typing Business,* that stirred my imagination. I had always wanted my own business. Since retirement is not too many years away, it seemed the right time to build something for retirement which would hold the fears of inflation, poverty, and boredom at bay.

I had a good secretarial job with a big company and many good benefits, but had no money saved to put into a business since we had just finished paying for my daughter's college education. There was the additional fear of "lack of cash" which plagues many businesses, so I decided to use my job as capital to start the business. This meant that it would not be possible to make any purchases for the business that could not be financed either out of the business or from my job. It also meant that there would be no need to draw from the business until it was strong enough to stand on its own feet. I knew that many new businesses fail because the demands made upon them are too great for them to bear. There is no such thing as "instant business." New businesses have to grow and become established. If they turn a profit after three years, that is considered good.

So, with all this in mind and with the help of an unpleasant boss who suddenly gave me an unwelcome "transfer," I said to myself, "No one is ever going to do that to me again!" What was I going to do about it? I decided to go into the secretarial business on a part-time basis. Having made this decision, I really felt terrible! Looking back to analyze what made me feel so bad, it was the closing of many doors—like the possibility of becoming a court reporter which had been a thought for over 20 years or the possibility of becoming a writer which had been a dream for even longer. Realistically, I had just so much energy. Once the decision was made to start a part-time business and work at a full-time job, be a wife and run a household, I would be lucky to have that much energy without expecting to have any surplus.

My business began on December 21, 1976, when I hired an answering service to take my daytime calls. I went through the Yellow Pages of my local phone book and sent out letters telling about my services to accountants, lawyers, architects, and engineers. This did not work very well; it took until March to get my first customer—a firm of architects still with me. Because there were colleges near me, I spent lunch hours walking around with thumbtacks and cards advertising my services, sticking them on any available bulletin boards. This brought business. My first year ended with about $4,000 gross. I considered that very good for a slow beginning!

One of the people I turned to for good advice was a man who ran a small temporary employment agency. He had employed my daughter while she was attending college. His good advice: "A letter only lasts about a week, but an ad in the Yellow Pages of the phone book lasts all year. It's your best advertisement."

I investigated this and found it necessary to change my telephone to a business phone, deposit $100, and meet the phone company's August deadline for insertion of listings. The new edition of the phone book with my listing in it came out in November of my first year. That was the best advertising investment made. My bill for Yellow Page listing has gone from around $5 to $60 a month, and it is money well spent. Perhaps 80% of my business comes from the Yellow Page listing.

My business began by offering a complete secretarial service which included dictation and typing of reports, letters, theses, manuscripts, and professional and technical typing. After typing some resumes, I decided I could do a much better job of writing them than those who wrote the ones that came across my typewriter and began to offer resume writing services. I had taken some very good personnel counseling courses and had worked for the Director of Industrial Relations in one of my previous jobs. My accumulated writing skills stood me in good stead. Since this service began, I have composed resumes for teachers, engineers, laboratory technicians, plant managers, medical technologists, managers, urban planners, computer operators, and others. The presentation of each client's information is a problem to be solved. I put a lot of time into writing a resume and have to be satisfied myself before considering it finished.

My clients have been very interesting; among them are lawyers, architects, engineers, scientists, sales managers, and industrial real estate firms. An author inscribed his book to me as a gift, and I have met people in interesting professions with whom I might never have come into contact in the usual course of my life.

My selling points are availability after business hours and during weekends, quality professional work done quickly, met deadlines, and reasonable charges current with the market in my area.

As time went by more equipment was added to my office; each piece was fully paid for when purchased. In this way, upon retirement, there will be no large unpaid items. At present, I have three types of word processors: IBM Mag Card I, IBM Memory 50, and QYX Intelligent Typewriter; three IBM Correcting Selectric II's; and eight dictating and transcribing machines. Two typewriters are in the homes of two women who type for me whenever there are jobs to give them. All typewriters are compatible. If changes or corrections are needed when the client comes to pick up work, the type for that job can be matched. These two women are paid as independent contractors and at the end of the year are given a 1099 form.

At the current cost of replacement, I have in the neighborhood of $15,000-$20,000 worth of equipment all paid for, and most of it by the business. With the word processors, automatic typing was added to my repertoire, and I do a very good business in employment search letters. I also have done programming on the QYX for a company with a compatible typewriter that wanted its purchase orders put into memory. If I had the time and energy, I would follow up on some of these different services, but at present, it is all I can do to keep up with the business at hand. Because of deadlines and other factors, it isn't that easy to give work out.

In the beginning, I was willing to take anything in the way of work. But as After 6 Secretarial grew and the Yellow Pages started bringing me a different type of business, I decided to get away from college typing. It is very trying, not too remunerative for the effort involved, and frequently frustrating dealing with students who are not always responsible or knowledgeable in the ways of the business world. It seems that when most business people start with a service like mine, they use it on a more or less regular basis, are grateful for good work, reasonable in their deadlines (sometimes), and understand that labor costs money.

As to the work—I do a great deal of the typing myself, make all of the planning, advertising, and purchasing decisions, and write resumes.

As mentioned, the end of the first year showed a cash intake of approximately $4,000; at the end of the second year, it had doubled to $8,000; and at the end of the third year, it was $12,000. The business showed a tiny profit at the end of the third year, but I have never taken any salary from the business. Each year, however, the business has contributed $750 to a Keogh retirement fund which is not currently taxed as income. When my husband lost his job and was ''retired'' for six months, the business also kept him pleasurably and profitably occupied. He had gone back to high school and had learned to type, and I taught him how to operate the IBM Memory typewriter. He was busy all day long. Now he is back to regular, full-time employment, and I have lost my typing help. I have also lost my package-taker-in-er, my maintenance-repairman-receiver and my taker-of-shoes-to-the-cobbler, but we are managing.

Many of the business benefits are intangible. The feeling of having created something that is wholly and totally my own is very satisfying. I am a good businesswoman, and it is satisfying to know that if I get very unhappy with my job, there is an alternative source of income. The knowledge that my husband can handle retirement, and that we have an ace-in-the-hole with income for our retirement years, is a great comfort. When people say, as they do all the time, ''How can you do it? I don't see how you can manage,'' my response is, ''It is mine, and I am motivated.''

Analysis of Letters and Questionnaires

For the past two years, women working from their homes have been writing letters describing their lives and home/work environments. We have compiled and analyzed several hundred of these fascinating letters and want to share the information gathered to date.

The ten top professions practiced from home, listed below in order of the number of women involved in each occupation are: Artists, Craftspersons, Writers, Consultants, Teachers, Advertising Agents, Attorneys, Salespersons, Therapists, and Secretaries/Typists. Horticulturists, Insurance Brokers, Interior Designers, and Manufacturers are next on our list out of a total of 111 occupations.

Ruth E. Delong
Artist
Photographer:
© *Terri P. Tepper 1977*

One-third of the women who wrote letters accompanying our questionnaires commented on their marital status. Of these, 80% are married, 20% are not married—and of this latter group, 3% are widowed and 12% are divorced or separated.

Many women wrote about their families. Their children's ages vary from infancy to adults in their forties. The women who have written on this subject have between one and seven children. 13% have one child; 33%, two children; 18%, three children; and 10%, four or more. Twenty-six percent have children, but did not relate how many.

The age brackets are as follows: 1-5 years, 18%; 6-10 years, 23%; 11-15 years, 26%; 16-20 years, 12%; and over 21 years, 21%. Of the respondents mentioning their ages, the largest group was in their forties.

In instances where families are supportive, the at-home business has had a much better opportunity to thrive. The years in business for individuals range from under one to over twenty-one. The percentages indicated run as follows: between 0-2 years, 18%; 2-5, 52%; 5-10, 15%; over 10, 15%.

The income stated ranges between pin money and $150,000 per year. The definition of success varies according to each letter but could be summarized by stating that the majority of women feel that earning a decent income (which varies according to each individual), combined with the ability to integrate work and home style harmoniously, is equivalent to success.

Reasons women have stated for wanting to work from their homes are numerous, but the main ones indicate: mothers are anxious to be present when their children return from school, adults find it necessary to be physically present to care for elderly parents, low overhead, no need to commute, and having materials readily accessible at all hours of the day and night.

Because the information gathered until now has fascinated and in some instances surprised us, we've decided to conduct a more comprehensive study. Included in this book you will find a questionnaire. If you are a woman working from home, please take the time to answer as many questions as possible and return the completed form. We hope to collect in-depth statistics through these questions and will compile the results and publish them in our next edition.

"I converted one level of my home to my office. I have a waiting room, two offices, and a bathroom. Also separate entry."

Hypnotist

"After birth of child, moved operation to my home where convenience and comfort outweighed outside-office advantages."

Attorney

"My definition of success? Well, I guess it's just the way each person feels about him or her self. I can't think of any cut-off point in terms of type of job or income level or even competency. I suppose I feel successful most of the time but never stop trying to raise my work to a higher level."

Music Teacher

Directory by State and Occupation

Wendy Krueger
Glass Blower
Photographer:
© *Terri P. Tepper 1978*

■ California

Barbara Abercrombie
2121 Palos Verdes Drive West
Palos Verdes, CA 90274
213-378-7374
Writer.

Nancy G. Binzen
The PR Center
253 Carl Street
San Francisco, CA 94117
415-566-6281
Public Relations Consultant.

Donna L. Cline
Cline-Garcia Day Care
373 Bowfin Street
Foster City, CA 94404
415-574-4670
Drop-in day care.

Andi Dalton
P.O. Box 222
14900 Canyon #2 Road
Rio Nido, CA 95471
707-869-0475
Rosewood crochet hooks, pens, and
chopsticks.

Ruth M. Ferm
3425 Alabama Street
San Diego, CA 92104
714-291-4576
Typing; bookkeeping.

Phyllis Garcia
Cline-Garcia Day Care
373 Bowfin Street
Foster City, CA 94404
415-574-4670
Drop-in day care.

Judith Gordon
Judith Gordon Associates
1111 Sierra Vista Way
Lafayette, CA 94549
415-284-9360
Records Management Consultant.

Sally Gradinger
800 Columbia Drive
San Mateo, CA 94402
415-343-6530
Interior Designer.

Gwen Haney-Webster
2921 Merian Drive
San Bruno, CA 94066
415-583-5435
San Francisco Street Artist—sand
paintings in glass.

Katherine Lee
Precision Unlimited
772 Faxon Avenue
San Francisco, CA 94112
415-239-6611
Proofreads and makes indexes for
book publishers.

Sunbow O'Brien
535 Hugo Street
San Francisco, CA 94122
415-731-7034
Watercolor buttons and framed
paintings.

Caryl Winter
Presentations with Impact
400 South Beverly Drive — Suite 312
Beverly Hills, CA 90212
213-933-0933
Conducts workshops on the art of
business writing, making effective
presentations, and developing policies
and procedures; Lecturer.

■ Connecticut

Aileen Bott
28 Rapids Road
Stamford, CT 06905
203-322-2120
Real Estate Broker.

Sandra S. Farrell
Peep Toad Mill
East Killingly, CT 06243
203-774-8967
Teams up with husband, Richard Farrell, creating contemporary stoneware
and porcelain. Work has been exhibited in numerous juried art festivals,
including Northeast Craft Fair in
Rhinebeck, NY, as well as museums,
galleries and shops. In 1979, with
grant aid from Connecticut Commission on the Arts, the Farrells designed
and developed a technique for forming dimensional tiles using a vacuum
process and porcelain.

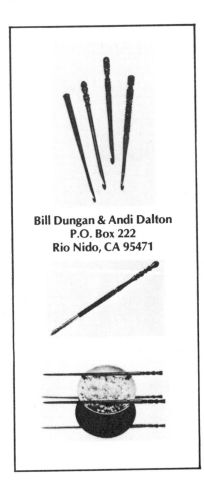

Bill Dungan & Andi Dalton
P.O. Box 222
Rio Nido, CA 95471

Marjorie E. Fox
Craftsperson

Marjorie E. Fox
Medieval Brass Rubbing Centre
Route 203, Box 299
Windham Center, CT 06280
203-423-2785
Craftsperson and Lecturer; conducts
workshops on brass rubbing; also
operates public relations business ad-
vising artists and craftspeople.

Marie Louise Gill
Gill Imports, Inc.
P.O. Box 73
Ridgefield, CT 06877
203-438-7409
Importer of fine handicrafts from
India: crewel fabrics and oriental rugs
sold wholesale and retail by mail
order.

Elayne Perry
11 Robin Lane
Milford, CT 06460
Avon Representative; Babysitter.

■ District of Columbia

Jacqueline K. Browner
JK Browner Associates
3712 Windom Place, NW
Washington, DC 20016
202-686-1696
Specialist in several areas of communication—public information,
marketing, public relations, and
publicity.

Marty Thomson
1933 Biltmore Street, NW
Washington, DC 20009
202-462-1285
Writing and editing—mainly for
business publications.

■ Idaho

Donna Lee Spencer
Route #1, Box 212A
Fruitland, ID 83619
208-452-3372
Drapery workrooms.

■ Illinois

Elizabeth Carr
664 Belleforte Avenue
Oak Park, IL 60302
312-848-3340
Antique Appraiser, Collector, Lecturer, and Writer. President of International Society of Fine Arts Appraisers, Ltd. Member: Chicago Rug
Society.

Maria Fiore
Latinos Unlimited
1701 West 69th Street
Chicago, IL 60636
312-922-0579
Film Producer.

Judith Hendershot
The Ceiling Lady
1408 Main Street
Evanston, IL 60202
312-475-6411
Stencilled decorations for ceilings,
walls, and floors.

Coralee Smith Kern
Maid-to-Order, Inc.
224 South Michigan Avenue
Chicago, IL 60604
312-939-6490
Serves homeowners, businesses, corporations, charitable organizations, building management firms, foreign consulates, trade associations, and moving companies with maid, party, vacation, nursing and companion services.

"I am single. Pottery is my only income source. I am thrilled with doing my favorite thing for a living and don't know if I could bear to work for someone else. I like being able to take vacations when I want and to set my own hours."

Craftsperson

Sharon A. Morgan
Sharon A. Morgan and Associates
4840 South King Drive
Chicago, IL 60615
312-266-0383
Communications, public relations, resource development, and specialized writing.

Terri P. Tepper
261 Kimberly
Barrington, IL 60010
312-381-2113
Photographer; Lecturer. Executive Director of Center for a Woman's Own Name and Consumer Credit Project, Inc. Counsels women on credit and name rights. Coauthor with mother, Nona Dawe Tepper, of *The New Entrepreneurs: Women Working from Home.*

Shirley Thomas-Hersh
3415 West Foster, #206
Chicago, IL 60625
312-583-6044
Advertising Copywriter; Guitar Teacher.

■ Kentucky

Barbara Gordon
2624 McCoy Way
Louisville, KY 40205
502-451-4150
Sells invitations, napkins, stationery, and accessories.

■ Maryland

Jill Groce
10904 Bucknell Drive, #1112
Silver Spring, MD 20902
301-942-0544
Writing, editing, and research.

Alison W. Heckler
5812 Maryhurst Drive
Hyattsville, MD 20782
301-559-6489
Editorial support services—editing, writing, indexing, and proofreading.

Claire Kincaid
13316 Old Forge Road
Silver Spring, MD 20904
301-384-2495
Editor.

Claudia Jan LaCovey
13701 Old Columbia Pike
Silver Spring, MD 20904
301-384-2856
Stained glass Artist.

■ Massachusetts

Katharine Barr
278 Elm Street
North Reading, MA 01864
617-664-2636
Advertising Consultant/Writer.

Peggy Z. Ehrman
Biblio Services
83 Bertwell Road
Lexington, MA 02173
617-862-8367
Sets up and maintains libraries for business and industry; also information research and retrieval by traditional methods or computer data bases.

Eva Glase
Words and Images
62 Turning Mill Road
Lexington, MA 02173
617-861-0484
Communication services—writing, editing, design, promotion, and public relations.

Dr. Susan H. Holton
Creative Potential Development
204 Central Street
Framingham, MA 01701
617-877-6278
Consultation; facilitation of groups focusing on significant life issues and problem solving.

Roz Shirley
4 Snyder Road
Medfield, MA 02052
617-359-2944
Fiber Artist—freestanding and dimensional wall pieces. Work exhibited in several juried shows—most recently at 1980 Northeast Craft Fair in Rhinebeck, NY, and in one- and two-artist and group shows in Massachusetts and California. Elected to Artists Advisory Council for Fiber Art Center in Boston. Member: American Crafts Council, Handweavers Guild of America and Massachusetts Association for the Crafts.

Erika Tauber
Words and Images
62 Turning Mill Road
Lexington, MA 02173
617-861-0484
Communication services—writing, editing, design, promotion, and public relations.

■ Michigan

Julie Shaw
Address Withheld
Birmingham, MI 48009
313-642-2808
Jewelry Designer. Work exhibited extensively in invitational shows, juried art festivals, galleries, and shops throughout U.S. Among many awards: Best in Show, First in Fine Crafts, and Purchase Award from Jordan Marsh at Lowe Museum Art Festival, Coral Gables, Florida, in 1978. Member: University of Michigan Artists and Craftsmens Guild, American Crafts Council, and Michigan Silversmiths Guild.

Susan C. Wright
909 Duncan Street
Ann Arbor, MI 48103
313-663-6015
Handwoven rugs, blankets, and
scarves.

■ New Jersey

Sylvia Allen
P.O. Box 272
Fair Haven, NJ 07701
201-741-8658
Responsible for design, development,
and/or implementation of marketing
programs for local and national accounts, including media selection and
placement, public relations, meeting
planning, employee communications,
dealer relations, training, and
promotion including trade shows and
exhibits. Editor of *Monmouth Magazine.* Author of *How to Prepare a
Production Budget for Film and
Videotape,* TAB Books, 1973 and *A
Manager's Guide to Audio-Visuals,*
McGraw-Hill, Inc., 1979.

Roz Shirley
Fiber Artist
Photographer: Ken Haywood

Jeannine Anderson
66 Hillside Road
Sparta, NJ 07871
201-729-6976
Rents condominium apartment on
Kaanapali Beach in western Maui,
Hawaii to vacationers.

Joan Arbeiter
58 Elm Avenue
Metuchen, NJ 08840
201-549-8917
Paints commissioned portraits; teaches
painting and drawing.

Fran Avallone
80 Hilltop Boulevard
East Brunswick, NJ 08816
201-254-8665
State Coordinator of Right to Choose,
abortion rights organization. Sends
out newsletters, writes literature for
use by schools and groups; speaks to
high school health and social studies
classes, college classes, women's and
church groups; lobbies legislators,
both state and national; sets up
booths at conventions.

Nancy T. Baarens
481 Tappan Road
Norwood, NJ 07648
201-768-5010
Oil paintings—horses and landscapes.

Dora Back
After 6 Secretarial Service
54 Johnson Street
Fords, NJ 08863
201-738-4670
Complete dictation and typing service, reports, letters, legal documents,
manuscripts, automatic typing, and
writing resumes.

Katherine F. Bailey
48 Baldwin Avenue
Somerset, NJ 08873
201-469-0464
Senior Sales Director for Mary Kay
Cosmetics.

Margaret L. Baller
226 Blake Avenue
Somerset, NJ 08873
201-246-1666
Attorney.

Stella Bari
716 Allen Avenue
Vineland, NJ 08360
609-691-4483
Ladies alterations.

Eleanor C. Beck
The Doll Dressmaker
56 Ronald Court
Ramsey, NJ 07446
201-327-2271
Restoration and repair; research for
the purpose of making authentic
costumes; also lectures about
America's First Ladies, with authentically dressed First Lady dolls.

Joyce Becker
Nourishing Nibbles
481 Grove Avenue
Edison, NJ 08817
201-549-4457
Health food snack service for college
campuses, schools, and private
individuals.

Peggy Bendel
113 Chestnut Avenue
Bogota, NJ 07603
201-343-3613
Free-lance Writer/Editor.

Rosemary Bennett
512 Middlesex Avenue
Colonia, NJ 07067
201-382-3412
Beauty Consultant for Mary Kay
Cosmetics.

Linda Benzaia
704 Wilson Court
River Vale, NJ 07675
201-666-7476
Personalized handpainted children's
shirts; custom orders.

Judy Caden
(201) 731-6461 · (201) 889-2182

Loretta Blessing
2931 Centre Street
Merchantville, NJ 08109
609-665-2353
Creates gold and silver jewelry; shows
at weekend fairs.

Tina Bobker
Rainbow Artisans, Inc.
19 Troy Drive
Livingston, NJ 07039
201-533-9081
Manufactures children's accessories.

Honey Bodenheimer
Country Crafts
17 Maple Stream Road
East Windsor, NJ 08520
609-443-3716
Candles, macramé, spice ropes, hobby horses, Christmas ornaments; also
operates crafts consignment shop;
teaches crafts to children.

Audrey J. Boerum
Ideas Unlimited
72 McNomee Street
Oakland, NJ 07436
201-337-7660
201-337-6449
Free-lance Writer for editorial and
promotional services.

Evelyn C. Breeden
182 Ridgewood Avenue
Glen Ridge, NJ 07028
201-743-8445
Paints in oil and watercolor; also Lab
Technician in husband's home office.

Barbara Broadbent
P.O. Box 145
Egg Harbor, NJ 08215
609-965-5107
Handcrafted leather goods.

Ellen Bruck
26 Park Street
Tenafly, NJ 07670
201-871-0832
Interior Designer.

Judy Caden
Judy Caden Marionettes
21 Glen Road
West Orange, NJ 07052
201-731-6461
201-889-5328
Performs at museums, clubs, libraries,
and home birthday parties; conducts
workshops in puppetry and crafts; exhibits her sculptures. Among other
awards, won Grumbacher Award for
Contribution to the Arts and
Curator's Prize for sculpture at Hunterdon, NJ Art Center.

Rosemary Cafasso
14 Morris Avenue
Riverdale, NJ 07457
201-839-1203
Collection Agent.

Anne R. Cantor
203 Second Avenue
Bradley Beach, NJ 07720
201-776-7088
Etchings and collographs. Has had
several one-artist shows and participa-
ted in numerous group exhibitions.
Work is represented in permanent
museum collections and has received
purchase prizes—the most recent,
National Association of Women Artists Graphics Award in 1974. Member: Artists Equity of NJ and National Association of Women Artists.

Peg Carey
771 Princeton-Kingston Road
Princeton, NJ 08540
609-921-1526
Demonstrates how to use the
newspaper as a textbook to teach
reading skills through presentations
and workshops for teachers,
newspaper personnel, and community
adult groups..

Barbara H. Carlbon
RD 1, Pattenburg Road
Pattenburg, NJ 08802
201-735-5764
Artist.

Laura E. Chenicek
42 Warren Court
South Orange, NJ 07079
201-763-7088
Her paintings have appeared in
numerous one-artist and group shows
since 1974.

E. Gioia Cipriano-Marciano
6 Gregory Avenue
West Orange, NJ 07052
201-731-6452
Attorney. Legal practice limited to
real estate and estates—by appointment only.

Nancy Coggins
3032 Cheesequake Road
Parlin, NJ 08859
201-727-3829
Creates crafts in a variety of materials; Road Tester of cars and mopeds;
Writer for cars and crafts magazines.

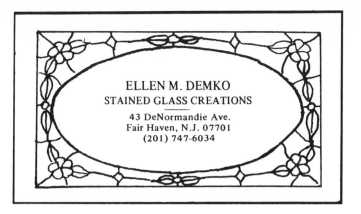

ELLEN M. DEMKO
STAINED GLASS CREATIONS
43 DeNormandie Ave.
Fair Haven, N.J. 07701
(201) 747-6034

Dorothy Cohen
5 Mountain Way South
West Orange, NJ 07052
201-736-4525
Educational Researcher.

Susan E. Collins
Through the Looking Glass
    Enterprises
32-33 Rockledge Road
Montville, NJ 07045
201-335-8748
Wholesale manufacturer of handmade quilted items.

Diane Colon
379 Lincoln Avenue
Cliffside Park, NJ 07010
201-943-6570
Creates one-of-a-kind three-
dimensional ric-rac flowers on
gingham in shadow box frames; also
Christmas ornaments.

"I love freedom of setting own hours

and find the selling/soliciting

aspect the most difficult....I

believe in scheduling, lists, and

strong self-discipline."

Marketing Consultant

Anne Connolly
94 Wells Court
Demarest, NJ 07627
201-768-0254
Has exhibited her work in numerous
one-artist shows throughout New
Jersey and has received over 100
awards in watercolor. Member:
American Artist Professional League
and Pascack, Hackensack, and Ridgewood Art Associations.

Anna Continos
315 Willowbrook Drive
North Brunswick, NJ 08902
201-821-7346
Has exhibited her paintings in
N.J.W.C.S. juried watercolor shows
at the Monmouth Museum and Morris Museum of Arts and Sciences;
winner of a number of awards in
1979, including Best of Show in
Dunellen-Greenbrook Art Show, first
place in Plainfield Festival of Art,
and first place in Franklin's Outdoor
Art Show. Member: New Jersey
Watercolor Society.

Penny Couphos
164 Hillside Avenue
Chatham, NJ 07928
201-635-5474
Distributes Shaklee natural food supplements, personal care and home
care products.

Annette B. Crema
Bardouille-Crema and Associates
P.O. Box 276
Edgewater, NJ 07020
201-224-2746
201-327-7462
Personal and Professional Develop-
ment Consultant.

Linda M. Cromarty
213 Central Avenue
West Caldwell, NJ 07006
201-228-3485
Horticultural interior design.

Elizabeth K. Cummins
The Cummins Garden
22 Robertsville Road
Marlboro, NJ 07746
201-536-2591
Retail mail-order plant business.

Ann M. Davis
157 Booth Avenue
Englewood, NJ 07631
201-567-8857
Makes silver jewelry: earrings, pins,
pendants, bracelets.

Vivian J. Day
1 Lincoln Place, Apt. 17C
North Brunswick, NJ 08902
201-297-2490
Professional typing.

Ann De Falco
102 Fairmount Avenue
Chester, NJ 07903
201-879-5556
Artist; Calligrapher; Sign Painter;
researches and creates coats of arms;
restores old paintings.

Ellen M. Demko
Stained Glass Creations
43 DeNormandie Avenue
Fair Haven, NJ 07701
201-747-6034
Designs and executes stained glass
articles.

Doris G. Dempster
35 Monmouth Junction Road
Dayton, NJ 08520
201-329-3092
Accountant; Bookkeeper.

Dee dePeralta
1387 Alvarado Avenue
Lakewood, NJ 08701
201-367-6697
Sells life and health insurance to individual families or small businesses.

Fran Derlinga
The Paperdoll
27 Heather Lane
Mahwah, NJ 07430
201-529-4081
Interior Decorator; Wallpaper
Hanger.

Sally Diaz
28 North 23rd Street
East Orange, NJ 07017
201-673-3245
Paints portraits, figures, landscapes.

Ursula S. Dinshah
513 Old Harding Highway
Malaga, NJ 08328
609-694-3639
Dried flower arrangements, weed
wreaths, pressed flower pictures,
framed wedding invitations, straw
weavings; also teaches her craft.

Pat Dixon
Face to Face
422 Beatrice Street
Teaneck, NJ 07666
201-836-5930
Sells color portrait business cards.

Carole Dlugasch
Rainbow Artisans, Inc.
35 Old Indian Road
West Orange, NJ 07052
201-731-6721
Manufactures children's accessories.

Rochelle H. Dubois
Merging Media
59 Sandra Circle, A-3
Westfield, NJ 07090
201-232-7224
Poetry therapy and creative counseling; Writer.

Pearl Ehrlich
233 Vivien Court
Paramus, NJ 07652
201-262-4810
Free-lance Writer; Public Relations
Consultant.

A. Valerie Eichen
Mayan Designs
120 North 3rd Avenue
Highland Park, NJ 08904
201-246-4007
Imports and wholesales accessories
and apparel.

Emily M. Eldridge
Copy Cats Limited
91 Main Street
Metuchen, NJ 08840
201-548-2369
Antique photographs: copied,
printed, brown-toned, or restored;
black-and-white and color portraits;
school portraits; transparencies;
duplication.

Judy Engstrom
216 White Horse Pike, Apt. 203
Collings Wood, NJ 08107
609-858-6141
Marketing management plans.

Kathleen Condon Enz
RD 1, Hidden Hollow Farm
Washington, NJ 07882
201-689-2306
Architectural Landscaper.

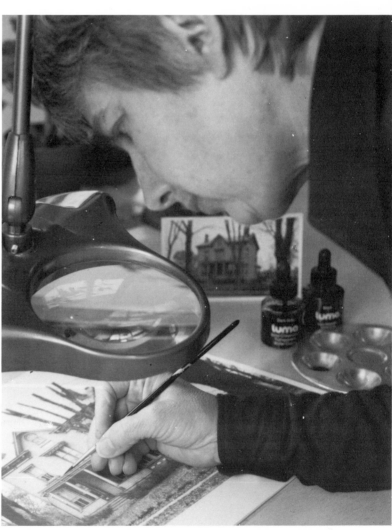

Emily Eldridge
Photographer
Self-Portrait

Sara Eyestone
20 Blair Court
Ocean Township, NJ 07712
201-922-4520
Painter and Textile Designer who
works with a batik wax-resist process
she developed in 1961 and has mar-
keted throughout the U.S. in
museums, galleries, and libraries; also
Lecturer; founder of the National
Association of Professional Artists and
Designer Craftspeople; included in
the Rockefeller Center Tribute to
American Women who have distin-
guished themselves with innovations
in their field. Member: American
Crafts Council.

Edith Fava
Pinch-Hitters, Inc.
4308 Cottage Avenue
North Bergen, NJ 07047
201-866-8938
212-662-4270
Singing telegrams, cookiegrams, balloongrams, special events.

Susan Feld
Paper Partners
33 Mistletoe Drive
Matawan, NJ 07747
201-583-5444
Personalized stationery; invitations,
announcements, lucite, personalized
jewelry, gifts.

'Workplace: consists of two desks...one

for thinking and one for doing,

with the advantage of alternating

from one to the other readily

with no-one to overseer my incen-

tive, keeping at my own pace,

where age and health are no

criteria for self-fulfillment.''

Inventor

Audree Feldman
Paper Partners
33 Mistletoe Drive
Matawan, NJ 07747
201-583-4654
Personalized stationery, invitations,
announcements, lucite, personalized
jewelry, gifts.

Name Withheld
Ferne Sales and Manufacturing Co.
P.O. Box 113 TCB
West Orange, NJ 07052
201-731-0967
Mail-order business; manufactures advertising specialty items: hand-
screened T-shirts, tote bags, bumper
stickers, buttons.

Kay Fialkoff
27-09 Romaine Street
Fair Lawn, NJ 07410
201-791-4320
Paintings: inks, watercolors, oils;
poetry readings and workshops; Producer of cultural events.

Elvira A. Fiducia
26 Collinwood Road
Maplewood, NJ 07040
201-763-3249
Oil paintings and enamels on copper;
also licensed Marriage Counselor.

Veona R. Finkelstein
22 Joline Road
Kendall Park, NJ 08824
201-297-1181
Advertising Representative for *The
Christian Science Monitor.*

Daria Finn
Finnishing Touch
164 Sargeant Avenue
Clifton, NJ 07013
201-473-1499
All-women painting and contracting
company—interior and exterior
work, including wallpaper and wall
graphics.

Lori Fischman
5 Knoll Terrace
West Caldwell, NJ 07006
201-575-9241
One-of-a-kind functional and/or
sculptural ceramics: teapots, vases,
bowls, weedpots, wall plaques. Member: N.J. Designer Craftsmen, First
Mountain Crafters.

Isabel Bogorad Fleiss
WomanSurance Advisory Services
P.O. Box 3034
Wayne, NJ 07470
201-956-1085
Insurance Broker; Executive Director
of WomanSurance and Phone Power
School of Insurance for People with
Disabilities, whose purpose is to
train, license, and employ individuals
to work from their homes as commis-
sioned sales representatives; also
Marketing Consultant to insurance in-
dustry.

Barbara Flood
421 Plainsfield Road
Edison, NJ 08817
201-549-6470
Typesetter.

Nina Forrest
246 Maple Street
Haworth, NJ 07641
201-387-1890
Vacuformed signs—stock items or
individually designed, professionally
crafted.

Hanna Fox
175 Hamilton Avenue
Princeton, NJ 08540
609-924-2990
Writes, tutors writers, and teaches
writing workshops. Books: *A Prism:
Fanny, Leonard, Elaine* and *Dorothea
Lynde Dix: Her Contribution to Mental Health.* Has also written
numerous short stories, poems,
essays, magazine and newspaper
articles.

Fern Galant
Grand Detours
P.O. Box 143
Tenafly, NJ 07670
201-871-0088
Designs and operates weekend or day
trips for private groups or for fund
raisers to galleries, gardens, estates,
gourmet restaurants, museums, and
cultural experiences.

Adrienne Gallo
JAM Co.
31 Winding Trail
Mahwah, NJ 07430
201-327-7858
Designs and coordinates a home
decorating line for resale.

LaVerne Hunt Gallob
19 Mac Arthur Avenue
Closter, NJ 07624
201-768-3057
Private piano lessons; music classes for
children.

Name Withheld
123 South Munn Avenue
East Orange, NJ 07018
201-675-0090
Free-lance Writer for ads, commercials, booklets.

Alma W. Garrison
435 Washington Avenue
Linden, NJ 07036
201-486-0079
Porcelain Painter; charcoal drawings,
pastels, oils.

Patti Genack
260 Park Avenue
Rutherford, NJ 07070
201-933-0724
Handpainted lithographs; handmade,
one-of-a-kind puppets and dolls.

"I take orders from stores and participate

in shows which effectively do this.

I have no set hours and often

find myself working at night and

find working at home most con-

venient for this. My studio used

to be away from home, and I

moved it to my home to facilitate

this working habit I learned I

have....I'm seldom bored and

have learned to do other things

when I find it impossible to work

at stained glass (such as thera-

peutic gardening) without guilt. I

feel life is too short to depend on

Saturday and Sunday as days for

recreation."

Craftsperson

Miriam Gershen
1 Norwood Road
Springfield, NJ 07081
201-376-5772
Repairs and restores antiques and objects of value in china, glass, and
porcelain.

Vera M.R. Giger
20 Garber Square, Apt. C2
Ridgewood, NJ 07450
201-447-4663
Printmaking by stencil method.

Norma Glessner
24 Evergreen Road
Somerset, NJ 08873
201-249-5038
Headline Typesetter.

Sylvia Glickman
15 Holly Street
Somerset, NJ 08873
201-249-9317
Attorney.

Trudy Glucksberg
14 Aiken Avenue
Princeton, NJ 08540
609-924-2061
Free-lance Illustrator and Printmaker.

Flo-Ann Goerke
Georgia Road
Freehold, NJ 07728
201-462-2785
Home repairs.

Marna Gold
Gold 'n Dot, Inc.
46 Alpine Drive
Closter, NJ 07624
201-768-8927
"Eat Your Heart Out"—inexpensive,
delicious, all-occasion boxed feasts;
also theme parties with coordinated
invitations, decorations, food,
flowers, music, serving staff, and
entertainment.

Rhoda S. Gold
35 Francis Place
Caldwell, 07006
201-226-7837
Psychotherapy, marriage and family
counseling.

Toni L. Goldfarb
586 Teaneck Road
Teaneck, NJ 07666
201-836-5030
Freelance Writer—medicine and
social sciences.

Susette Gould-Malloy
Jasmine Artisans
475 North 5th Street
Newark, NJ 07107
201-483-5554
Quiltwork, applique, motifs, and
assorted paraphernalia for children.

Joyce Graichen
P.O. Box 42
Seaside Heights, NJ 08751
201-793-1395
Cake decorating.

Cecilia Greco
611 North Washington Avenue
Dunellen, NJ 08812
201-968-7037
Sells Mary Kay Cosmetics.

Jean Greenbaum
57 County Road
Demarest, NJ 07627
201-768-5096
Organizes, catalogs, classifies, preserves, and restores books; also advises on acquisitions, shelving, and
technical problems of small private or
institutional book collections.

Barbara J. Guile
12 Farrington Ave.
Closter, NJ 07624
201-767-8075
Types intermediate copy manuscript
for Translation Department, American Bible Society.

Claire Gulman
Nourishing Nibbles
481 Grove Avenue
Edison, NJ 08817
201-494-1266
Health food snack service for college
campuses, schools, and private
individuals.

Marilou Hamer
Discovery Art Galleries
1191 Valley Road
Clifton, NJ 07013
201-746-2291
Art Dealer.

Suzanne Haviv
72 Ross Avenue
Demarest, NJ 07627
201-768-2665
Amway Distributor.

Faith Heisler
Address Withheld
Paramus, NJ 07652
Fiber Artist.

Rose Hertzberg
27 Buckingham Drive
Ramsey, NJ 07446
201-327-5288
Her work in oil, watercolor, and collage exhibited nationally and interna-
tionally in numerous group and one-
artist exhibitions, in private and
public collections. Most recent award:
Irene Sickle Feist Award, 1977,
National Association of Women
Artists. Member: Artist's Equity of
N.J., National Association of Women
Artists, Art Students League, Painters
and Sculptors Society of N.J.

Sharon Hodges
1315 East 7th Street
Plainfield, NJ 07062
201-753-0514
Poet.

Dot Hofmann
Gold 'n Dot, Inc.
120 Maplewood Avenue
Bogota, NJ 07603
201-342-1984
"Eat Your Heart Out"—inexpensive,
delicious all-occasion boxed feasts;
also theme parties with coordinated
invitations, decorations, food,
flowers, music, serving staff, and
entertainment.

Roslyn Hollander
5 Dogwood Drive
Newton, NJ 07860
201-383-4966
Artist.

Luz Holvenstot
100 Naughright Road
Long Valley, NJ 07853
Solar Consultant.

Ellyn Hopkins
La Chariettes
2400 Hudson Terrace
Fort Lee, NJ 07024
201-592-1535
Private valet parking service for weddings, graduations, Bar Mitzvahs,
parties.

Marian Howard
Fine Ethnic Prints
150 Woodlawn Avenue
Jersey City, NJ 07305
Original watercolor, pencil drawing,
silkscreen, etching, collages, mixed-
media works, and hand-sculptured
pieces.

Marian Howard
Artist

Judy Ignall
127 Howard Terrace
Leonia, NJ 07605
201-461-8223
Cooking lessons to children and
adults.

Theodora Ilowitz
15 Central Avenue
Demarest, NJ 07627
Exhibited work in New York, New
Jersey, and Illinois. Most recent award
from The Painters and Sculptors
Society of NJ, 1979.

Janet Indick
428 Sagamore Avenue
Teaneck, NJ 07666
201-836-0211
Welded steel sculpture shown in one-
artist and group exhibitions, in galleries and museums, and in numerous
private collections in the U.S. and
Israel. Fellowship: NJ State Council
on the Arts, 1981. Most recent
awards: Sculpture Prizes at National
Association of Painters and Sculptors,
1978, 1980.

Nancy Irons
337 Chestnut Street
Audubon, NJ 08106
609-546-4812
Makes original sterling jewelry.

Barbara Isaac
Riding High Farms
P.O. Box 229, Route 526
Allentown, NJ 08501
609-259-3884
Horses boarded, sold, trained, and exhibited; English and Western instruction; riding instruction for the handicapped.

Doranne Jacobson
290 Demarest Avenue
Closter, NJ 07624
201-767-7241
Anthropological Consultant, Photographer, and Researcher.

Marion E. Josephson
650 Prospect AVenue
West Orange, NJ 07052
201-325-8366
Potter, Designer of creative note paper, Bread Baker. Member: First Mountain Crafters of N.J.

Sarah Kaplan, R.N., M.S., C.S.
B17 David's Court
Dayton, NJ 08810
201-329-8007
Clinical consultation and psychotherapy.

Elizabeth Marsha Kendall
1620 Monmouth Avenue
Lakewood, NJ 08701
201-364-5571
"Clementine, The Classroom Clown"—creates and performs skill skits; children's educational dramatic programs for schools, organizations, and children's parties.

Wendy King, R.N., M.S.
53 Kossuth Street
Somerset, NJ 08873
201-828-9317
Nutritional awareness and self-improvement courses; health-related services.

Yvette M.L. King
22 Ernest Street
Nutley, NJ 07110
201-667-6756
Party planning, shopping, fashion counseling, research, management assistance, travel arrangements.

Chana Ann Kirschner
18 Oakcrest Road
West Orange, NJ 07052
201-736-1960
Wall hangings, soft sculpture, and wearable art: batik and direct dye on fabric, stitched and stuffed. Invitational shows: Society of Arts and Crafts, Boston; Images in Fiber and Metal, Nabisco, Inc. Headquarters, Hanover, NJ; Fiber Works, YM-YWHA, West Orange, NJ. Juried exhibitions in NY, NJ, and Washington, D.C., including Northeast Craft Fair—Bennington, VT, and Rhinebeck, NY, 1970-1977, Winners' Circle 1970, 1973, 1974. One-artist shows in NY and NJ.

Carolyn S. Jacoby
Carolyn's Curiousities
194 John Street
Englewood, NJ 07631
201-871-4970
Sells antique photographs and prints.

Jan Johnson
1339 Highland Avenue
Plainfield, NJ 07060
201-753-5417
Media Consultant; Amway Distributor.

Margaret W. Johnson
Figure Mates, Inc.
P.O. Box 218
East Hanover, NJ 07936
201-386-9314
Manufactures skating apparel.

Indian Women Grinding Wheat
Photographer: Doranne Jacobson

Rhoda Kelner
Fill 'Em Up
47 Jamaica Street
Edison, NJ 08817
201-549-8044
Lucite and ceramic gift items filled with nuts, fruits, and candy.

Susan Kelner
Fill 'Em Up
47 Jamaica Street
Edison, NJ 08817
201-549-8044
Lucite and ceramic gift items filled with nuts, fruits, and candy.

Ruth M. Krieger
33 Winding Way
West Orange, NJ 07052
201-731-5644
Painter; Printmaker.

Carol Kroupa
Carol's Alterations and Sewing
23 Roberta Drive
Howell, NJ 07731
201-458-2915
Custom sewing and alterations.

Marjorie Shaw Kubach
308 Lacey Drive
New Milford, NJ 07646
201-261-1650
Painter; Printmaker.

"I work for myself because I enjoy being
totally responsible for what I do
and produce. My former
job . . . was very much that way,
but the ultimate power rested
with someone else, which I found
frustrating. I enjoy the freedom
of self-employment and find the
hardest aspect of it is self-
motivation. My former job was
largely self-motivating, but the
tasks were much more defined. I
work best under pressure and
have learned to set up deadlines
for myself."

Craftsperson

Betsy Kuga
Beihon Trade Co.
406 3rd Street
Hoboken, NJ 07030
201-656-8711
Imports handmade rice paper for
printmaking and bookbinding; exports books, greeting cards, and frisbees; also consultation and translation
service relating to retail marketing
trends.

Sally Moran Kugelmeyer
Box 107
Port Murray, NJ 07865
201-689-1297
Printmaker (etchings); dried flowers,
herb wreaths.

Joan M. Kurtzman
1641 Southbrook Drive
Bridgewater, NJ 08807
201-722-4533
Sells all types of social and commercial printing—invitations, stationery, business forms.

Barbara Lafer
44 Mandeville Drive
Wayne, NJ 07470
201-694-8013
Conducts personal growth workshops
for adolescents and adults on decision
making, sexuality, assertiveness, self-
awareness, values clarification, death,
and dying.

Jayne L. Lahti
Through the Looking Glass
   Enterprises
32-33 Rockledge Road
Montville, NJ 07045
201-263-5417
Wholesale Manufacturer of hand-
made quilted items.

Beverly Lane
Graphics Lane, Inc.
22 University Road
East Brunswick, NJ 08816
201-257-8778
Typesetter.

Marilynn Larson
Chevré Associates
5 Deer Trail Road
Saddle River, NJ 07458
201-327-1438
Manufacturer of women's sportswear.

Beverly LeBeau
708 West Park Avenue
Oakhurst, NJ 07755
Engravings on used roofing slate:
farm scenes, sports figures, animals,
sailboats, homes.

Alice S. Leventhal, Ph.D.
28 Sunset Drive
Summit, NJ 07901
201-277-2190
Clinical Psychologist.

Marion Levine
304 Sea Isle Key
Secaucus, NJ 07094
201-866-5929
Does research, layout, design, and
correspondence for *Health Career*
Digest, a digest of nationwide high-
level career opportunities in the
health field.

Rae Lindsay
364 Mauro Road
Englewood Cliffs, NJ 07632
201-567-8986
Writer; Literary Agent.

Francine S. Litofsky
13 Rambling Brook Drive
Holmdel, NJ 07733
201-946-4463
Production Weaver.

Kay Longo
Pinch-Hitters, Inc.
Address Withheld
201-866-8938
212-662-4270
Singing telegrams, cookiegrams,
balloongrams, special events.

Saralee Luchansky
120 RD 2
Freehold, NJ 07728
Private investing.

Helen Lurie
127 Lincoln Place
Waldwick, NJ 07463
201-652-5144
Travel Agent.

Jackie Lynn
34 Warwick Road
Edison, NJ 08817
201-548-8452
Teacher and Director of dance studio.

Marie MacBride
412 North Monroe Street
Ridgewood, NJ 07450
201-652-7833
Free-lance writing, copy editing,
proofreading—from ideas to printed
form.

Marzetta G. Madge
470 Farmer Road
Bridgewater, NJ 08807
201-526-6973
Three-dimensional palette knife
painting with oil on velvet.

Gabriella Mancini
1 Koster Boulevard, 5A
Edison, NJ 08817
201-494-8013
Piano Teacher and Piano Accompanist for performing artists—
classical music only.

Lea-Claire M. Mascio
Cosmic Star Enterprises, Inc.
1600 Woodland Avenue
South Plainfield, NJ 07080
201-755-0058
Produces "The Cosmos—Solar System
Sundial" game; also sells the game
wholesale and retail.

Sara McAulay
Box 52
Mountain Lakes, NJ 07046
201-263-2197
Writer of fiction and nonfiction; also
Editor.

Mona McCormack
30 Woodside Avenue
Trenton, NJ 08618
609-695-2635
Calligraphy—handlettering, design,
and illumination.

"The only real inconvenience I've found

in having my office at home is

that I don't have clients come to

see me—I feel that seeing me in

a home setting would diminish

my professional status; also, I

wouldn't feel comfortable having

my corporate contacts in my

home."

Public Relations Consultant

Marie L. Menichini
21 Stratford Drive
Old Bridge, NJ 08857
201-679-3115
Bookkeeping-accounting services.

Georgine A. Meyer
18 Horizon Drive
Mendham, NJ 07945
201-543-4286
Secretarial service—stenography,
typing of resumes, letters,
manuscripts, mailing lists, billings.

Beverly Michael
Bev Michael Promotions
P.O.Box 382
Fair Lawn, NJ 07410
201-791-3145
Organizes antique shows, flea
markets, street fairs, mall promotions,
craft shows.

Bascha Mon
7 Coleman Road
Long Valley, NJ 07853
201-876-4697
Her oil paintings have appeared in
many one-artist, group, and juried
shows, both local and national, and
in galleries and museums in New
York, New Jersey, Pennsylvania, In-
diana, and Illinois.

June R. Monnier
Feathers in Wood
1 Scenic Drive
Highlands, NJ 07732
201-291-2411
Birds carved in wood.

Dorothy M. Mortenson
5 Euclid Place
Montclair, NJ 07042
201-746-6870
Proprietor of "Nantucket Landfall."
Takes reservations for seasonal guest
house on Nantucket in Massachusetts.

Barbara Moskowitz
The Sleepless Needle
7 Sherwood Road
Edison, NJ 08817
201-548-0591
Sells needlepoint supplies; also
teaches needlepoint and pulled-
thread techniques.

Hannah D. Mott
125 Bartine Street
Somerville, NJ 08876
201-685-1910
Silkscreen graphics, textile printing,
framing.

Bonny E. Mulvey
30 Orchard
Bernardsville, NJ 07924
201-766-7343
Macramé, stained glass, pen-and-ink
sketches, sculpture, and paintings.

Marianna Murphy
5 Clinton Avenue
Maplewood, NJ 07040
201-763-5339
Copywriting, public relations, print
production; Project Coordinator.

Frances E. Mustard
At the Sign of the Thistle
Fairmont Road
Pottersville, NJ 07979
201-439-2089
Manufactures naturally dyed wool
embroidery kits.

Phyllis M. Myers
139 Taylor Avenue
Sommerville, NJ 08876
201-725-0563
Branch Manager, Artcraft Concepts—sales and teaching.

Gabrielle Nappo
715 West Bay Avenue
Barnegat, NJ 08005
Weaving: placemats, jackets,
blankets, wall hangings.

Leslie Nerz
P.O. Box 145
Egg Harbor, NJ 08215
609-965-5107
Handcrafted leather goods.

Janice Newman
115 Sunset Avenue
Newark, NJ 07106
201-373-4063
Beauty Consultant for Mary Kay
Cosmetics.

Peggy Nugent
74 Hamilton Avenue
Leonardo, NJ 07737
201-872-0192
Crochets afghans, pillows, table accessories, plant holders, tissue covers.

Catherine Oetjen
40 Lincoln Avenue
Metuchen, NJ 08840
201-494-3184
Party Plan Demonstrator-Manager.

Roberta O'Hanlon
Pinch-Hitters, Inc.
Address Withheld
201-866-8938
212-662-4270
Singing telegrams, cookiegrams,
balloongrams, special events.

Greek Woman
Photographer: Pat Q

Gwen O'Neill
The Music Learning Place
44 Oakridge Road
Verona, NJ 07044
201-239-0631
Music Specialist for pre-schoolers;
group lessons for all ages.

Kate O'Shea-Gillen
39 Seneca Avenue
Rockaway, NJ 07866
201-625-1009
Fiber Artist.

Pat Owens
1760 Forest Drive
Williamstown, NJ 08094
609-629-0856
Recipe development; educational
mailing service.

Mary Beth Pappas
KMH Productions
Box 1231
Edison, NJ 08817
201-287-3347
Account Executive—broadcast
advertising and production agency.

Anna M. Parciak
54 Smith Street
Belleville, NJ 07109
201-751-2237
Typing, paper work, clerical duties,
Dictaphone transcriptions.

Diana Wilkoc Patton
497 Stony Brook Drive
Bridgewater, NJ 08807
201-722-0562
Watercolors; pen-and-ink architectural renderings.

Jean Perlmutter
200 Devon Road
Westwood, NJ 07675
201-664-4753
Paper toile, gold inlay, mini-
repoussé, tinsel painting; invitations,
announcements, awards, honors specially preserved; classes at home.

Judith Pierson
26 Lincoln Avenue
Highland Park, NJ 08904
201-249-2820
Consultation, training, speaking
engagements and conference planning. Social work/mental health practice with women and general
women's issues.

Susanne Pitak
65 Swan Street
Lambertville, NJ 08530
609-397-2541
Hypnotist—treats weight, smoking,
and personal problems.

Lydia Pizzute
27 Sieber Court
Bergenfield, NJ 07621
201-384-4929
One-of-a-kind, three-dimensional ric-
rac flowers on gingham in shadow
box frames; also Christmas
ornaments.

Barbara Procino
561 Branch Avenue
Little Silver, NJ 07739
201-741-4764
Welfare Director—Borough of Little
Silver.

Dr. Penny Pypcznski
Penfield Associates
26 Brenwal Avenue
Ewing, NJ 08618
609-882-4657
Information Consultant.

Patricia Q
Coronet Studio
2004 Lincoln Highway
Edison, NJ 08817
201-287-1234
Master of Photography; Photographic
Craftsman; Associate Fellow of Pho-
tography; star exhibitor, Photographic
Society of America; Fassbander Cup
Award, 1976.

869

...tant.

...Drive
Edison, ... 08817
201-494-7127
Field Organizer for Common Cause,
citizens' lobby group.

"I work at home because I'm basically a

night person and have the free-

dom of working all night on a

piece of art if I want to. I also

feel very comfortable and creative

in my own surroundings, with

everything in the house readily

available....I have never felt that

working at home is any less pro-

fessional since doctors, dentists,

salesmen, accountants, architects

are known to prefer the same

work environment. I surely have

the best of both worlds."

Artist

III   (201) 731-1200

Julie Rogers
FINANCIAL PLANNER
III

MEMBER   200 EXECUTIVE DRIVE
INTERNATIONAL ASSOCIATION   SUITE 340
OF FINANCIAL PLANNERS   WEST ORANGE, N.J. 07052

Polly Reilly
520 Sherwood Parkway
Westfield, NJ 07090
201-233-2510
Creates whimsical handpainted
wooden tree ornaments; also runs
Christmas and Spring Boutiques.

Reni
720 East 2nd Avenue
Roselle, NJ 07203
201-245-1218
Free-lance Artist—fine arts and
graphics. Work commissioned for
private collections and for posters,
book covers, T-shirts, business cards,
and toy designs. Member: Summit
and Somerset Art Associations.

Patricia Ricci
26 Niamoa Drive
Cherry Hill, NJ 08003
609-424-9611
Advertising and public relations.

Bernice Richmond
863 Carleton Road
Westfield, NJ 07090
201-654-3370
Commercial art; ceramic sculpture;
creative writing.

Margaret P. Roeske
5 Meade Court
Somerset, NJ 08873
201-828-8632
Free-lance editing, writing, indexing,
proofreading.

Julie Rogers
115 Wells Drive
South Plainfield, NJ 07080
201-731-1200
Insurance Agent; financial and estate
planning.

Rose Rogozinski
Seneca Coal and Coke Corporation
Jomark Corporation
Harlingen-Dutchtown Road
Belle Mead, NJ 08502
201-359-8860
Exporter.

Barbara Bryan Rojas
646 Lalor Street
Trenton, NJ 08611
609-989-8817
Translations—mostly medical into
Spanish; also from Spanish, French,
and English to English and Spanish.

Janet Romandetta
JAM Co.
39 Winding Trail
Mahwah, NJ 07430
201-825-1035
Designs and sells fabric accessories for
the home, wholesale and retail.

Rosalyn Rose
457 Baldwin Road
Maplewood, NJ 07040
201-763-5655
Printmaker.

Carol Rosen
Beavers Road, RR 3, Box 57
Califon, NJ 07830
201-832-7780
Artist.

Ellen Rosko
73 Normandy Road
Colonia, NJ 07067
201-382-2543
Complete design shop-at-home service for custom furniture, drapes,
blinds, shades, slipcovers, with floor
plans.

Marion Ruane
40 Forest Hill Drive
Howell, NJ 07731
201-367-9489
Custom drapes.

Bea Rubin
429 Woodland Place
Leonia, NJ 07605
201-461-6957
Pantyhose Distributor/Salesperson.

Cathie Ruppi
398 Tenafly Road
Englewood, NJ 07631
201-871-1643
Music studio: piano and guitar lessons
—ages 6-66.

Ann Rutten
78 Elbert Street
Ramsey, NJ 07446
201-327-7197
Antique Dealer; mail order, shows,
lectures—specializes in sewing and
needlework collectibles, Depression
Era glassware and china, post cards,
and advertising items.

Sue Sachs
40 Camelot Road
Parsippany, NJ 07054
201-884-2734
Makes silver and gold jewelry and
handcrafted vegetable paper
sculptures.

"We converted a utility room in the back of our home into an office and covered the hole from the washer-dryer connection with an attractive framed print. It's not the ritziest office in the world, but it's comfortable, functional, and it's mine."

Writer

Carolyn L. Sadowski
2376 Birch Place
Manasquan, Park, NJ 08736
201-528-6322
Designer of mixed-media batik paintings.

Sarah A. Saltus
Pleasant Hill Road
Chester, NJ 07930
201-879-6281
Designs and creates batik T-shirts, pillows, and calico animals.

Josephine Santillo, M.S.W.
14 West End Avenue
Pompton Plains, NJ 07444
201-835-4710
Psychotherapist.

Pamela Sarett
Little Red School
48 Carter Road
Princeton, NJ 08450
609-466-2873
Owns and operates a child care center.

Name Withheld
Importers and Traders of Assorted
  European Goods
Little Ferry, NJ 07643
201-440-4907
Imports high quality Irish goods.

Marilyn Schiffman
10 Heritage Court
Demarest, NJ 07627
201-768-8996
Secretary for husband's home optometrist office.

Sonia E. Schlenger
Organizational Systems
6 Aberdeen Place
Fair Lawn, NJ 07410
201-791-2396
201-943-3700
Helps businesses and individuals get organized.

Sherry Schuster
1565 North Lake Drive
Lakewood, NJ 08701
201-364-9586
Creates kiln-fired glass objects d'art.

Dorene Schwartz-Weitz
147 Harbinson Place
East Windsor, NJ 08520
609-443-5549
Air brushing/photo-silkscreen designs on T-shirts, fabrics, and wallpaper. Example of her work in *Cosmopolitan Living* in 1981.

Sandy Schwarz
Sandesigns
142 Van Houton Avenue
Chatham, NJ 07928
201-635-9212
Designs and creates a collection of needlepoint boutique kits sold throughout U.S., Puerto Rico, Guam, Australia, and Canada.

Barbara Schwinn
754 Belvidere Avenue
Westfield, NJ 07090
201-232-7058
Free-lance Artist.

Ruth Seligman
Metamorphics, Inc.
5 Drummond Road
Westfield, NJ 07090
201-654-3200
Consultant in scientific hypnosis.

Isabelle Selikoff
P.O. Box 884
Hightstown, NJ 08520
609-448-7560
Public relations, editing, advertising.

Helen Seymour
Personally Puzzled
69 Edgemere Avenue
Plainsboro, NJ 08536
609-799-0845
Creates wooden jigsaw puzzles from photographs submitted by customers.

Barbara M. Sharman
176 West Shore Road
Harrington Park, NJ 07640
201-768-1947
Piano Teacher.

Jane Sharp
33 Engle Street
Tenafly, NJ 07670
201-567-0644
Acts, directs, and produces under stage name of Jane Sharp; teaches under married name of Jane Cornet.

Ann Shepard
Shepard's Garden Center
P.O. Box 2094
Edison, NJ 08817
201-549-4330
Horticulturist.

Adele Shinder
Living Arts Studio
41-65 Rys Terrace
Fair Lawn, NJ 07410
201-796-1728
Teaches home management skills, including food preparation and sewing for the home.

Helen Simon
24 Birkendene Road
Caldwell, NJ 07006
201-226-9255
Coding and editing service for market research.

Dorothy Sinclair
JoDot Creations and Eudora
848 Woodmere Drive
Cliffwood Beach, NJ 07735
201-566-4704
Custom embroidered trapunto pictures, "Eudora" dolls, bread-dough sculptures.

Marian Slepian
5 Overlook Drive
Bridgewater, NJ 08807
201-526-5856
Cloisonné enamel paintings.

Barbara J. Sloan
1425 Cedarview Avenue
Lakewood, NJ 08701
201-363-5424
Marketing coordination to the building industry: publicity, advertising, promotions, graphic design, public relations counsel.

Lisa Steinberg
1 Beechtree Road
Roseland, NJ 07068
201-226-4385
Crafts; fine arts; tutoring; art lessons.

Irene Stella
Stella Shows
162 Stuart Street
Paramus, NJ 07652
201-262-3063
Produces antique shows and exhibitions for fund raising and promotions.

Gail Strauss
54 Stoneham Place
Metuchen, NJ 08840
201-494-3653
Caters hor d'oeuvres for home parties.

Lee Strauss
Ampersand
16 Forest Drive
Morris Plains, NJ 07950
201-538-9407
Public relations, advertising and communications services: needs assessments, program/project planning, management consulting, data gathering and analysis, concept development, editorial services, art direction, graphics services, production supervision, special events and program management.

Elsa Sullivan
4 Laurel Place Plaza
Upper Montclair, NJ 07043
201-783-9405
Free-lance Artist—Watercolorist.

"I think one reason I have been able to continue doing the glass and produce as much as I do is my ability to feel the frustration and hopelessness and to act against those feelings by holding a positive direction that my work is important."

Artist

Zilla Sussman
42 Fairview Avenue
West Orange, NJ 07052
201-731-2325
Painter; Printmaker; also teaches art.

Anne Sutera
La Chariettes
2400 Hudson Terrace
Fort Lee, NJ 07024
201-592-1535
Private valet parking service for weddings, graduations, Bar Mitzvahs, parties.

Emilie Taylor
189 Kaywin Road
Paramus, NJ 07652
201-265-4145
Teaches meat buying, cutting, and cookery.

Myra Terry-Meisner
370 Central Avenue
Mountainside, NJ 07092
201-232-6054
Interior Designer.

Suzanne Tillman, M.S.W.
67 Pageant Lane
Willingboro, NJ 08046
609-877-3973
Voice Teacher.

Midge Touw
104 Lake Park Terrace
Hewitt, NJ 07421
201-728-2133
Collection Agent.

Joan Tracey
Something Creative
237 Spruce Drive
Bricktown, NJ 08723
201-920-1314
Advertising, promotions, public relations, business cards, letterheads, logo design, brochures, catalogs, direct mail, flyers.

Joan Bannigan Walsh
Bannigan Basics Inc.
RD 2, Box 403
Flemington, NJ 08822
201-782-0066
Personnel placement/career counseling.

Phyllis Walsh
10 Von Steuben Lane
South Bound Brook, NJ 08880
201-469-2005
Trains, breeds, and shows Golden Retrievers (Corbec Goldens) for field, show, obedience.

Marilyn Joan Wander
88 Audubon Road
Teaneck, NJ 07666
201-833-0539
Potter.

Susan Warn
Pinch-Hitters, Inc.
Address Withheld
201-866-8938
212-662-4270
Singing telegrams, cookiegrams, balloongrams, special events.

Marianne Wehrenberg
The Key Directory, Inc.
P.O. Box 562
East Brunswick, NJ 08816
201-254-6448
Publishes directories, magazines, journals, direct mail.

Ann Weiner
Victorian Vintage
P.O. Box 761
Clark, NJ 07066
201-382-2135
Arts, crafts, miniatures, dolls.

Edith Weiss
Cooking Sisters, Inc.
632 Sagamore Avenue
Teaneck, NJ 07666
201-836-5544
Gourmet catering.

Nadine H. Weiss
Weiss Studio and Craft Workshop
161 Culberson Road
Basking Ridge, NJ 07920
201-766-5228
Pottery, sculpture, rug hooking, stitchery, weaving without a loom, copper enameling, fused and leaded stained glass; also conducts special interest tours. Work exhibited in one-artist shows, invitational and group exhibitions and shown in New Jersey in Trenton, Newark, Montclair, and Morris County Museums, as well as in art galleries and universities. Work also accepted in juried World Craft Exhibition in South America.

Carol D. Westfall
162 Whitford Avenue
Nutley, NJ 07110
Fiber Artist.

Malle N. Whitaker
The Design Workshop
152 Paulison Avenue
Passaic, NJ 07055
201-778-9360
Creative graphic service—advertising, design, and illustration.

Working from the home is ideal as you really do not have to punch a clock, so to speak. You are very busy, but you can set your own pace. Sometimes it is more hectic than others, but it all irons out....However, it is most enjoyable and rewarding.

So far, in 1980, we continue to strive successfully and have developed many regular production items, a home decorating service, and a Christmas line. We hope to continue to expand and grow."

Home Decorator

Robin Whitely
46 Colonial Way
Short Hills, NJ 07078
201-467-1704
Translator of nontechnical material—Russian-English / English-Russian.

Sharon Rudman Williams
54 Pennsylvania Avenue
Carteret, NJ 07008
201-969-2028
Free-lance writing for newspapers and public relations for organizations; also sells women's clothes from home.

Reggi Y. Wilson
26 Briarcliff Road
Livingston, NJ 07039
201-992-5456
Artists' Representative: photographs, paintings, lithographs, batiks, stained glass, weaving, afghans, wall murals, wood-block invitations.

Jane Wind
596 Piermont Road
Demarest, NJ 07627
201-767-7695
Amway Distributor.

Gail Wisneski
13 Hampshire Road
Midland Park, NJ 07432
201-447-6457
Makes calico Christmas decorations.

Margaret Faith Wolverton
289 Riverbrook Avenue
Lincroft, NJ 07738
201-747-9354
Designs and creates puppets; also ink drawings of homes and businesses, paintings, crafts.

Madlyn-Ann C. Woolwich
473 Marvin Drive
Long Branch, NJ 07740
201-229-3752
Oils, pastels, batiks.

Martha Otis Wright
84 Maclean Circle
Princeton, NJ 08540
609-924-8016
Teaches and sells ceramics. Has exhibited her pottery and sculpture in many juried and invitational shows, including NJ State Museum, Voorhees Gallery of Rutgers University, Hunterdon Art Center, Stockton State College, and Newark Museum, as well as Greenmeadow Invitational Show. Works with three kilns—stoneware, raku, and sawdust—and many different kinds of clay. Member: NJ Designer-Craftsmen, American Crafts Council, World Crafts Council.

Gail Zavian
175 Manhattan Avenue
Jersey City, NJ 07307
201-795-3050
Free-lance Designer—Promoter.

Renee Zimrin
Program Development Associates
3 Rosemont Drive
West Orange, NJ 07052
201-731-1013
201-325-8221
Creates and implements special projects for business organizations, educators, and community groups.

Ruthi Zinn
11 Athens Road
Short Hills, NJ 07078
201-467-2356
Public relations, advertising.

Vivian J. Ziomek
1 Cambridge Drive
Jackson, NJ 08527
201-364-6696
Spanish Translator and Interpreter.

Adrienne Zoble
Adrienne Zoble Advertising
P.O. Box 238
Martinsville, NJ 08836
201-560-0010
Owns marketing/advertising agency; speaks and consults on marketing/advertising—all geared to small businesses.

■ **New York**

Judith Abaroa
RD 5, Lovell Street
Mahopac, NY 10541
914-248-5406
Beauty Consultant—Mary Kay Cosmetics.

Linda Abrams
15 Carstensen Road
Scarsdale, NY 10583
914-723-9067
Management Consultant/Trainer.

Patricia S. Ardizzone
A.N.D. Engine Company 3 Corp.
1144 Mamaroneck Avenue
White Plains NY 10605
914-428-1452
Operates a party, promotional, and limousine service using a fire engine.

Carol Desoe
Party Planner
Photographer: Arey Photo

Toby Baron
Window Designs
21 Cohawney Road
Scarsdale, NY 10583
914-725-2633
Sells window treatments.

Rochelle Bender
Window Designs
1042 Webster Avenue
New Rochelle, NY 10804
914-235-8076
Sells window treatments.

Maureen Berkman
30 Farragut Street
Scarsdale, NY 10583
914-723-7823
Catering; also teaches cookery.

Lori K. Boden
8 Dannybrook Place
Yonkers, NY 10710
914-337-3444
Gift Distributor; Importer; sales
agency.

Mary Brooks
Something Special
37 Barnwell Drive
White Plains, NY 10607
914-997-0373
Unique designs in sequins and
rhinestones on sportswear.

Sybil Conrad
30 Edgewood Road
Scarsdale, NY 10583
914-725-2360
Communications Consultant.

Patricia de Haan
25 Sammis Lane
White Plains, NY 10605
914-761-1681
914-761-1648
Painter.

Judith M. Delaney
7 Spinet Drive
Rochester, NY 14625
716-385-4729
Shaklee natural food supplements,
personal care and home care
products.

128

Carol Desoe
A.N.D. Engine Company 3 Corp.
14 Fern Way
Scarsdale, NY 10583
914-723-2267
Operates a party, promotional, and
limousine service using a fire engine.

Linda Blair Doescher
Linda Blair Associates
11 Fox Meadow Road
Scarsdale, NY 10583
914-472-5690
Interior Designer.

Carole Ferster
Handcrafted Wearables
125 Ramona Court
New Rochelle, NY 10804
914-235-5699
Original handpainted and embroidered designs on fabric,
predominantly clothing.

Dvora Fields
50 Brite Avenue
Scarsdale, NY 10583
914-472-5988
Interior Designer.

Madelene Fink
Witty Ditty
29 Cornell Street
Scarsdale, NY 10583
914-GR 2-GRAM
Singing telegrams, custom-written
songs.

Barbara R. Fogel
86 Carthage Road
Scarsdale, NY 10583
914-723-1272
Free-lance writer for foundations and
educational organizations.

Gail Francis
800 Grand Concourse
Bronx, NY 10451
212-665-8753
Crochet apparel.

Nancy A. Fuller
Projects Unlimited
626 East 20th Street, 6D
New York, NY 10009
212-228-1758
Personalized administrative service
bureau assisting individuals and
organizations: meeting arrangements,
relocation assistance, parties and
tours, special purchases, editing and
transcription services, research.

Mary Jo Gatti
Dayspring
322 Abbey Road
Manhasset, NY 11030
516-627-2891
Mail-order sales of personalized
business gifts.

Phyllis Gebert
Carrie Lauren Designs
35 Avon Road
New Rochelle, NY 10804
914-576-2286
Country decorations with natural and
dried materials.

Gale Kramer Goldman
8 Tam O'Shanter Drive
Purchase, NY 10577
914-428-7822
Clothing and costume design.

Joanne Goverman
14 Dellwood Road
White Plains, NY 10605
914-761-2014
Quilting—teaching and sale of goods.

'...I can make my own hours. Since I

sometimes have surges of energy

at 5 AM, I can take advantage of

this situation. I can put on my

robe, walk across the hall, and

spend a few hours expending

energy in a creative and profitable

manner."

Educational Consultant

Marjorie Gross
Mail Bag, Too
Address Withheld
914-723-0859
Sells personalized stationery, an-
nouncements, and invitations.

Laura Gurton
785 West End Avenue
New York, NY 10025
212-663-9180
Stained glass Artist.

Phyllis Baker Hammond
285 Scarborough Road
Scarborough, NY 10510
914-762-4194
Clay sculpture.

Roberta Hershenson
35 Hampton Road
Scarsdale, NY 10583
914-723-1891
Photographer.

Sandi F. Howell
554 South 10th Avenue
Mount Vernon, NY 10550
914-699-4372
Pottery, ceramics, sewing, knitting;
Herbalist.

Joan Israel
17 Horseguard Lane
Scarsdale, NY 10583
914-723-6579
Sculptor.

Ann Jacobson
Planters Plus
11 Floren Place
Scarsdale, NY 10583
914-472-5540
Custom mirrored furniture.

Geri Jefferson
35 Midwood Street
Brooklyn, NY 11225
212-462-1638
Communications Consultant and
Writer: varying topics for children
and adults in audio and print media.
Recognized as Outstanding Young
Woman of America in 1977 and
1978. Cited for television work by
National Academy of Television Arts
and Sciences and Brooklyn Model
Cities. Member: Authors Guild and
New York Press Club.

Martha Kantor
Pajama Party
40 Cornell Road
Scarsdale, NY 10583
914-723-4550
Sells designer lingerie for fund raising
and at house parties.

Michele A.F. Kidwell
495 West End Avenue
New York, NY 10024
212-724-6391
Art consultations, writing, lectures,
fund-raising events for individuals,
organizations, and colleges.

Fran Klingsberg
5 Westview Lane
Scarsdale, NY 10583
914-725-4489
Calligrapher.

Naomi Kolstein
''Goat Lady''
7 Faist Drive
Spring Valley, NY 10977
914-352-6917
Lectures on subject of goats and
brings pet goat, Flash, with her.

Stephanie Kovarnik
CPO Box 1385
Kingston, NY 12401
914-331-0089
Stained glass Artist.

Fredda Kray
Sheridan Road
Scarsdale, NY 10583
914-723-2997
Diet control/weight maintenance.

Randi Kreiss
983 East Prospect Street
Woodmere, NY 11598
516-374-0504
Free-lance Writer.

Gail Lehmann
2365 Loring Place
Yorktown Heights, NY 10598
914-962-4578
Career Counseling Consultant.

Lucy Little
225 Sprain Road
Scarsdale, NY 10583
914-693-6746
Astrologer; also teaches astrology.

Meri Lobel
11 Lake Street, 7C
White Plains, NY 10603
914-761-1049
Flute, piano, recorder, and music
theory.

Arlene K. Lucas
217 Smith Street
Peekskill, NY 10566
914-739-8471
Shaklee natural food supplements,
personal care and home care
products.

Diane Mahon
89 Metropolitan Oval
Bronx, NY 10462
212-892-1904
Custom-tailored clothing; dolls; all-occasion cards.

"I work from my dining room table and even had notepaper made up which says 'From the dining room table of…'"

Organization Coordinator

Charlotte Malten
193 Germonds Road
West Nyack, NY 10994
914-623-3235
Pottery and ceramic sculpture.

Charlotte Malten
Potter

Susan Graham Mann
SGM Marketing Services
224 Falmouth Road
Scarsdale, NY 10583
914-723-8632
Public relations/marketing services.

Joan Marmor
Images
1019 North Avenue
New Rochelle, NY 10804
914-235-2960
Photographer.

Jeanne Mattson
Route 82
LaGrangeville, NY 12540
914-223-3056
Senior Sales Director, Mary Kay Cosmetics.

DJ Mazer
Projects Unlimited
626 East 20th Street, 6D
New York, NY 10009
212-228-1758
Personalized administrative service bureau assisting individuals and organizations: meeting arrangements, relocation assistance, parties and tours, special purchases, editing and transcription services, research.

Juliette McGinnis
114 Pinecrest Drive
Hastings-on-Hudson, NY 10706
914-478-1696
Creates and designs stress-management programs, products, and concepts.

Vicki Mechner
OmniQuest Inc.
P.O. Box 15
Chappaqua, NY 10514
914-238-9646
Operates as free-lance research department locating any product, service, or information needed.

Mimi Mendelson
100 Secor Road
Scarsdale, NY 10583
914-723-5981
Interior Designer.

Helaine Messer
535 West 113th Street, #22
New York, NY 10025
212-864-0765
Photographer/Photojournalist. Art world subject specialty: editorial photography, including annual reports and portraits.

Deborah B. Miller
6 Sargent Place
Manhasset, NY 11030
516-627-6337
Translater—French, German, Italian, Spanish.

Sandra Miller
50 Brite Avenue
Scarsdale, NY 10583
914-725-5070
Interior Designer.

Mara Mills
335 East 10th Street
New York, NY 10009
212-254-5173
Writer and Researcher; also does copy editing and text editing.

Wendy E. Moldovan
3826 Old Crompond Road
Peekskill, NY 10566
914-739-3448
Apartment Contractor—renovation and rental.

Eleanor Moss
16 Butler Road
Scarsdale, NY 10583
914-725-0693
Personal shopping—women's wardrobes and gifts.

Helaine Messer
Photographer
Photographer: Michael Boodro

Susan Newman
400 East 52nd Street
New York, NY 10022
212-935-0293
Writer; also owner of gift package
company, ''Cities to Go''.

Toni Gloria Novick, M.D.
621 Pine Brook Boulevard
New Rochelle, NY 10804
914-235-1526
Gynecology and family planning.

Diane Owen
27 Fieldstone Drive
Hartsdale, NY 10530
914-948-8007
Macramé Fiber Artist.

Murielle Peters-Davis
Mama Mimi Embroidery
2661 Marion Avenue, #5B
Bronx, NY 10458
914-295-7823
Children's underwear and T-shirts.

Jean Phillips
360 West 22nd Street
New York, NY 10011
Free-lance writing, public relations,
interviewing.

Joan Picket
In Good Taste
12 Cooper Road
Scarsdale, NY 10583
914-725-5646
Party Planner.

Carolyn Pine
376 Old Mamaroneck Road
White Plains, NY 10605
914-946-3788
Repairs, rebuilds, and tunes pianos.

Marlene Piturro
B.J. Silverman & Co.
3 Wagner Place
Hastings, NY 10706
914-478-1199
Computerized financial services,
mailings.

Hildegard N. Pleva
197 Main Street
Kingston, NY 12401
914-331-5466
Quilting; also teaches her craft.

Wilma O. Reid
81 Bruce Avenue
Yonkers, NY 10705
914-965-2332
Custom silver jewelry.

Beverly Rich
Special Summers
8 Richbell Road
Scarsdale, NY 10583
914-472-9199
Summer camp trip advisory service—
plans cross-country and European
trips, as well as camp alternatives.

Emily Rosen
Witty Ditty
29 Cornell Street
Scarsdale, NY 10583
914-GR 2-GRAM
Singing telegrams; custom-written
songs.

Linda Rosensweig
116 Carthage Road
Scarsdale, NY 10583
914-722-3992
Tennis and paddle tennis instruction.

Marion J. Rosley
41 Topland Road
Hartsdale, NY 10530
914-682-9718
Secretarial, transcription, and translation service.

Sarelle Rosner
Handcrafted Wearables
205 Devoe Avenue
Yonkers, NY 10705
914-968-0573
Original handpainted and embroidered designs on fabric, predominantly clothing.

Marian Rubin
Planters Plus
14 Short Lane
New Rochelle, NY 10804
914-235-1746
Custom mirrored furniture.

Nancy Rubin
35 Broadfield Road
New Rochelle, NY 10804
914-632-1052
Free-lance Journalist/Writer, specializing in sociological trends and education. Work has appeared in *The New York Times* and in various other periodicals, magazines and newspapers.

Susan Rubin
302 West 79th Street, #7C
New York, NY 10024
212-877-3614
Makes color xerographic postcards.

Susan Sarlin, C.S.W.
22 Kempster Road
Scarsdale, NY 10583
914-723-7646
Individual and family therapy.

Joan M. Scobey
9 Lenox Place
Scarsdale, NY 10583
914-723-2747
Writer.

Shalome′
111 North Pine Avenue
Albany, NY 12203
518-489-3320
Massage therapy and hypnotherapy; also Writer.

Susan Sheinlin
111 Tennyson Drive
Nanuet, NY 10954
914-623-7969
Roller skate sales.

Kayla J. Silberberg
Chappaqua College Counseling
  Service
83 Old Lyme Road
Chappaqua, NY 10514
914-238-5257
Educational counseling.

Maggy Simony
Freelance Publications
230 McConnell Avenue—Box 8
Bayport, NY 11705
516-472-1799
Typesetter and independent
Publisher.

Linda Singer
In Good Taste
12 Cooper Road
Scarsdale, NY 10583
914-723-1731
Party Planner.

Kim Wilder
Artist
Joan Morell
Designer
Photographer: Chester Hasbrouk

Harriet Langsam Sobol
10 Claremont Road
Scarsdale, NY 10583
914-472-2248
Writer.

Stephanie Urso Spina
Tudor Graphics
866 Lincoln Avenue
Baldwin, NY 11510
516-546-2373
Illustrations, ad copy, logos and trademarks; also advertising consultations for new campaigns and program revision.

Amy Stein
49 Clubway
Hartsdale, NY 10530
914-472-6730
Director of children's summer camp.

Judith Stein
175 Castlebar Road
Rochester, NY 14610
716-271-2585
Fibercrafts: weaving, dye painting, printmaking on fabric.

Carolyn G. Streicher
37 Montrose Road
Scarsdale, NY 10583
914-725-5781
Flute Teacher.

Cynthia Wallach
Pajama Party
2 Hickory Lane
Scarsdale, NY 10583
914-472-3808
Sells designer lingerie for fund raising and at house parties.

Lynn Walter
48 Sargent Road
Scarsdale, NY 10583
914-472-1475
Works with husband importing and
exporting machinery.

Rita Wasserman
5 Briarwood Lane
Pleasantville, NY 10570
914-769-2098
Shaklee natural food supplements,
personal care and home care
products.

Kimberly Wilder
Denver-Vega Road
Denver, NY 12421
607-326-7933
Mother-daughter team: mother, Joan
Morell, does all designs for daughter
Kim Wilder's stained glass work.

Cynthia Winika
P.O. Box 906
New Paltz, NY 12561
914-255-9338
Pillows with prints and paintings she
designs—sold wholesale and retail.

"Our home is an old Mill. The renovation of the Mill, the upkeep and direction of the Mill gallery, and the design and production of our ceramic works are a large undertaking and all interrelated.

It is obvious that the completed integration of work, play, and lifestyle which is our goal, could not be accomplished without the opportunity to work at home."

Artist

Katie Winterstein
Little Moon Studio, Inc.
12 Morrison Drive
New Rochelle, NY 10804
914-428-7571
Graphic design, illustration,
advertising.

Ina Wishner
10 Knollwood Drive
Portchester, NY 10573
914-937-2020
Artist—watercolors, graphics,
needlework.

Myrna R. Youdelman
Gift Finders International
7 Tennyson Street
Hartsdale, NY 10530
914-948-6121
Designs, manufactures, and
distributes gifts.

Suzanne H. Zilenziger
270 Nelson Road
Scarsdale, NY 10583
914-472-4676
Beauty Consultant for Mary Kay
Cosmetics.

Sandra Zook
Unbeaten Paths
P.O. Box 78
Village Station, NY 10014
212-677-5674
Operates a telephone tape directory
of unique, out-of-the-way shops,
restaurants, galleries and theaters in
New York City area, plus special services and weekend retreats. Directory
number: 212-677-0337.

■ Ohio

Mariam Eikenberry
The Book Cart
4082 Kilbourn Road
Arcanum, OH 45304
513-548-8582
Mail order book sales business —
how-to informational materials.

Dorothy M. Ranney
11820 Edgewater Drive, #210
Lakewood, OH 44107
216-521-5171
Writer.

Deborah K. Rauh
5634 Rauh Road
Coldwater, OH 45828
419-942-1821
Amway Distributor.

■ Oregon

Meredith Morehead
204 Eureka Avenue
Silverton, OR 97381
503-873-6503
Fiber Artist and Designer—stitchery,
weaving, macramé, patchwork, and
quilting.

Georgia Terry
Collector's Cranny
840 NE Cochran Avenue
Gresham, OR 97030
503-667-0950
Sells autographs and documents to
collectors and dealers in 28 states.

■ Pennsylvania

Joan Devon
Poemetrics
228 Standish Road
Merion, PA 19066
215-667-5896
Original poetry and calligraphy for
cards, invitations, etc.

Bobbi Wolf
Poemetrics
228 Standish Road
Merion, PA 19066
215-667-5896
Original poetry and calligraphy for
cards, invitations, etc.

Joan Wortis
89 West Bridge Street
New Hope, PA 18938
215-862-2121
Handweaving.

■ Rhode Island

Linda Blaney
3 Abalone Road
Narragansett, RI 02822
401-783-8180
Grows and sells herbs, their by-
products, and vegetables.

Joan Wortis
Weaver
Photographer: Rosemary Ranck

Sondra Medwin
Simply Sondra
116 Dellwood Road
Cranston, RI 02920
401-943-1142
Stationer.

■ Tennessee

Buton Whicker
102 Melrose
Greenfield, TN 38230
901-235-2429
Painter.

■ Texas

Miriam Cohen
Special Occasions
7706 Yamini Drive
Dallas, TX 75230
214-363-4744
Party rental service—cloths,
napkins, table skirting, centerpieces.

Leslie Smith Collier
8727 Fawn Drive
Dallas, TX 75238
512-341-5166
Caterer.

Marlene F. Kehler
405 Ridge Crest Drive
Richardson, TX 75080
214-238-9204
Executive Recruiter.

Antoinette C. Lowe
7830 Eagle Trail
Dallas, TX 75238
214-349-8586
Tutoring and consulting in reading.

Cynthia S. Lowe
Rainbow Squared
   Communications, Inc.
7830 Eagle Trail
Dallas, TX 75238
214-349-8586
Provides following services: editing
art, speeches, stories, and poems,
writing audio-visual presentations and
radio scripts, planning multi-media
presentations, editing academic
theses, researching, copywriting,
writing individualized wedding and
christening ceremonies, preparing
resumes, and addressing and mailing
holiday and special occasion cards.

Joyce Mohr-Aicklen
10826 Stone Canyon Road, Apt. 2318
Dallas, TX 75230
214-692-6013
Secretarial service—typing, word
processing.

Margaret Charlene Newlin
8526 Thunderbird Lane
Dallas, TX 75238
214-341-2795
Custom dressmaking and design
(women and children's clothing); also
needlework and toys.

Ann Olesky
Special Occasions
7706 Yamini Drive
Dallas, TX 75230
214-748-3189
Party rental service—cloths,
napkins, table skirting, centerpieces.

Jody Robbins
7805 Deer Trail
Dallas, TX 75238
Calligrapher.

■ Utah

Connie Chris Marshall
Home Uniqueness Enterprises
P.O. Box 36
Minersville, UT 84752
801-386-2266
Home Uniqueness Consultant; Lec-
turer. Conducts seminars. Has
monthly newsletter.

■ Vermont

Jill Marvin
Box 258
Shaftsbury, VT 05262
802-375-6316
Stained glass Artist.

■ Virginia

Barbara Anderson
6002 Hibbling Avenue
Springfield, VA 22150
703-569-9062
Publications Manager.

Name Withheld
Address Withheld
Centreville, VA 22020
702-631-1280
Typist.

Elizabeth Cassady
5917 Brookland Road
Alexandria, VA 22310
703-971-0360
Bookkeeper.

Laura Horowitz
Editorial Experts
5905 Pratt Street
Alexandria, VA 22310
703-971-7350
Editorial services company providing writing, editing, research, indexing, proofreading, and manuscript typing and specializing in education, government, consumer, and urban/community affairs. Uses both free-lance professional journalists and what Ms. Horwitz calls "that great under-used pool of talent—college-educated housewife-mothers" who work from home. From this large group of more than 200 experienced writers, editors, typists, and researchers, Editorial Experts directs teams of skilled workers assigned to each project; also publishes *The Editorial Eye*, a newsletter focusing on editorial standards and practices.

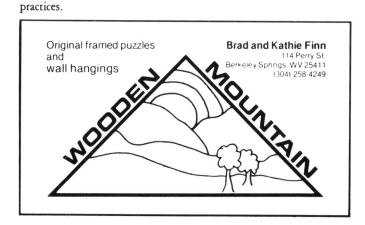

Original framed puzzles and wall hangings

Brad and Kathie Finn
114 Perry St.
Berkeley Springs. WV 25411
(304) 258-4249

WOODEN MOUNTAIN

Eleanor Johnson
8433 Willow Forge Road
Springfield, VA 22152
703-451-6814
Administrative/editorial work— newsletter marketing, correspondence, research, and proofreading.

Bernadette Knoblauch
9617 Beach Mill Road
Great Falls, VA 22066
703-759-2255
Technical editing.

Elaine Sullivan
6100 Larkspur Drive
Alexandria, VA 22310
703-971-4916
Proofreader.

Margaret C. Tobin
4209 Olley Lane
Fairfax, VA 22032
703-323-0073
Typing and transcribing.

■ Washington

Linda Carey
4306 73rd Avenue, NW
Gig Harbor, WA 98335
206-265-3887
Macramé, flower arrangements, ceramics, plaster craft, découpage, picture-pressed flower arrangements.

Charlotte Chester
Route 1, Box 53
Reardon, WA 99029
509-796-4787
Printmaker, Painter, Gallery Owner, and Teacher-Critic.

■ West Virginia

Kathleen A. Finn
Wooden Mountain
114 Perry Street
Berkeley Springs, WV 25411
304-258-4249
Works with husband making original wood-framed puzzles and wall hangings.

■ Wyoming

Margo Brown
457 North Main
Buffalo, WY 82834
307-684-9406
Makes stoneware and porcelain pottery.

Remember the children's occupational nonsense rhyme that started with "rich man, poor man, beggar man, thief...?" As women now establish their places in the business world, it's high time we updated that nonsense with another rhyme. Perhaps, this one:

Doctor, lawyer, publicist, furrier,
Caterer, writer, plumber,
couturiere...Our point is made! Women are doing anything and everything to earn an income from home-based businesses. The only limits are an individual's time, talents, imagination, and energy.

Initially, we attempted to categorize the occupations, but many were so unique that they really didn't fit in any one place. Thus, we have simplified matters by listing them alphabetically.

The one group that continues to perplex us is the creative arts, for it represents all individuals who have combined their intelligence with a totally individual spirit to produce an original work of art. In many instances it has been very difficult to separate the artist from the craftsperson. While visiting the Northeast Craft Fair in Rhinebeck to distribute questionnaires, we discovered that in nearly all instances the crafted items were works of art! In our occupational titles of Artist and Craftsperson we have generally represented individuals as they themselves chose to be identified.

The following list is a sampling of what can be done—and what is being done—by enterprising women at home.

Occupations

■ Accessories Manufacturer

Tina Bobker
Rainbow Artisans, Inc.
19 Troy Dr.
Livingston, NJ 07039
201-533-9081
Children's accessories.

Susan E. Collins
Through the Looking Glass
    Enterprises
32-33 Rockledge Rd.
Montville, NJ 07045
201-335-8748
Quilted accessories.

Carole Dlugasch
Rainbow Artisans, Inc.
35 Old Indian Rd.
West Orange, NJ 07052
201-731-6721
Children's accessories.

Jayne L. Lahti
Through the Looking Glass
    Enterprises
32-33 Rockledge Rd.
Montville, NJ 07045
201-263-5417
Quilted accessories.

■ Accountant

Doris G. Dempster
35 Monmouth Junction Road
Dayton, NJ 08520
201-329-3092

■ Advertising Consultant

Katharine Barr
278 Elm Street
North Reading, MA 01864
617-664-2636

Mary Beth Pappas
KMH Productions
Box 1231
Edison, NJ 08817
201-287-3347

Patricia Ricci
26 Niamoa Drive
Cherry Hill, NJ 08003
609-424-9611

Stephanie Urso Spina
866 Lincoln Avenue
Baldwin, NY 11510
516-546-2373

Joan Tracey
237 Spruce Drive
Bricktown, NJ 08723
201-920-1314

Adrienne Zoble
Adrienne Zoble Advertising
P.O. Box 238
Martinsville, NJ 08836
201-560-0010

■ Advertising Representative

Veona R. Finkelstein
22 Joline Road
Kendall Park, NJ 08824
201-297-1181
Advertising Representative for *The Christian Science Monitor*.

■ Animal Breeder

Phyllis Walsh
10 Von Steuben Lane
South Bound Brook, NJ 08880
201-469-2005
Golden Retrievers.

■ Anthropologist

Doranne Jacobson
290 Demarest Avenue
Closter, NJ 07624
201-767-7241
Anthropological Photographer, Consultant, and Researcher.

■ Antique Appraiser

Elizabeth Carr
664 Belleforte Avenue
Oak Park, IL 60302
312-848-3340
President of International Society of Fine Arts Appraisers, Ltd.

■ Antique Dealer

Ann Rutten
78 Elbert Street
Ramsey, NJ 07446
201-327-7197
Sewing and needlework collectibles, Depression Era glassware and china, post cards, and advertising items.

■ Antique Restorer

Miriam Gershen
Restorations Unlimited
1 Norwood Road
Springfield, NJ 07081
201-376-5772

■ Art Consultant

Michele A.F. Kidwell
495 West End Avenue
New York, NY 10024
212-724-6391

■ Art Dealer

Charlotte W. Chester
Route 1, Box 53
Reardon, WA 99029
509-796-4787

Marilou Hamer
Discovery Art Galleries
1191 Valley Road
Clifton NJ 07013
201-746-2291

Doranne Jacobson
Anthropologist
Photographer:
Pamela W. Sartorelli

■ Artist

Joan Arbeiter
58 Elm Avenue
Metuchen, NJ 08840
201-549-8917
Painter.

Nancy T. Baarens
481 Tappan Road
Norwood, NJ 07648
201-768-5010
Medium: oil.

Evelyn Breeden
182 Ridgewood Avenue
Glen Ridge, NJ 07028
201-743-8445
Media: oil and watercolor.

Anne R. Cantor
203 Second Avenue
Bradley Beach, NJ 07720
201-776-7088
Media: etchings and collographs.

Barbara H. Carlbon
RD 1, Pattenburg Road
Pattenburg, NJ 08802
201-735-5764

Laura E. Chenicek
42 Warren Court
South Orange, NJ 07079
201-763-7088

Charlotte W. Chester
Route 1, Box 53
Reardan, WA 99029
509-796-4787
Printmaker; Painter.

Ann Connolly
94 Wells Court
Demarest, NJ 07627
201-768-0254
Medium: watercolor.

Anna Continos
315 Willowbrook Drive
North Brunswick, NJ 08902
201-821-7346
Medium: watercolor.

Patricia de Haan
25 Sammis Lane
White Plains, NY 10605
914-761-1681
914-761-1648
Painter.

Ellen M. Demko
43 DeNormandie Avenue
Fair Haven, NJ 07701
201-747-6034
Medium: Stained glass.

Sally Diaz
28 North 23rd Street
East Orange, NJ 07017
201-673-3245
Portraits, figures, landscapes.

Sara Eyestone
20 Blair Court
Ocean Township, NJ 07712
201-922-4520
Medium: batik.

Sandra Farrell
Peep Toad Mill
East Killingly, CT 06243
203-774-8967
Media: stoneware and porcelain.

Kay Fialkoff
27-09 Romaine Street
Fair Lawn, NJ 07410
201-791-4320
Media: inks, watercolor, oil.

Judith Hendershot
Stencil Artist
Photographer:
North Shore Magazine
Winnetka, IL

Elvira A. Fiducia
26 Collinwood Road
Maplewood, NJ 07040
201-763-3249
Media: oil and enamel.

Lori Fischman
5 Knoll Terrace
West Caldwell, NJ 07006
201-575-9241
Medium: clay.

Alma W. Garrison
435 Washington Avenue
Linden, NJ 07036
201-486-0079
Media: charcoal, pastel, oil.

Patti Genack
260 Park Avenue
Rutherford, NJ 07070
201-933-0724
Lithographs.

Vera M.R. Giger
20 Garber Square, Apt. C2
Ridgewood, NJ 07450
201-447-4663
Printmaker.

Trudy Glucksberg
14 Aiken Avenue
Princeton, NJ 08540
609-924-2061
Free-lance Illustrator and
Printmaker.

Laura Gurton
785 West End Avenue
New York, NY 10025
212-663-9180
Medium: stained glass.

Gwen Haney-Webster
2921 Merian Drive
San Bruno, CA 94066
415-583-5435
Medium: sand.

Faith Heisler
Address Withheld
Paramus, NJ 07652
Medium: fiber.

Judith Hendershot
The Ceiling Lady
1408 Main Street
Evanston, IL 60202
312-475-6411
Stencilled decorations for ceilings,
walls, and floors.

Rose Hertzberg
27 Buckingham Drive
Ramsey, NJ 07446
201-327-5288
Media: oil, watercolor, collage.

Rosalyn Hollander
5 Dogwood Drive
Newton, NJ 07860
201-383-4966

Marian Howard
Fine Ethnic Prints
150 Woodlawn Avenue
Jersey City, NJ 07305
Media: watercolor, pencil drawings,
silkscreen, etchings, collages, sculpture.

Theodora Ilowitz
15 Central Avenue
Demarest, NJ 07627

Janet Indick
428 Sagamore Avenue
Teaneck, NJ 07666
201-836-0211
Medium: welded steel.

Joan Israel
17 Horseguard Lane
Scarsdale, NY 10583
914-723-6579
Sculptor.

Chana Ann Kirschner
18 Oak Crest Road
West Orange, NJ 07052
201-736-1960
Media: batik and direct dye on fabric.

Stephanie Kovarnik
CPO Box 1385
Kingston, NY 12401
914-331-0089
Medium: stained glass.

Ruth M. Krieger
33 Winding Way
West Orange, NJ 07052
201-731-5644
Painter; Printmaker.

Marjorie Shaw Kubach
308 Lacey Drive
New Milford, NJ 07646
201-261-1650
Painter; Printmaker.

Sally Moran Kugelmeyer
Box 107
Port Murray, NJ 07865
201-689-1297
Media: etching, dried flowers.

Claudia Jan LaCovey
13701 Old Columbia Pike
Silver Spring, MD 20904
301-384-2856
Medium: stained glass.

"At this point in time, the advantages

of running a homebased business

outweigh the disadvantages. I en-

joy the flexibility of schedules

and not having to 'dress up' for

work every day. If the pace gets

too hectic, if my son gets sick, or

if I just need the time to work on

projects unrelated to my

business...I simply refer new

clients to other free lancers in the

area. I disconnect our home

phone during working hours to

eliminate the constant

interruptions."

Writer

Marzetta G. Madge
470 Farmer Road
Bridgewater, NJ 08807
201-526-6973
Medium: oil on velvet.

Jill Marvin
Box 258
Shaftsbury, VT 05262
802-375-6316
Medium: stained glass.

Bascha Mon
7 Coleman Road
Long Valley, NJ 07853
201-876-4697
Medium: oil.

Meredith Morehead
204 Eureka Avenue
Silverton, OR 97381
503-873-6503
Medium: fiber.

Hannah D. Mott
125 Bartine Street
Somerville, NJ 08876
201-685-1910
Media: silkscreen and textiles.

Sunbow O'Brien
535 Hugo Street
San Francisco, CA 94122
415-731-7034
Medium: watercolor.

Kate O'Shea-Gillen
39 Seneca Avenue
Rockaway, NJ 07866
201-625-1009
Medium: fiber.

Diana Wilkoc Patton
497 Stony Brook Drive
Bridgewater, NJ 08807
201-722-0562
Media: watercolor, pen and ink.

Reni
720 East 2nd Avenue
Roselle, NJ 07203
201-245-1218
Free-lance Artist—fine art and
graphics.

Bernice Richmond
863 Carleton Road
Westfield, NJ 07090
201-654-3370
Commercial art; ceramics.

Rosalyn Rose
457 Baldwin Road
Maplewood, NJ 07040
201-763-5655
Artist; Printmaker.

Carol Rosen
Beavers Road
RR3, Box 57
Califon, NJ 07830
201-832-7780

Carolyn L. Sadowski
2376 Birch Place
Manasquan Park, NJ 08736
Medium: batik.

Barbara Schwinn
754 Belvidere Avenue
Westfield, NJ 07090
201-232-7058
Free-lance Artist.

Roz Shirley
4 Snyder Road
Medfield, MA 02052
617-359-2944
Medium: fiber.

Marian Slepian
5 Overlook Drive
Bridgewater, NJ 08807
201-526-5856
Medium: enamel—cloisonné.

Elsa Sullivan
4 Laurel Place Plaza
Upper Montclair, NJ 07043
201-783-9405
Medium: watercolor.

Zilla Sussman
42 Fairview Avenue
West Orange, NJ 07052
201-731-2325
Painter; Printmaker.

Carol D. Westfall
162 Whitford Avenue
Nutley, NJ 07110
Medium: fiber.

Buton Whicker
102 Melrose
Greenfield, TN 38230
901-235-2429
Painter.

Kimberly Wilder
Denver-Vega Road
Denver, NY 12421
607-326-7933
Medium: stained glass.

Ina Wishner
10 Knollwood Drive
Portchester, NY 10573
914-937-2020
Media: watercolor, graphics,
needlework.

Madlyn-Ann C. Woolwich
473 Marvin Drive
Long Branch, NJ 07740
201-229-3752
Media: oil, pastel, batik.

"The reason I work at home is so that I can be here when my children return from school....I can do my work whenever it suits me (although translations seem to almost always be rush jobs!) which is the biggest advantage of working at home."

Translator

■ Artists' Rep

Reggie Y. Wilson
26 Briarcliff Road
Livingston, NJ 07039
201-992-5456

■ Arts & Crafts Instructor

Joan Arbeiter
58 Elm Avenue
Metuchen, NJ 08840
201-549-8917
Painting and drawing.

Honey Bodenheimer
Country Crafts
17 Maple Stream Road
East Windsor, NJ 08520
609-443-3716
Crafts for children.

Ursula S. Dinshah
513 Old Harding Highway
Malaga, NJ 08328
609-694-3639
Dried flower arrangements, weed wreaths, pressed flower pictures, straw weavings.

Marjorie E. Fox
Medieval Brass Rubbing Centre
Route 203, Box 299
Windham Center, CT 06280
203-423-2785
Workshops on brass rubbing.

Joanne Goverman
14 Dellwood Road
White Plains, NY 10605
914-761-2014
Quilting.

Barbara Moskowitz
The Sleepless Needle
7 Sherwood Road
Edison, NJ 08817
201-548-0591
Needlepoint and pulled-thread techniques.

Phyllis M. Myers
139 Taylor Avenue
Somerville, NJ 08876
201-725-0563

Jean Perlmutter
200 Devon Road
Westwood, NJ 07675
201-664-4753
Craft classes.

Hildegard N. Pleva
197 Main Street
Kingston, NY 12401
914-331-5466
Quilting.

Lisa Steinberg
1 Beechtree Road
Roseland, NJ 07068
201-226-4385
Art lessons.

Zilla Sussman
42 Fairview Avenue
West Orange, NJ 07052
201-731-2325
Art lessons.

Martha Otis Wright
84 Maclean Circle
Princeton, NJ 08540
609-924-8016
Ceramics.

■ Astrologer

Lucy Little
225 Sprain Road
Scarsdale, NY 10583
914-693-6746
Consulting Astrologist; also teaches astrology.

■ Attorney

Margaret L. Baller
226 Blake Avenue
Somerset, NJ 08873
201-246-1666

E. Gioia Cipriano-Marciano
6 Gregory Avenue
West Orange, NJ 07052
201-731-6452
Practice limited to real estate and estates.

Sylvia Glickman
15 Holly Street
Somerset, NJ 08873
201-249-9317

■ Beauty Consultants

Judith Abaroa
RD 5, Lovell Street
Mahopac, NY 10541
914-248-5406
Mary Kay cosmetics.

Rosemary Bennett
512 Middlesex Avenue
Colonia, NJ 07067
201-382-3412
Mary Kay cosmetics.

Cecilia Greco
611 North Washington Avenue
Dunellen, NJ 08812
201-968-7037
Mary Kay cosmetics.

Janice Newman
115 Sunset Avenue
Newark, NJ 07106
201-373-4063
Mary Kay cosmetics.

Elayne Perry
11 Robin Lane
Milford, CT 06460
Avon cosmetics.

Suzanne H. Zilenziger
270 Nelson Road
Scarsdale, NY 10583
914-472-4676
Mary Kay cosmetics.

■ Bookkeeper

Elizabeth Cassady
5917 Brookland Road
Alexandria, VA 22310
703-971-0360

Doris G. Dempster
35 Monmouth Junction Road
Dayton, NJ 08520
201-329-6535

"As for my jewelry, I usually work in two directions at once, one which is spontaneous, funny, colorful, and playful, while the other is more subdued in color and straightforward. Both styles are important to me, and tend to regenerate and feed off one another. Most of my pieces...are designed on paper first, refined, and transferred to the metal. Often after I've started cutting the metal (which are pieces usually soldered or riveted together), I'll start to alter my original design and change it as it takes shape. Sometimes I feel as if the piece is making itself."

Jewelry Designer

Ruth M. Ferm
3425 Alabama Street
San Diego, CA 92104
714-291-4576

Marie L. Menichini
21 Stratford Drive
Old Bridge, NJ 08857
201-679-3115

■ Cake Decorator

Joyce Graichen
P.O. Box 42
Seaside Heights, NJ 08751
201-793-1395

■ Calligrapher

Joan Devon
Poemetrics
228 Standish Road
Merion, PA 19066
215-667-5896

Fran Klingsberg
5 Westview Lane
Scarsdale, NY 10583
914-725-4489

Mona McCormack
30 Woodside Avenue
Trenton, NJ 08618
609-695-2635

Jody Robbins
7805 Deer Trail
Dallas, TX 75238

■ Camp Consultant

Beverly Rich
Special Summers
8 Richbell Road
Scarsdale, NY 10583
914-472-9199

■ Camp Director

Amy Stein
49 Clubway
Hartsdale, NY 10530
914-472-6730

■ Career Counseling Consultant

Gail Lehmann
2365 Loring Place
Yorktown Heights, NY 10598
914-962-4578

■ Caterer

Joyce Becker
Nourishing Nibbles
481 Grove Avenue
Edison, NJ 08817
201-494-1266
Health-food snack service.

Maureen Berkman
30 Farragut Street
Scarsdale, NY 10583
914-723-7823

Leslie Smith Collier
8727 Fawn Drive
Dallas, TX 75238
512-341-5166

Claire Gulman
Nourishing Nibbles
481 Grove Avenue
Edison, NJ 08817
201-494-1266
Health-food snack service.

Gail Strauss
54 Stoneham Place
Metuchen, NJ 08840
201-494-3653
Hors d'oeuvres for home parties.

Edith Weiss
Cooking Sisters, Inc.
632 Sagamore Avenue
Teaneck, NJ 07666
201-836-5544
Gourmet catering.

■ Child Care Specialist

Donna L. Cline
Cline-Garcia Day Care
373 Bowfin Street
Foster City, CA 94404
415-574-4670
Day care providers—drop-in day care.

Phyllis Garcia
Cline-Garcia Day Care
373 Bowfin Street
Foster City, CA 94404
415-574-4670
Day care providers—drop-in day care.

Elayne Perry
11 Robin Lane
Milford, CT 06460
Babysitter.

Pamela Sarett
Little Red School
48 Carter Road
Princeton, NJ 08450
609-466-2873
Child care center.

■ Children's Entertainer

Elizabeth Marsha Kendall
"Clementine, The Classroom Clown"
1620 Monmouth Avenue
Lakewood, NJ 08701
201-364-5571

Judy Caden
21 Glen Road
West Orange, NJ 07052
201-731-6461
201-889-5328
Puppet shows and workshops.

■ Clothing Designer/Manufacturer

Mary Brooks
Something Special
37 Barnwell Drive
White Plains, NY 10607
914-997-0373
Unique designs in sequins and
rhinestones on sportswear.

Carole Ferster
Handcrafted Wearables
125 Ramona Court
New Rochelle, NY 10804
914-235-5699
Handpainted and embroidered
designs on clothing.

Gail Francis
800 Grand Concourse
Bronx, NY 10451
212-665-8753
Crochet apparel.

Gale Kramer Goldman
8 Tam O'Shanter Drive
Purchase, NY 10577
914-428-7822
Clothing and costume design.

"I travel to Guatemala about 2-3 times a year to prepare for each different season. Most of my business comes from exhibitions at the National Fashion and Boutique Show twice a year at the New York Coliseum. Forty thousand retailers attend."

Importer

Margaret W. Johnson
P.O. Box 218
East Hanover, NJ 07936
201-386-9314
Manufactures skating apparel.

Chana Ann Kirschner
18 Oak Crest Road
West Orange, NJ 07052
201-736-1960
Wearable art—batik and direct dye
on fabric.

Marilynn Larson
Chevré Associates
5 Deertrail Road
Saddle River, NJ 07458
201-327-1438
Manufactures women's sportswear.

Murielle Peters-Davis
Mama Mimi Embroidery
2661 Marion Avenue—#5B
Bronx, NY 10458
914-295-7823
Children's underwear and T-shirts.

Sarelle Rosner
Handcrafted Wearables
205 Devoe Avenue
Yonkers, NY 10705
914-968-0573
Handpainted and embroidered
designs on clothing.

■ Collection Agent

Rosemary Cafasso
14 Morris Avenue
Riverdale, NJ 07457
201-839-1203

Midge Touw
104 Lake Park Terrace
Hewitt, NJ 07421
201-728-2133

■ Communications Consultant

Jacqueline K. Browner
JK Browner Associates
3712 Windom Place, NW
Washington, DC 22016
202-686-1696
Public information, public relations,
marketing, publicity.

Sybil Conrad
30 Edgewood Road
Scarsdale, NY 10583
914-725-2360

Eva Glase
Words and Images
62 Turning Mill Road
Lexington, MA 02173
617-861-0484
Writing, editing, design, promotion,
and public relations.

Geri Jefferson
35 Midwood Street
Brooklyn, NY 11225
212-462-1638
Audio tapes: children and adults;
brochures, feature articles, grants
counseling, proposals, teaching
guides.

Sharon A. Morgan
Sharon A. Morgan and Associates
4840 South King Drive
Chicago, IL 60615
312-266-0383
Special promotions and events,
newsletter development and writing,
speech-writing, press releases,
marketing and sales materials.
Program planning, funding strategies,
foundation and procurement research. Position and strategy papers,
presentations, program descriptions.

Lee Strauss
Ampersand
16 Forest Drive
Morris Plains, NJ 07950
201-538-9407
Program/project planning, data
gathering and analysis, concept
development, editorial and graphics
services, special events and program
management.

Erika Tauber
Words and Images
62 Turning Mill Road
Lexington, MA 02173
617-861-0484
Writing, editing, design, promotion,
and public relations.

Caryl Winter
Presentations with Impact
400 South Beverly Drive, Suite 312
Beverly Hills, CA 90212
213-933-0933
Conducts workshops on the art of
business writing, making effective
presentations, and developing policies
and procedures.

■ Contractor

Wendy E. Moldovan
3826 Old Crompond Road
Peekskill, NY 10566
914-739-3448
Apartment Contractor—renovation
and rental.

'I am also lucky in having friends and family who understand that if I am home, there are times I'm available and times I'm working. They take my business seriously and respect my working hours just as they would if I went out to an office. Maybe the reason is that I take what I do seriously. That's important, too."

Advertising Consultant

■ Copywriter

Marianna Murphy
5 Clinton Avenue
Maplewood, NJ 07040
201-763-5339

Shirley Thomas-Hersh
3415 West Foster, #206
Chicago, IL 60625
312-583-6044
Advertising Copywriter.

■ Craftsperson

Eleanor C. Beck
The Doll Dressmaker
56 Ronald Court
Ramsey, NJ 07466
201-327-2271
Repair and restoration of dolls; also
doll dressmaking.

Linda Benzaia
704 Wilson Court
River Vale, NJ 07675
201-666-7476
Personalized handpainted children's
shirts; custom orders.

Honey Bodenheimer
Country Crafts
17 Maple Stream Road
East Windsor, NJ 08520
609-443-3716
Candles, macramé, spice ropes,
hobby horses, Christmas ornaments,
doll clothes, and pillows.

Barbara Broadbent
P.O. Box 145
Egg Harbor, NJ 08215
609-965-5107
Handcrafted leather goods.

Margo Brown
457 North Main
Buffalo, WY 82834
307-684-9406
Stoneware and porcelain pottery.

Linda Carey
4306 73rd Avenue NW
Gig Harbor, WA 98335
206-265-3887
Macramé, flower arrangements,
ceramics, and plastercraft.

Nancy Coggins
3932 Cheesequake Road
Parlin, NJ 08859
201-727-3829
Handicrafts in fabric, glass, leather,
metal, plastics, plaster, wax, and
wood.

Diane Colon
379 Lincoln Avenue
Cliffside Park, NJ 07010
201-943-6570
One-of-a-kind three-dimensional
ric-rac flowers on gingham in shadow
box frames; also Christmas
ornaments.

Andi Dalton
P.O. Box 222
14900 Canyon #2 Road
Rio Nido, CA 95471
707-869-0475
Rosewood crochet hooks, pens,
chopsticks.

Ann De Falco
102 Fairmount Avenue
Chester, NJ 07930
201-879-5556
Artist; Sign Painter; Restorer of old
paintings; Calligrapher.

Ursula S. Dinshah
513 Old Harding Highway
Malaga, NJ 08328
609-694-3639
Dried flower pictures and
arrangements.

Name Withheld
Ferne Sales and Manufacturing Co.
P.O. Box 133 TCB
West Orange, NJ 07052
201-731-0967
Advertising specialty items: hand-
screened T-shirts, tote bags.

Kathleen A. Finn
Wooden Mountain
114 Perry Street
Berkeley Springs, WV 25411
304-258-4249
Wooden puzzles and wall hangings.

Nina Forrest
246 Maple Street
Haworth, NJ 07641
201-387-1890
Vacuformed signs—stock items or
individually designed, professionally
crafted.

Marjorie E. Fox
Medieval Brass Rubbing Centre
Route 203, Box 299
Windham Center, CT 06280
203-423-2785
Brass rubbings.

Phyllis Gebert
Carrie Lauren Designs
35 Avon Road
New Rochelle, NY 10804
914-576-2286
Country decorations with natural and
dried materials.

Susette Gould-Malloy
Jasmine Artisans
475 North 5th Street
Newark, NJ 07107
201-483-5554
Quiltwork, appliqué, motifs, and
assorted paraphernalia for children.

Joanna Goverman
14 Dellwood Road
White Plains, NY 10605
914-761-2014
Quilting.

Phyllis Baker Hammond
285 Scarborough Road
Scarborough, NY 10510
914-762-4194
Clay sculpture.

"My office is separate enough from the

mainstream of the house but not

completely private. It is my oasis

and special place. I have fixed it

up to be cozy, comfortable, and

pleasing to my aesthetic taste."

Psychologist

Sandi F. Howell
554 South 10th Avenue
Mount Vernon, NY 10550
914-699-4372
Pottery, ceramics, sewing, knitting;
Herbalist.

Marion Josephson
650 Prospect Avenue
West Orange, NJ 07052
201-325-8366
Potter; also designs note paper.

Beverly LeBeau
708 West Park Avenue
Oakhurst, NJ 07755
Engravings on used roofing slate.

Francine S. Litofsky
13 Rambling Brook Drive
Holmdel, NJ 07733
201-946-4463
Production Weaver.

Diane Mahon
89 Metropolitan Oval
Bronx, NY 10462
212-892-1904
Dolls; all-occasion cards.

Charlotte Malten
193 Germonds Road
West Nyack, NY 10994
914-623-3235
Pottery and ceramic sculpture.

June R. Monnier
1 Scenic Drive
Highlands, NJ 07732
201-291-2411
Birds carved in wood.

Bonny E. Mulvey
30 Orchard
Bernardsville, NJ 07924
201-766-7343
Macramé, stained glass, pen-and-ink
sketches, sculpture, painting.

Frances E. Mustard
At the Sign of the Thistle
Fairmont Road
Pottersville, NJ 07979
201-439-2089
Manufactures naturally dyed wool
embroidery kits.

Gabrielle Nappo
715 West Bay Avenue
Barnegat, NJ 08005
Weaving.

Leslie Nerz
P.O. Box 145
Egg Harbor, NJ 08215
609-965-5107
Handcrafted leather goods.

Peggy Nugent
74 Hamilton Avenue
Leonardo, NJ 07737
201-872-0192
Crochets afghans, pillows, accessories.

Dianne Owen
27 Fieldstone Drive
Hartsdale, NY 10530
914-948-8007
Macramé fiber art.

Jean Perlmutter
200 Devon Road
Westwood, NJ 07675
201-664-4753
Paper toile, gold inlay, mini-
repoussé, tinsel painting—invitations,
announcements, awards, honors
specially preserved; classes at home.

Lydia Pizzute
27 Sieber Court
Bergenfield, NJ 07621
201-384-4929
One-of-a-kind three-dimensional ric-
rac flowers on gingham in shadow
box frames; also Christmas
ornaments.

Hildegard N. Pleva
197 Main Street
Kingston, NY 12401
914-331-5466
Quilting.

Polly Reilly
520 Sherwood Parkway
Westfield, NJ 07090
201-233-2510
Handpainted wooden tree ornaments.

Bernice Richmond
863 Carleton Road
Westfield, NJ 07090
201-654-3370
Ceramic sculpture.

Susan Rubin
302 West 79th Street, #7C
New York, NY 10024
212-877-3614
Color xerographic post cards.

Sarah A. Saltus
Pleasant Hill Road
Chester, NJ 07930
201-879-6281
Batik T-shirts, pillows, calico animals.

Sherry Schuster
1565 North Lake Drive
Lakewood, NJ 08701
201-364-9586
Kiln-fired glass objects d'art.

Sandy Schwarz
Sandesigns
142 Van Houton Avenue
Chatham, NJ 07928
201-635-9212
Designs and creates a collection of
needlepoint boutique kits sold
throughout U.S., Puerto Rico, Guam,
Australia, and Canada.

Helen Seymour
Personally Puzzled
69 Edgemere Avenue
Plainsboro, NJ 08536
609-799-0845
Wooden jigsaw puzzles.

Dorothy Sinclair
JoDot Creations and Eudora
848 Woodmere Drive
Cliffwood Beach, NJ 07735
201-566-4704
Embroidered trapunto pictures,
"Eudora" dolls, bread dough
sculptures.

Judith Stein
175 Castlebar Road
Rochester, NY 14610
716-271-2585
Fibercrafts: weaving, dye painting,
printmaking on fabric.

Lisa Steinberg
1 Beechtree Road
Roseland, NJ 07068
201-226-4385

Nadine A. Weiss
161 Culberson Road
Basking Ridge, NJ 07920
201-766-5228
Pottery, sculpture, rug hooking,
stitchery, weaving without a loom,
copper enameling, stained glass.

Cynthia Winika
P.O. Box 906
New Paltz, NY 12561
914-255-9338
Pillows—printed and painted.

Joan Wortis
89 West Bridge Street
New Hope, PA 18938
215-862-2121
Handweaving.

Martha Otis Wright
84 Maclean Circle
Princeton, NJ 08540
609-924-8016
Pottery and sculpture.

Raku Pot
Martha Otis Wright
Potter
Photographer: Nina Alexander

Marilyn Joan Wander
88 Audubon Road
Teaneck, NJ 07666
201-833-0539
Potter.

Ann Weiner
Victorian Vintage
P.O. Box 761
Clark, NJ 07066
201-382-2135
Miniatures and dolls.

Gail Wisneski
13 Hampshire Road
Midland Park, NJ 07432
201-447-6457
Calico Christmas decorations.

Margaret Faith Wolverton
289 Riverbrook Avenue
Lincroft, NJ 07738
201-747-9354
Puppets; also ink drawings of homes
and businesses.

Susan C. Wright
909 Duncan Street
Ann Arbor, MI 48103
313-663-6015
Handwoven rugs, blankets, scarves.

■ Creative Consultant

Edith Fava
Pinch-Hitters, Inc.
4308 Cottage Avenue
North Bergen, NJ 07047
201-866-8938
212-662-4270
Singing telegrams, cookiegrams,
balloongrams, special events.

Madelene Fink
Witty Ditty
29 Cornell Street
Scarsdale, NY 10583
914-GR 2-GRAM
Singing telegrams, custom-written
songs.

Kay Longo
Pinch-Hitters, Inc.
Address Withheld
201-866-8938
212-662-4270
Singing telegrams, cookiegrams,
balloongrams, special events.

Roberta O'Hanlon
Pinch-Hitters, Inc.
Address Withheld
201-866-8938
212-662-4270
Singing telegrams, cookiegrams,
balloongrams, special events.

Emily Rosen
Witty Ditty
29 Cornell Street
Scarsdale, NY 10583
914-GR 2-GRAM
Singing telegrams, custom-written
songs.

Susan Warn
Pinch-Hitters, Inc.
Address Withheld
201-866-8938
212-662-4270
Singing telegrams, cookiegrams,
balloongrams, special events.

■ Custom Drapery Designer

Marion Ruane
40 Forest Hill Drive
Howell, NJ 07731
201-367-9489

Donna Lee Spencer
Route 1, Box 212A
Fruitland, ID 83619
208-452-3372
Drapery workrooms.

■ Dance Instructor

Jackie Lynn
34 Warwick Road
Edison, NJ 08817
201-548-8452
Teacher and Director of dance studio.

Jackie Lynn
Dance Instructor
Photographer:
Frank Wojciechowski

■ Data Processor

Marlene Piturro
B.J. Silverman & Co., Inc.
3 Wagner Place
Hastings, NY 10706
914-478-1199
Computerized financial services,
mailings.

■ Designer

Gail Zavian
175 Manhattan Avenue
Jersey City, NJ 07307
201-795-3050
Free-lance Designer—Promoter.

■ Diet Consultant

Fredda Kray
Sheridan Road
Scarsdale, NY 10583
914-723-2997
Diet control and weight maintenance.

■ Doctor

Toni Gloria Novick, M.D.
621 Pine Brook Boulevard
New Rochelle, NY 10804
914-235-1526
Gynecology and family planning.

■ Drama Coach

Jane Sharp
33 Engle Street
Tenafly, NJ 07670
201-567-0644

■ Dressmaker

Stella Bari
716 Allen Avenue
Vineland, NJ 08360
201-691-4483

Carol Kroupa
Carol's Alterations & Sewing
23 Roberta Drive
Howell, NJ 07731
201-458-2915

Diane Mahon
89 Metropolitan Oval
Bronx, NY 10462
212-892-1904
Custom-tailored clothing.

"Since I love to sew, I have a machine for each process in making draperies and bedspreads. Have 20 machines. Nearly every interior job needs window coverings. We have them all.

Have a 28-foot motor home that is a great help on out of town and state jobs. Also have three vans for local work. Have a pick-up for larger deliveries such as carpet, besides a Lincoln for personal use.

My home is 5 miles from the nearest town. There are 5 towns within 10 miles from me, 4 others within 16 miles."

Interior Designer

Margaret Charlene Newlin
8526 Thunderbird Lane
Dallas, TX 75238
214-341-2795

■ Editor

Peggy Bendel
113 Chestnut Avenue
Bogota, NJ 07603
201-343-3613
Free-lance Editor/Writer.

Jill Groce
10904 Bucknell Drive, #1112
Silver Spring, MD 20902
301-942-0544

Alison W. Heckler
5812 Maryhurst Drive
Hyattsville, MD 20782
301-559-6489
Editorial support services—editing, writing, indexing, proofreading.

Laura Horowitz
Editorial Experts
5905 Pratt Street
Alexandria, VA 22310
703-971-7350
Editorial services company providing writing, editing, research, indexing, proofreading, and manuscript typing: specializing in education, government, consumer and urban/community affairs.

Eleanor Johnson
8433 Willow Forge Road
Springfield, VA 22152
703-451-6814
Administrative editorial work—newsletter marketing, correspondence, research, proofreading.

Claire Kincaid
13316 Old Forge Road
Silver Spring, MD 20904
301-384-2495

Bernadette Knoblauch
9617 Beach Mill Road
Great Falls, VA 22066
703-759-2255

Katherine Lee
Precision Unlimited
722 Faxon Avenue
San Francisco, CA 94112
415-239-6611
Proofreader.

Cynthia S. Lowe
Rainbow Squared
  Communications, Inc.
7830 Eagle Trail
Dallas, TX 75238
214-349-8586
Editing and writing service.

Marie MacBride
412 North Monroe Street
Ridgewood, NJ 07450
201-652-7833
Copy editing, proofreading.

Sara McAulay
Box 52
Mountain Lakes, NJ 07046
201-263-2197

Mara Mills
335 East 10th Street
New York, NY 10009
212-254-5173

Margaret P. Roeske
5 Meade Court
Somerset, NJ 08873
201-828-8632
Free-lance editing, indexing.

Helen Simon
24 Birkendene Road
Caldwell, NJ 07006
201-226-9255
Coding and editing service for market research.

Elaine Sullivan
6100 Larkspur Drive
Alexandria, VA 22310
703-971-4916
Proofreading.

Marty Thomson
1933 Biltmore Street NW
Washington, DC 20009
202-462-1285
Writing and editing—mainly for business publications.

■ Educational Consultant

Peg Carey
771 Princeton-Kingston Road
Princeton, NJ 08540
609-921-1526
Newspaper in education Consultant.

Peg Carey
Newspaper in Education
Consultant

Kayla J. Silberberg
Chappaqua College Counseling
  Service
83 Old Lyme Road
Chappaqua, NY 10514
914-238-5257
Educational counseling.

■ Educational Researcher

Dorothy Cohen
5 Mountain Way South
West Orange, NJ 07052
201-736-4525

■ Exhibition Producer

Beverly Michael
P.O. Box 382
Fair Lawn, NJ 07410
201-791-3145
Organizes antique shows, flea
markets, street fairs, mall promotions,
craft shows.

Irene Stella
Stella Shows
162 Stuart Street
Paramus, NJ 07652
201-262-3063
Antique shows and exhibitions for
fund raising and promotions.

■ Fabric and Wallpaper Designer

Dorene Schwartz-Weitz
147 Harbinson Place
East Windsor, NJ 08520
609-443-5549

■ Fashion Consultant

Eleanor Moss
16 Butler Road
Scarsdale, NY 10583
Personal shopping—women's wardrobes and gifts.

■ Field Organizer

Mimi Rabois
29 Jonathan Drive
Edison, NJ 08817
201-494-7127
Field Organizer for Common Cause,
citizens lobby group.

■ Film Producer

Maria Fiore
Latinos Unlimited
1701 West 69th Street
Chicago, IL 60636
312-922-0579

■ Food and Cooking Instructor

Maureen Berkman
30 Farragut Street
Scarsdale, NY 10683
914-723-7823

Judy Ignall
127 Howard Terrace
Leonia, NJ 07605
201-461-8223
Cooking lessons to children and
adults.

Adele Shinder
Living Arts Studio
41-65 Rys Terrace
Fair Lawn, NJ 07410
201-796-1728
Food preparation.

Emilie Taylor
189 Kaywin Road
Paramus, NJ 07652
201-265-4145
Meat buying, cutting, cookery.

■ Furniture Designer/Manufacturer

Ann Jacobson
Planters Plus
11 Floren Place
Scarsdale, NY 10583
914-472-5540
Mirrored furniture.

Marian Rubin
Planters Plus
14 Short Lane
New Rochelle, NY 10804
914-235-1746
Mirrored furniture.

■ Gift Designer/Manufacturer

Rhoda Kelner
Fill 'Em Up
47 Jamaica Street
Edison, NJ 08817
201-549-8044
Lucite and ceramic gift items.

Emilie Taylor
Food Instructor
Photographer: Jack Anderson

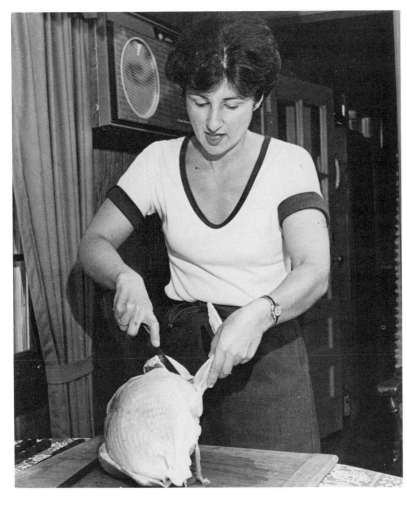

Susan Kelner
Fill 'Em Up
47 Jamaica Street
Edison, NJ 08817
201-549-8044
Lucite and ceramic gift items.

Myrna R. Youdelman
Gift Finders International
7 Tennyson Street
Hartsdale, NY 10530
914-948-6121
Designs, manufactures, and
distributes gifts.

■ Graphic Designer

Malle N. Whitaker
The Design Workshop
152 Paulison Avenue
Passaic, NJ 07055
201-778-9369
Advertising, design, and illustration.

Katie Winterstein
Little Moon Studio, Inc.
12 Morrison Drive
New Rochelle, NY 10804
914-428-7571
Advertising, design, and illustration.

■ Growth Counsellor

Dr. Susan A. Holton
Creative Potential Development
204 Central Street
Framingham, MA 01701
617-877-6278
Consultation; facilitation of groups
focusing on significant life issues and
problem solving.

Wendy King, R.N., M.S.
53 Kossuth Street
Somerset, NJ 08873
201-828-9317
Nutritional awareness and self-
improvement courses; health-related
services.

Barbara Lafer
44 Mandeville Drive
Wayne, NJ 07470
201-694-8013
Conducts personal growth workshops
for adolescents and adults.

Judith Pierson
26 Lincoln Avenue
Highland Park, NJ 08904
201-249-2870
Consultation and training: social
work/mental health practice with
women.

■ Home Decorator

Adrienne Gallo
JAM Co.
31 Winding Trail
Mahwah, NJ 07430
201-327-7858
Designs and coordinates a home
decorating line sold wholesale and
retail.

Janet Romandetta
JAM Co.
39 Winding Trail
Mahwah, NJ 07430
201-825-1035
Designs and coordinates a home
decorating line sold wholesale and
retail.

■ Home Economist

Adele Shinder
Living Arts Studio
41-65 Rys Terrace
Fair Lawn, NJ 07410
201-796-1728
Courses in food preparation, sewing,
home management.

■ Home Repairer/Restylist

Fran Derlinga
The Paperdoll
27 Heather Lane
Mahwah, NJ 07430
201-529-4081
Wallpaper Hanger.

"My workplace is a lovely little workshop

all set up in my den closet. I

open the folding doors and

whala! a carpenters bench—com-

plete with vise, saws, knives, and

foredom tool."

Craftsperson

Daria Finn
Finnishing Touch
164 Sargeant Avenue
Clifton, NJ 07013
201-473-1499
All-women painting and contracting
company—interior and exterior work,
including wallpaper and wall
graphics.

Flo-Ann Goerke
Georgia Road
Freehold, NJ 07728
201-462-2785
Home repairs.

■ Horticulturist

Linda Blaney
3 Abalone Road
Narragansett, RI 02822
401-783-8180
Grows and sells herbs, their by-
products, and vegetables.

Elizabeth K. Cummins
22 Robertsville Road
Marlboro, NJ 07746
201-536-2591
Retail mail-order plant business.

Linda M. Cromarty
213 Central Avenue
West Caldwell, NJ 07006
201-228-3465
Horticultural interior design.

Ann Shepard
Shepard's Garden Center
P.O. Box 2094
Edison, NJ 08817
201-549-4330

■ Hypnotist

Susanne Pitak
65 Swan Street
Lambertville, NJ 08530
609-397-2541

Ruth Seligman
Metamorphics, Inc.
5 Drummond Road
Westfield, NJ 07090
201-654-3200

■ Importer/Exporter

Lori K. Boden
8 Dannybrook Place
Yonkers, NY 10710
914-337-3444
Gift Distributor; Importer; sales
agency.

Valerie A. Eichen
274 Livingston Avenue
New Brunswick, NJ 08901
201-246-4007
Imports accessories and apparel sold
wholesale.

Marie Louise Gill
Gill Imports, Inc.
P.O. Box 73
Ridgefield, CT 06877
203-438-7409
Imports fine handicrafts from India:
crewel fabrics and oriental rugs sold
wholesale and retail by mail order.

Betsy Kuga
Beihon Trade Co.
406 3rd Street
Hoboken, NJ 07030
201-656-8711
Imports handmade rice paper for
printmaking and bookbinding; exports books, greeting cards, frisbees.

Rose Rogozinski
Seneca Coal and Coke Corp.
Jomark Corp.
Harlingen-Dutchtown Road
Belle Mead, NJ 08502
201-359-8860

Name Withheld
Importers & Traders of Assorted
European Goods
Little Ferry, NJ 07643
201-440-4907
Imports high quality Irish goods.

Lynn Walter
48 Sargent Road
Scarsdale, NY 10583
914-472-1475
Imports and exports machinery.

■ Information Consultant

Dr. Penny Pypcznski
Penfield Associates
26 Brenwal Avenue
Ewing, NJ 08618
609-882-4657

■ Instructor for the Handicapped

Barbara Isaac
Riding High Farms
P.O. Box 229, Route 526
Allentown, NJ 08501
609-259-3884
Horseback riding instruction.

■ Insurance Agent/Broker

Dee de Peralta
1387 Alvarado Avenue
Lakewood, NJ 08701
201-367-6697
Insurance Broker.

Isabel Bogorad Fleiss
WomanSurance Advisory Services
P.O. Box 3034
Wayne, NJ 07470
201-956-1085
Insurance Broker.

Julie Rogers
115 Wells Drive
South Plainfield, NJ 07080
201-731-1200
Insurance Agent: financial and estate
planning.

■ Interior Designer

Toby Baron
Window Designs
21 Cohawney Road
Scarsdale, NY 10583
914-725-2633

Rochelle Bender
Window Designs
1042 Webster Avenue
New Rochelle, NY 10804
914-235-8076

Ellen Bruck
26 Park Street
Tenafly, NJ 07670
201-871-0832

Dvora Fields
50 Brite Avenue
Scarsdale, NY 10583
914-472-5988

Sally Gradinger
800 Columbia Drive
San Mateo, CA 94402
415-343-6530

Mimi Mendelson
100 Secor Road
Scarsdale, NY 10583
914-723-5981

Sandra Miller
50 Brite Avenue
Scarsdale, NY 10583
914-725-5070

Myra Terry-Meisner
370 Central Avenue
Mountainside, NJ 07092
201-232-6054

■ Inventor

Lea-Claire M. Mascio
1600 Woodland Avenue
South Plainfield, NJ 07080
201-755-0058

■ Investment Counsellor

Saralee Luchansky
120 RD #2
Freehold, NJ 07728
Private investing.

Fran Derlinga
Interior Decorator
Photographer: Al Paglione

Fran Derlinga
The Paperdoll
27 Heather Lane
Mahwah, NJ 07430
201-529-4081
Interior Decorator.

Linda Blair Doescher
Linda Blair Associates
11 Fox Meadow Road
Scarsdale, NY 10583
914-472-5690
Home furnishings Consultant.

Ellen Rosko
73 Normandy Road
Colonia, NJ 07067
201-382-2543

Donna Lee Spencer
Route #1, Box 212A
Fruitland, ID 83619
208-452-3372
Drapery workroom.

■ Jewelry Designer/Manufacturer

Loretta Blessing
2931 Centre Street
Merchantville, NJ 08109
609-665-2353
Gold and silver jewelry.

Ann M. Davis
157 Booth Avenue
Englewood, NJ 07631
201-567-8857
Silver jewelry.

Nancy Irons
337 Chestnut Street
Audubon, NJ 08106
609-546-4812
Original silver jewelry.

Wilma O. Reid
81 Bruce Avenue
Yonkers, NY 10705
914-965-2332
Custom silver jewelry.

Sue Sachs
40 Camelot Road
Parsippany, NJ 07054
201-884-2734
Gold and silver jewelry.

Julie Shaw
Address Withheld
Birmingham, MI 48009
313-642-2808

■ Landscape Architect

Kathleen Condon Enz
RD #1, Hidden Hollow Farm
Washington, NJ 07882
201-689-2306

■ Lecturer

Eleanor C. Beck
The Doll Dressmaker
56 Ronald Court
Ramsey, NJ 07446
201-327-2271
Subject: America's First Ladies, with
authentically dressed First Lady dolls.

Elizabeth Carr
664 Belleforte Avenue
Oak Park, IL 60302
312-848-3340
Antique Appraiser and Collector.

Sara Eyestone
20 Blair Court
Ocean Township, NJ 07712
201-922-4520
Painter and Textile Designer.

Marjorie E. Fox
Medieval Brass Rubbing Centre
Route 203, Box 299
Windham Center, CT 06280
203-423-2785
Subject: brass rubbings

Naomi Kolstein
"Goat Lady"
7 Faist Drive
Spring Valley, NY 10977
914-352-6917
Subject: goats—and brings pet goat,
Flash, with her.

■ Librarian

Peggy Z. Ehrman
Biblio Services
83 Bertwell Road
Lexington, MA 02173
617-862-8367
Sets up and maintains libraries for
business and industry; also
information research and retrieval by
traditional methods or computer
data bases.

Jean Greenbaum
57 County Road
Demarest, NJ 07627
201-768-5096
Organizes, catalogs, classifies,
preserves, and restores books; also advises on acquisitions, shelving, and
technical problems of small private or
institutional book collections.

■ Literary Agent

Rae Lindsay
364 Mauro Road
Englewood Cliffs, NJ 07632
201-567-8986

■ Mail-Order Sales Director

Elizabeth K. Cummins
The Cummins Garden
22 Robertsville Road
Marlboro, NJ 07746
201-536-2591
Retail plant business.

Mariam Eikenberry
The Book Cart
4082 Kilbourn Road
Arcanum, OH 45304
513-548-8582
Books—how-to and informational
materials.

Ferne Sales and Manufacturing Co.
P.O. Box 113 TCB
West Orange, NJ 07052
201-731-0967
Advertising specialty items: T-shirts,
tote bags, bumper stickers, buttons.

Mary Jo Gatti
Dayspring
322 Abbey Road
Manhasset, NY 11030
516-627-2891
Personalized business gifts.

Marie Louise Gill
Gill Imports, Inc.
P.O. Box 73
Ridgefield, CT 06877
203-438-7409
Fine handicrafts from India: crewel
fabrics and oriental rugs sold
wholesale and retail.

Ann Rutten
78 Elbert Street
Ramsey, NJ 07466
201-327-7197
Antiques: sewing and needlework collectibles, Depression Era Glassware
and china, post cards, and advertising
items.

■ Management Consultant

Linda Abrams
15 Carstensen Road
Scarsdale, NY 10583
914-723-9067

Sonia E. Schlenger
Organizational Systems
6 Aberdeen Place
Fair Lawn, NJ 07410
201-791-2396
201-943-3700

■ Marketing/Media Consultant

Sylvia Allen
P.O. Box 272
Fair Haven, NJ 07701
201-741-8658

Katherine F. Bailey
48 Baldwin Avenue
Somerset, NJ 98873
201-469-0464
Senior Sales Director, Mary Kay
Cosmetics.

Judy Engstrom
316 White Horse Pike, Apt. 203
Collings Wood, NJ 08107
609-858-6141

Sylvia Allen
Marketing Consultant

Judith Gordon
Judith Gordon Associates
111 Sierra Vista Way
Lafayette, CA 94549
415-284-9360

Jan Johnson
1339 Highland Avenue
Plainfield, NJ 07060
201-753-5417

Sarah Graham Mann
SGM Marketing Services
224 Falmouth Road
Scarsdale, NY 10583
914-723-8632

Jeanne Mattson
Route 82
LaGrangeville, NY 12540
914-223-3056
Senior Sales Director, Mary Kay
Cosmetics.

Barbara S. Sloan
1425 Cedarview Avenue
Lakewood, NJ 08701
201-363-5424

■ Masseuse

Shalomé
111 North Pine Avenue
Albany, NY 12203
518-489-3320
Massage therapy and hypnotherapy.

■ Medical Lab Technician

Evelyn Breeden
182 Ridgewood Avenue
Glen Ridge, NJ 07028
201-743-8445

■ Music Teacher/Performer

LaVerne Hunt Gallob
19 MacArthur Avenue
Closter, NJ 07624
201-768-3057
Private piano lessons; music classes for children.

Meri Lobel
11 Lake Street, 7C
White Plains, NY 10603
914-761-1049
Flute, piano, recorder, and music theory.

Gabriella Mancini
1 Koster Boulevard, Apt. 5A
Edison, NJ 08817
201-494-8013
Piano Accompanist for performing artists; also Piano Teacher—classical music only.

Gwen O'Neill
The Music Learning Place
44 Oakridge Road
Verona, NJ 07044
201-239-0631
Music Specialist for pre-schoolers; group lessons for all ages.

Cathie Ruppi
398 Tenafly Road
Englewood, NJ 07631
201-871-1643
Music studio: piano and guitar lessons.

Barbara M. Sharman
176 West Shore Road
Harrington Park, NJ 07640
201-768-1947
Piano Teacher.

Carolyn G. Streicher
37 Montrose Road
Scarsdale, NY 10583
914-725-5781
Flute Teacher.

Shirley Thomas-Hersh
3415 West Foster, #206
Chicago, IL 60625
312-583-6044
Guitar Teacher.

Suzanne Tillman
67 Pageant Lane
Willingboro, NJ 08046
609-877-3973
Voice Teacher.

■ Organization Coordinator

Fran Avallone
80 Hilltop Boulevard
East Brunswick, NJ 08816
201-254-8665
State Coordinator, Right to Choose.

■ Party Planner

Patricia S. Ardizzone
A.N.D. Engine Company 3 Corp.
114 Mamaroneck Avenue
White Plains, NY 10605
914-428-1452
Uses fire engine for parties, promotions, and limousine service.

Miriam Cohen
Special Occasions
7706 Yamini Drive
Dallas, TX 75230
214-363-4744
Party rental service.

Carol Desoe
A.N.D. Engine Company 3 Corp.
14 Fern Way
Scarsdale, NY 10583
914-723-2267
Uses fire engine for parties, promotions, and limousine service.

Marna Gold
Gold 'N Dot, Inc.
46 Alpine Drive
Closter, NJ 07624
201-768-8927
"Eat Your Heart Out"—boxed feasts and coordinated theme parties.

Dot Hofmann
Gold 'N Dot, Inc.
120 Maplewood Avenue
Bogota, NJ 07603
201-342-1984
"Eat Your Heart Out"—boxed feasts and coordinated theme parties.

Ellyn Hopkins
La Chariettes
24 Hudson Terrace, Apt. 6W
Fort Lee, NJ 07024
201-592-1535
Private valet parking service for weddings, graduations, Bar Mitzvahs.

Ann Olesky
Special Occasions
7706 Yamini Drive
Dallas, TX 75230
214-748-3189
Party rental service.

Joan Picket
In Good Taste
12 Cooper Road
Scarsdale, NY 10583
914-725-5646

Linda Singer
In Good Taste
12 Cooper Road
Scarsdale, NY 10583
914-723-1731

Ann Sutera
La Chariettes
2400 Hudson Terrace, Apt. 6W
Fort Lee, NJ 07024
201-592-1535
Private valet parking service for weddings, graduations, Bar Mitzvahs.

■ Personal and Professional Development Consultant

Annette B. Crema
Bardouille-Crema & Associates
P.O. Box 276
Edgewater, NJ 07020
201-224-2746
201-327-7462

Nancy A. Fuller
Projects Unlimited
626 East 20th Street, 6D
New York, NY 10009
212-228-1758
Personalized administrative service bureau assisting individuals and organizations: meeting arrangements, relocation assistance, parties and tours, special purchases, editing and transcription services, research.

Connie Chris Marshall
Home Uniqueness Enterprises
PO Box 36
Minersvillle, UT 84752
801-386-2266
Home Uniqueness Consultant.

DJ Mazer
Projects Unlimited
626 East 20th Street, 6D
New York, NY 10009
212-228-1758
Personalized administrative service bureau assisting individuals and organizations: meeting arrangements, relocation assistance, parties and tours, special purchases, editing and transcription services, research.

■ Personal Services Consultant

Yvette M.L. King
22 Ernest Street
Nutley, NJ 07110
201-667-6756

■ Personnel Placement Specialist

Marlene F. Kehler
405 Ridge Crest Drive
Richardson, TX 75080
214-238-9204
Executive recruiting.

Coralee Smith Kern
Maid-to-Order, Inc.
224 South Michigan Avenue
Chicago, IL 60604
312-939-6490
Maid, party, vacation, nursing and companion services.

Joan Bannigan Walsh
RD 2, Box 403
Flemington, NJ 08822
201-782-0066
Personnel placement/career counselling.

■ Photographer

Emily M. Eldridge
Copy Cats Limited
91 Main Street
Metuchen, NJ 08840
201-548-2369
Antique photographs—copied, printed, brown-toned, or restored; also portraits, transparencies, duplication.

Wall Flowers for Indian Wedding
Photographer: Doranne Jacobson

Roberta Hershenson
35 Hampton Road
Scarsdale, NY 10583
914-723-1891

Doranne Jacobson
290 Demarest Avenue
Closter, NJ 07624
201-767-7241

Joan Marmor
Images
1019 North Avenue
New Rochelle, NY 10804
914-235-2960

Helaine Messer
535 West 113th Street, #22
New York, NY 10025
212-864-0765
Photographer/Photojournalist. Art
world subject specialty: editorial
photography, including annual
reports and portraits.

Patricia Q
Coronet Studio
2004 Lincoln Highway
Edison, NJ 08817
201-287-1234
Master of Photography; Photographic
Craftsman.

Terri P. Tepper
261 Kimberly
Barrington, IL 60010
312-381-2113

■ Piano Technician

Carolyn Pine
376 Old Mamaroneck Road
White Plains, NY 10605
914-946-3788
Repairs, rebuilds, and tunes pianos.

■ Producer of Cultural Events

Kay Fialkoff
27-09 Romain Street
Fair Lawn, NJ 07410
201-791-4320

■ Psychologist

Alice S. Leventhal, Ph.D.
28 Sunset Drive
Summit, NJ 07901
201-277-2190
Clinical Psychologist.

■ Public Relations Consultant

Nancy G. Binzen
The PR Center
253 Carl Street
San Francisco, CA 94117
415-566-6281

Pearl Ehrlich
233 Vivien Court
Paramus, NJ 07652
201-262-4810

Marjorie E. Fox
Medieval Brass Rubbing Centre
Route 203, Box 299
Windham Center, CT 06280
203-423-2785
Advises artists and craftspeople.

Sarah Graham Mann
SGM Marketing Services
224 Falmouth Road
Scarsdale, NY 10583
914-723-8632

Marianna Murphy
5 Clinton Avenue
Maplewood, NJ 07040
201-763-5339

Patricia Ricci
26 Niamoa Drive
Cherry Hill, NJ 08003
609-424-9611

Isabelle Selikoff
P.O. Box 884
Hightstown, NJ 08520
609-448-7560

Ruthi Zinn
11 Athens Road
Short Hills, NJ 07078
201-467-2356

■ Publications Manager

Barbara Anderson
6002 Hibbling Avenue
Springfield, VA 22150
703-569-9062

■ Publisher

Maggy Simony
Freelance Publications
230 McConnell Avenue, Box 8
Bayport, NY 11705
516-472-1799

Marianne Wehrenberg
The Key Directory, Inc.
P.O. Box 562
East Brunswick, NJ 08816
201-254-6448
Publishes directories, magazines, journals, direct mail.

■ Puppeteer

Judy Caden
21 Glen Road
West Orange, NJ 07052
201-731-6461
201-889-5328
Puppet shows and workshops.

■ Reading Consultant

Antoinette C. Lowe
7830 Eagle Trail
Dallas, TX 75238
204-349-8586
Also tutors reading.

Judy Caden
Puppeteer

Miriam Raber
5 Bayberry Lane
Randolph, NJ 07869
201-366-1511

■ Real Estate Broker

Aileen Bott
28 Rapids Road
Stamford, CT 06905
203-322-2120

■ Recipe Developer

Pat Owens
1760 Forest Drive
Williamstown, NJ 08094
609-639-0856

■ Researcher

Ann De Falco
102 Fairmount Avenue
Chester, NJ 07930
201-879-5556
Researches and creates coats of arms.

Peggy Z. Ehrman
Biblio Services
83 Bertwell Road
Lexington, MA 02173
617-862-8367
Information research and retrieval by traditional methods or computer data bases.

Jill Groce
10904 Bucknell Drive, #1112
Silver Spring, MD 20902
301-942-0544

Doranne Jacobson
290 Demarest Avenue
Closter, NJ 07624
201-767-7241
Anthropological Researcher.

Marion Levine
304 Sea Isle Key
Secaucus, NJ 07094
201-866-5929
Research Analyst for nationwide
digest of career opportunities in
health field.

Vicki Mechner
OmniQuest, Inc.
P.O. Box 15
Chappaqua, NY 10514
914-238-9646
Finds resources such as products, ser-
vices, information, consultants; also
market studies.

Mara Mills
335 East 10th Street
New York, NY 10009
212-254-5173

■ Reservations/Rental Manager

Jeannine Anderson
66 Hillside Road
Sparta, NJ 07871
201-729-6976
Rents condominium in Maui, Hawaii.

Dorothy M. Mortenson
5 Euclid Place
Montclair, NJ 07042
201-746-6870
Rents seasonal guest house in
Nantucket, Massachusetts.

"Translating is a type of work where

total concentration is required—

making it ideally suited to a quiet

home environment."

Translator

■ Riding Instructor

Barbara Isaac
Riding High Farms
Route 526, Box 229
Allentown, NJ 08501
201-259-3884

■ Salesperson

Linda Blaney
3 Abalone Road
Narragansett, RI 02882
401-783-8180
Herbs, their by-products, and
vegetables.

Honey Bodenheimer
Country Crafts
17 Maple Stream Road
East Windsor, NJ 08520
609-443-3716
Crafts consignment shop.

Penny Couphos
164 Hillside Avenue
Chatham, NJ 07928
201-635-5474
Shaklee natural food supplements,
personal care and home care
products.

Judith M. Delaney
7 Spinet Drive
Rochester, NY 14625
716-385-4726
Shaklee natural food supplements,
personal care and home care
products.

Patricia F. Dixon
422 Beatrice Street
Teaneck, NJ 07666
201-836-5930
Color portrait business cards.

Suzanne Haviv
72 Ross Avenue
Demarest, NJ 07627
201-768-2665
Amway household products.

Carolyn S. Jacoby
Carolyn's Curiosities
194 John Street
Englewood, NJ 07631
201-871-4970
Antique photographs and prints.

Jan Johnson
1339 Highland Avenue
Plainfield, NJ 07060
201-753-5417
Amway household products.

Martha Kantor
Pajama Party
40 Cornell Road
Scarsdale, NY 10583
914-723-4550
Designer lingerie for fund raising and
at house parties.

Arlene K. Lucas
217 Smith Street
Peekskill, NY 10566
914-739-8471
Shaklee natural food supplements,
personal care and home care
products.

Barbara Moskowitz
7 Sherwood Road
Edison, NJ 08817
201-548-0591
Needlepoint supplies.

Susan Newman
400 East 52nd Street
New York, NY 10022
212-935-0293
"Cities to Go"—Souvenir gift pack-
ages geared to major cities.

Catherine Oetjen
40 Lincoln Avenue
Metuchen, NJ 08840
201-494-3184

Deborah K. Rauh
5634 Rauh Road
Coldwater, OH 45828
419-942-1821
Amway household products.

Bea Rubin
429 Woodland Place
Leonia, NJ 07605
201-461-6957
Pantyhose.

Susan Sheinlin
111 Tennyson Drive
Nanuet, NY 10954
914-623-7969
Roller skates.

Georgia Terry
Collector's Cranny
840 NE Cochran Avenue
Gresham, OR 97030
503-667-0950
Sells autographs and documents to
collectors and dealers in 28 states.

Cynthia Wallach
Pajama Party
2 Hickory Lane
Scarsdale, NY 10583
914-472-3808
Designer lingerie for fund raising and
at house parties.

Rita Wasserman
5 Briarwood Lane
Pleasantville, NY 10570
914-769-2098
Shaklee natural food supplements,
personal care and home care
products.

"My main reason for working at home is

that what I do is traditionally

done there and much prefer

teaching here to renting a studio

somewhere. It does have draw-

backs, however. It is hard on a

house to have people trooping in

and out in all kinds of weather; it

sometimes interferes with activi-

ties of the rest of the family."

Music Teacher

Sharon Rudman Williams
54 Pennsylvania Avenue
Carteret, NJ 07008
201-969-2028
Clothing.

■ Secretarial Services Director

Dora Back
After 6 Secretarial Service
54 Johnson Street
Fords, NJ 08863
201-738-4670

Georgine A. Meyer
18 Horizon Drive
Mendham, NJ 07945
201-543-4286

Joyce Mohr-Aicklen
10826 Stone Canyon Road,
  Apt. 2318
Dallas, TX 75230
214-692-6013

Marion J. Rosley
41 Topland Road
Hartsdale, NY 10530
914-682-9718

Margaret C. Tobin
4209 Olley Lane
Fairfax, VA 22032
703-323-0073

■ Secretary/Typist

Name Withheld
Address Withheld
Centreville, VA 22020
703-631-1280
Typing.

Vivian J. Day
1 Lincoln Place, Apt. 17C
North Brunswick, NJ 08902
201-297-2490
Typing.

Ruth M. Ferm
3425 Alabama Street
San Diego, CA 92104
714-291-4576
Typing.

Barbara J. Guile
12 Farrington Avenue
Closter, NJ 07624
201-767-8075
Typing.

Anna M. Parciak
54 Smith Street
Belleville, NJ 07109
201-751-2237
Typing, clerical duties, Dictaphone
transcriptions.

Marilyn Schiffman
10 Heritage Court
Demarest, NJ 07627
201-768-8996
Secretary in husband's home
optometrist office.

■ Social Services Counselor

Terri P. Tepper
261 Kimberly
Barrington, IL 60010
312-381-2113
Executive Director of Center for a
Woman's Own Name and Consumer
Credit Project, Inc. Counsels women
on credit and name rights.

■ Solar Consultant

Luz Holvenstot
100 Naughright Road
Long Valley, NJ 07853

■ Special Projects Coordinator

Renee Zimrin
3 Rosemont Drive
West Orange, NJ 07052
201-731-1013
201-325-8221
Creates and implements special projects for business organizations,
educators, and community groups.

■ Sports Instructor

Linda Rosensweig
116 Carthage Road
Scarsdale, NY 10583
914-722-3992
Tennis and paddle tennis instruction.

■ Stationer

Susan Feld
Paper Partners
33 Mistletoe Drive
Matawan, NJ 07747
201-583-5444
Personalized stationery, invitations,
announcements.

Audree Feldman
Paper Partners
33 Mistletoe Drive
Matawan, NJ 07747
201-583-4654
Personalized stationery, invitations,
announcements.

Barbara Gordon
2624 McCoy Way
Louisville, KY 40205
502-451-4150
Invitations and accessories.

Marjorie Gross
Mail Bag, Too
Address Withheld
914-723-0859
Personalized stationery, invitations,
announcements.

"I have made my garage into a pottery

and built a gas kiln. I really like

to work on a simple saw horse

8' x 4' plywood board table in

my backyard."

Craftsperson

Joan M. Kurtzman
1641 Southbrook Drive
Bridgewater, NJ 08807
201-722-4533
Stationery, invitations, business
forms.

Sondra Medwin
Simply Sondra
116 Dellwood Road
Cranston, RI 02920
401-943-1142
Stationery, invitations, accessories.

■ Stress Management Consultant

Juliette McGinnis
114 Pinecrest Drive
Hastings-on-Hudson, NY 10706
914-478-1696
Creates and designs stress-management programs, products, and
concepts.

■ Therapist

Rochelle H. Dubois
Merging Media
59 Sandra Circle, A-3
Westfield, NJ 07090
201-232-7224
Poetry therapy.

Elvira A. Fiducia
26 Collinwood Road
Maplewood, NJ 07040
201-763-3249
Licensed Marriage Counsellor.

Rhoda S. Gold
35 Francis Place
Caldwell, NJ 07006
201-226-7837
Psychotherapy.

Sarah Kaplan, R.N., M.S., C.S.
B17 David's Court
Dayton, NJ 08810
201-329-8007
Psychotherapy.

Josephine Santillo, M.S.W.
14 West End Avenue
Pompton Plains, NJ 07444
201-835-4710
Psychotherapy.

Susan Sarlin, C.S.W.
22 Kempster Road
Scarsdale, NY 10583
914-723-7646
Individual and family therapy.

■ Translator

Deborah B. Miller
6 Sargent Place
Manhasset, NY 11030
516-627-6337
French, German, Italian, Spanish.

Barbara Bryan Rojas
646 Lalor Street
Trenton, NJ 08611
609-989-8817
Spanish, French, and English to
English and Spanish.

Marion J. Rosley
41 Topland Road
Hartsdale, NY 10530
914-682-9718
French, German, Portuguese,
Spanish.

Robin Whitely
46 Colonial Way
Short Hills, NJ 07078
201-467-1704
Russian-English/English-Russian.

■ Travel Agent/Consultant

Fern Galant
Grand Detours
P.O. Box 143
Tenafly, NJ 07670
201-871-0088
Designs and operates weekend or day
trips for private groups or for fund
raisers to galleries, gardens, estates,
gourmet restaurants, museums, and
cultural experiences.

Helen Lurie
127 Lincoln Place
Waldwick, NJ 07463
201-652-5144

Nadine A. Weiss
161 Culberson Road
Basking Ridge, NJ 07920
201-766-5228
Conducts special interest tours.

Sandra Zook
Unbeaten Paths
P.O. Box 78
Village Station, NY 10014
212-677-5674
Operates a telephone tape directory
of unique, out-of-the-way shops,
restaurants, galleries, and theaters in
the New York City area, plus special
services and weekend retreats. Directory number: 212-677-0337.

■ Typesetter

Barbara Flood
421 Plainfield Road
Edison, NJ 08817
201-549-6470

Norma Glessner
24 Evergreen Road
Somerset, NJ 08873
201-249-5038
Headline Typesetter.

Beverly Lane
Graphics Lane, Inc.
22 University Road
East Brunswick, NJ 08816
201-257-8778

Maggy Simony
Freelance Publications
230 McConnell Avenue, Box 8
Bayport, NY 11705
516-472-1799

"I love my work which is basically typing manuscripts and transcribing hearings from cassette tapes. My goal originally was to earn $500 a month which was about what I was earning working 30 hours a week in offices for others. I have averaged over these past 13 months a bit in excess of $500 and have kept so busy that I often have to turn down work in order to keep up with what work I have accepted."

Typist

■ Vehicle Tester

Nancy Coggins
3932 Cheesequake Road
Parlin, NJ 08859
201-727-3829
Road tests cars and mopeds.

"My business is strictly referral—whether from physicians or satisfied clients."

Hypnotist

■ Welfare Director

Barbara J. Procino
561 Branch Avenue
Little Silver, NJ 07739
201-741-4764

■ Writer

Barbara Abercrombie
2121 Palos Verdes Drive West
Palos Verdes, CA 90274
213-378-7374

Peggy Bendel
113 Chestnut Avenue
Bogota, NJ 07603
201-343-3613
Free-lance Writer.

Audrey J. Boerum
72 McNomee Street
Oakland, NJ 07436
201-377-7660
201-377-6449
Publicity, advertising, promotions, speeches, articles, letters, newsletters, brochures, public relations.

Elizabeth Carr
664 Belleforte Avenue
Oak Park, IL 60302
312-848-3340

Nancy Coggins
3932 Cheesequake Road
Parlin, NJ 08859
201-727-3829
Writes about cars and craft projects.

Rochelle H. Dubois
Merging Media
59 Sandra Circle, A-3
Westfield, NJ 07090
201-232-7224

Pearl Ehrlich
233 Vivien Court
Paramus, NJ 07652
201-262-4810

Kay Fialkoff
27-09 Romaine Street
Fair Lawn, NJ 07410
201-791-4320
Poetry.

Barbara R. Fogel
86 Carthage Road
Scarsdale, NY 10583
914-723-1272
Free-lance writing for foundations, educational organizations.

Hanna Fox
175 Hamilton Avenue
Princeton, NJ 08540
609-924-2990
Author of *A Prism; Fanny, Leonard, Elaine* and *Dorothea Lynde Dix: Her Contribution to Mental Health.* Also tutors writers and conducts writing workshops.

Name Withheld
123 South Munn Avenue
East Orange, NJ 07018
201-675-0090
Free-lance Writer—ads, commercials, booklets.

Toni L. Goldfarb
586 Teaneck Road
Teaneck, NJ 07666
201-836-5030
Free-lance Writer—medicine and social sciences.

Jill Groce
10904 Bucknell Drive, #1112
Silver Spring, MD 20902
301-942-0544

Sharon Hodges
1315 East 7th Street
Plainfield, NJ 07062
201-753-0514
Poetry.

Randi Kreiss
983 East Prospect Street
Woodmere, NY 11598
516-374-0504
Free-lance Writer.

Rae Lindsay
364 Mauro Road
Englewood Cliffs, NJ 07632
201-567-8986

Marie MacBride
412 North Monroe Street
Ridgewood, NJ 07450
201-652-7833

Sara McAulay
Box 52
Mountain Lakes, NJ 07046
201-263-2197

Mara Mills
335 East 10th Street
New York, NY 10009
212-254-5173

Susan Newman
400 East 52nd Street
New York, NY 10022
212-935-0293
Magazine Writer—parent/child and home-related topics.

Jean Phillips
360 West 22nd Street
New York, NY 10011
Freelance writing, public relations,
interviewing.

"I am a great appreciator of peace and

quiet and greatly enjoy working

on quiet contemplative work

(proofreading and indexing are

that!) in a peaceful house. I

appreciate not having to get

dressed up every day for work

downtown and not having to

hassle with public

transportation."

Proofreader

"I love freedom of setting own hours

and find the selling / soliciting

aspect the most difficult. . . . I

believe in scheduling, lists, and

strong self-discipline."

Marketing Consultant

Dorothy M. Ranney
11820 Edgewater Drive, #210
Lakewood, OH 44107
216-521-5171

Bernice Richmond
863 Carleton Road
Westfield, NJ 07090
201-654-3370

Nancy Rubin
35 Broadfield Road
New Rochelle, NY 10804
914-632-1052
Free-lance Journalist/Writer.

Joan M. Scobey
9 Lenox Place
Scarsdale, NY 10583
914-723-2747

Shalomé
111 North Pine Avenue
Albany, NY 12203
518-489-3320
Poetry and novels.

Harriet Langsam Sobol
10 Claremont Road
Scarsdale, NY 10583
914-472-2248

Terri P. Tepper
261 Kimberly
Barrington, IL 60010
312-381-2113
Coauthor with mother, Nona Dawe
Tepper, of *The New Entrepreneurs:
Women Working from Home.*

Marty Thomson
1933 Biltmore Street NW
Washington, DC 20009
202-462-1285
Writes for business publications.

Sharon Rudman Williams
54 Pennsylvania Avenue
Carteret, NJ 07008
201-969-2028
Free-lance Writer for newspapers.

Bobbi Wolf
Poemetrics
228 Standish Road
Merion, PA 19066
215-667-5896
Poetry.

A-Z Idea List

The following list of possibilities is set forth as a springboard for your imagination. These ideas are, for the most part, not listed elsewhere in the book—ideas to set you off on your own wondrous flights of fancy from A to Z.

Think about them. Think of what you can do that others cannot do (or cannot do as well). Think of saving people time, money, effort, or aggravation. Are any of the ideas potential moneymakers in your area? Are any of special interest to you?

Answering service—"Hello, Central!"
Appliances—fix-it shop for small items
Appraisals—antiques, books, collectibles, objects d'art
Aprons—different strokes for different folks—carpenters, cooks, gardeners, kids, painters, etc.
Aquariums—design and installation
Architectural design—blueprints, drafts, renderings
Awnings and shades—custom design and sales

Baby items—buntings, diaper bags, carryalls, bibs, toys
Babysitters—daytime sitters, especially—a working mother's best friend!
Bagels 'n lox—personal delivery for Sunday brunches
Beauty services—hairstyling, manicures, pedicures, electrolysis
Bedding—handcrafted linens, quilts, pillows; coordinating accessories
Bees—keeping hives, selling honey, making beeswax candles
Birds—fancy feeders and cages—a feather in your cap!
Books—binding, collecting, trading, publishing, and sales
Boxes—big and little designs, but only big sales
Bridal services—gowns and accessories
Buttons—design and sales

Camps—information specialist and broker
Candy—homemade sweets for the sweet—who can resist?
Caricatures and cartooning—children's and adults' parties
Cars—driver education; customized interior and exterior decoration
Cellars—cleaning and organization
Chairs—caning, needlepoint seats and backs
Chickens and eggs—breeding, but which comes first?
China—painting
Clocks—collecting and sales; repairs
Cloisonné—jewelry, belt buckles, pictures
Coins—collecting and sales

Copper—hand-tooled artifacts
Costumes—rental
Crafts—supplies

Dagwoods—hero sandwiches for parties, lunch hours, etc.
Découpage—furniture, boxes, and accessories
Decoys—carving, painting, and sales
Detectives—private eyes
Dinner deliveries—definitely delicious!
Designer—dog houses, doll houses, and what have you!
Dolls—unique dolls, clothing, and repairs

Ear piercing and earring sales
Eggs—blowing, decorating, and sales
English—teaching English as a second language for conversation
or citizenship; tutoring in composition and creative writing

Fabric—specialty fabrics, sales
Felt—designs for dolls, mobiles, pillows, puppets
Fish—breeding
Flies—designing and creating fishing flies
Flowers—preservation, arrangement, and instruction; creating
artificial flowers
Foreigners—helping them resettle, adjust, become familiar with
American systems (being bilingual is important)
Frames—one-of-a-kind frames for pictures and mirrors; also
framing
Frozen foods—specialty items
Furniture—designing, building, stripping, refinishing
Furs—remodeling and repairing

Garage sales—organization and management
Garden furniture—rewebbing, repainting, repadding,
reupholstering
Gifts—buying, wrapping, and mailing
Greenhouses—design and installation
Greeting cards—handcrafted
Groups—Lose Weight, Stop Smoking, Improve Your
Memory, etc.

Hair—design and creation of unique combs, barrettes, clasps
Hammocks—handmade of rope, cord, canvas, webbing
Handwriting—analysis
Health foods—homegrown
Herbs—homegrown, dried or fresh, mixed or matched, creatively
packaged
Hiking—guide and outfitter

Illusion—pantomime and magic
Indians—baskets, carvings, and handicrafts
Instruction—bridge, cooking, dance, fencing, gymnastics, judo,
karate, languages, needlework, painting, sculpting, sewing, speed
reading, shorthand, slimnastics, swimming, tennis, typing, etc.

Jams and jellies—homemade and creatively packaged
Jewelry—repairs, restyling, and sales

Kids—child care, play groups, trips
Kitchen—planning and organization
Kites—handcrafted
Kits—crafts, butterfly breeders, needlework, holiday items, doll house furniture and accessories

Lampshades—custom designed; handpainted lamp globes to match bases
Letters—correspondence for busy people who don't have secretaries, for elderly or ill
Linens—handmade and coordinated napkins, tablecloths, placemats, and aprons

Mail—direct-mail marketing and lists
Maps and globes—antique and contemporary—collecting and sales
Marzipan—mouth-watering, edible art
Messenger service
Miniatures—handcrafted landmarks and doll house items
Mobile homes—rental or leasing
Monograms—personalized bags, aprons, handkerchiefs, clothing
Movies—8mm film or videotape biographies for special occasions
Murals—custom designed on walls and ceilings

Needlework—appliqué, crewel, crochet, embroidery, knitting, needlepoint, patchwork, sewing, stitchery, string art, trapunto

Omens—astrologers, nephrologists, palmists, tea-leaf readers

Paperweights—collecting and sales
Papier maché—toys and accessories
Pattern maker and tester
Pets—vacation care, grooming, supplies
Pillow furniture—handcrafted
Pillows—in lace, ribbons, fabric, needlepoint, batik — designed and created in patterned motifs, also with flowers, in seasonal or holiday themes, in sailing codes
Plants—propagating, potting, and sales
Portraits—painted or needlepointed—pets, people, residences

Quackers—breeding ducks (!)
Quilts—original designs, handcrafted

Rentals—Rent-a-picture, -plant, -sculpture
Restorations—antiques, artifacts, cars, homes
Roommates—matchmaking service
Rugs—custom designed—braided, hooked, and woven

"Friends ask me how I do it, too. I have an inner drive—I'm an over-achiever and have always been. I can't sit still without feeling as though I should be doing some-thing. There's always something that needs to be completed or started."

Artist

Scarves—batiked, embroidered, handpainted, knitted, silk-screened
Scrimshaw—jewelry and belt buckles
Sewing—specialty clothes for hard-to-fit people; novelty items for special occasions
Shells—shell craft novelties
Shoes—repair and sales
Shopping services—groceries, gifts, clothing, whatever
Speech—therapy, dialect, inflection, pattern correction, diction
Spices—mixed or matched, creatively packaged
Stencils—on tin, wall plaques, floors
Surveys—by mail or phone
Sweaters—knitted and crocheted; also mittens, socks, hats, scarves

Ties—handsewn of elegant or unusual materials
Totes—handcrafted designs
Tours—theme tours of your town or region
Transportation—for children, elderly, handicapped; to car inspection; service to airports

Umbrellas—handpainted, personalized
Unicorns and other stuffed animals in a variety of fabrics and fake furs
Upholstery—repair, recovering

Valuables—photographic records to provide householders with proof of ownership
Vans—customized
Vegetables—excess produce from home garden sold at roadside stand
Voice—teaching musical comedy and opera

Wastebaskets—painted, beribboned, découpaged, custom designed
Wigs—design, refurbishing and sales
Windows and screens—cleaning service

X-otic foods—specially prepared

Yarn—imports; naturally-dyed sheep's wool

Zoot suits and zo forth—period clothing—restyling and sales

I find that my business and professional colleagues are delighted to have our conferences and work sessions here, because the atmosphere is so pleasing—so refreshingly 'uncorporate.'...

The large dining room table is a perfect conference set-up, the kettle is always on...

I've worked in corporate offices; I've worked in bustling institutions. But for me, there's nothing like being my own boss and most assuredly...there's no workplace like home."

Communications Consultant

The Bitter End

Since you have reached this point in the book, you have read the variety of feelings and experiences of women who are now working from home. They are taking a visible stand, being counted proudly among the millions of working American women, making a name for themselves, and making money as well. They have shared with us their joys and frustrations, their problems and problem-solving techniques. Hundreds of women have written to us and most of them are listed within our directory. Some, however, have given us permission to publish everything *but* names or addresses or phone numbers. Others have not allowed us to publish any information at all. That is the other side of this unfolding story.

"My neighbors know I have dogs, but they don't know I'm a breeder. It's not allowed in this Class A zone!"

"Do you realize how much garbage I contribute to the municipal system?," asked a caterer.

An artist who exhibits at occasional weekend shows was told by her husband: "Paint if you like, but keep your nose clean and stay out of trouble!"

"I only sell my jams and jellies during the summer to just a few places. I don't want to be listed because I don't want more business. My husband doesn't want us in a higher tax bracket."

"You may use any of my statements, but keep my name out of it!"

The IRS and the local zoning boards are both protagonists and antagonists in these stories, but they need not be. Zoning ordinances are designed for everybody's peace of mind. The artist, craftsperson, writer, and designer may not have much of a problem because the business is a quiet one and will cause no neighborhood disturbance. On the other hand, any business which brings patients, clients, or customers to the door may arouse suspicion and be a nuisance to the neighbors. Put yourselves in their position. If you lived close to the house next door, you wouldn't like a stream of cars moving down your residential street and cars parked on all sides!—or business signs obliterating the beauty of trees and shrubs! Seeing it from the other point of view, helps puts things in perspective. Visitors aren't the only bone of contention, though. A business that creates noise or foul odors would also be unwelcome in residential areas. That seems reasonable, doesn't it? Furthermore, the use of combustibles and hazardous substances are not only a matter of safety, but could also invalidate a homeowner's insurance policy.

Carefully check local zoning laws before opening a

homebased business. Don't risk being closed down because of an illegal operation. You can apply for—and perhaps receive—a variance allowing you to operate a business from home. If it's important, maybe you'd rather fight than switch. It's worth a try. It has been done.

A music teacher, threatened with closure of her home studio because she was violating a zoning law, discovered through careful research that the ordinance was put into effect after she had opened her studio. She's still in business at home!

A woman in an affluent New York suburb recently sued her town's Zoning Board of Appeals and the Town Board after she had been denied permission to keep her pet goat. After hearing an impressive array of testimony, the judge ruled in the goat's favor! Since we read about this case in the papers, this woman may not have a business centered around that animal, but for those who do have family pets within the business, the ruling is a positive one.

"I had to get a specific variance for the home to be built because of the studio and teaching combination. Some neighbors thought the studio would deteriorate the neighborhood. It's not easy for someone to have their family and something they enjoy doing, which is economically beneficial to the family situation, and open it up to the public in a residential neighborhood. We looked three years for a good location. When we were building and put in the kitchen window, a neighbor came in and asked if I was going to put a neon sign in the window. That's how upset and uptight they were…"

Taxes are a different matter. The law of the land is that anyone earning a certain sum of money must pay taxes, and that is that, like it or not! There's no way to get away from it. We are a nation of laws, and we must abide by them. We know there are individuals who do not declare an income and therefore do not pay taxes; we've been to craft fairs, purchased handicrafts, and paid no sales taxes. Be it known, however, that failure to file returns and to collect sales tax when appropriate constitutes tax evasion or fraud, and that is a serious offense.

After reading through this book, we hope you now understand that there is a great deal to be gained from having a business at home. In addition to the intangible pleasures of flexibility, convenience, comfort, fulfillment, and achievement, there is that one big, real tangible—money! The need for it never seems to diminish. "Money can't buy happiness," someone once wisely stated, "but it sure helps!"

Every business is entitled to tax benefits for start-up losses. If a businesswoman does not declare till somewhat later, she has lost these benefits. Moreover, she risks losing her business at that later date because of illegal operation. There are certain legitimate deductions that may be taken by a woman in a home-based business, and these should be thoroughly researched. We cannot stress often enough the importance of good advice from both an accountant and an attorney. In addition, the IRS has agents to help with tax questions and many pamphlets available, free of charge, for taxpayers.

Some women claim not to have a "business" but "just a little hobby." We asked the IRS to explain at what point "just a little hobby" becomes a "business." The answer was simple and direct: if the individual is soliciting business through any means, the hobby is no longer a hobby. A business, we were told, is an activity engaged in for profit.

The Small Business Administration defines it this way: when you open your doors to customers, you are legally in business if you have complied with licenses, permits, unemployment, insurance coverage, social security coverage, and sales, income, and personal property taxes—all of which depend upon state and county regulations. These differ in accordance with the locality and the nature of the business.

There are thousands of women working from home who measure their successes in dollar signs and emotional well-being. They have dealt with the problems of taxes and zoning and their businesses are growing. The bitter end need not be bitter, and the end will hopefully signify merely the end of the beginning to a career that brings wealth, health, and happiness.

Arleen Priest, Wendy Lazar, Marion Behr
Photographer: Doranne Jacobson

Here we are—Arleen Priest, Wendy Lazar, and Marion Behr—three women, each working from her own home to produce *Women Working Home: The Homebased Business Guide and Directory.*

It began with an idea of Marion's: to find out who were the women working at home, why were they there, and what was the nature of their business/home environment. As the study developed and grew, Marion, a fine artist, and Wendy, a writer, again joined forces as they had done a few years ago when they collaborated on a children's book. As *Women Working Home* took shape, Arleen added her business expertise.

Thus, as the study has grown, so, too, have we—personally, professionally, and academically. The association has been a pleasant one, as expected. We have known each other many years, as childhood friends in Rochester, New York and as students at Syracuse University. Careers and marriage initially scattered us to the four winds, but, happily, we are together again.

168

Do You Have a Homebased Business?

By filling out this questionnaire, you will enable us to collect statistics on women who produce goods or provide services from their homes.

We would also appreciate letters describing your work at home—reasons you chose a home environment, hours, workplace, problems, frustrations, how you manage it all, your definition of success. These additional comments add dimension to our findings.

Please print or type the answers. Some or all of the information may be published, so please sign the permission paragraph at the end and indicate what information you wish to be held confidential. Return the completed form to Women Working Home, Inc., 24 Fishel Road, Edison, NJ 08820.

Name: _____

Street Address: _____

City/State _____ Zip_____ Phone_____

1. Occupation: _____
2. What products are produced or services rendered? _____
_____
3. When did you start your business? _____
4. Why did you start your business?_____
_____
5. How much did you know about your business before you started?
a. nothing ☐   b. a little ☐   c. a great deal ☐
6. A. Was "start-up" capital needed?   a. Yes ☐   b. No ☐
B. If yes, did you take out a loan from a bank or
other financial institution?   a. Yes ☐   b. No ☐
C. If not, how did you finance the "start-up"? _____
_____
7. Do you enjoy what you are doing?   a. Yes ☐   b. No ☐
8. Why do you work from home?_____
_____
9. Do you like working from home?   a. Yes ☐   b. No ☐
10. Would you move the business out of your home if
you could?   a. Yes ☐   b. No ☐
11. Do you consider your business primarily
a. a business ☐   b. a hobby ☐   c. self-fulfillment ☐
d. other ☐ (Please explain) _____
_____
12. Does your business now support you or do you intend to
make it support you?   a. Yes ☐   b. No ☐

13. Is your neighborhood
a. urban ☐   b. suburban ☐   c. rural ☐   d. small town? ☐
14. Do you   a. own ☐   b. rent ☐   your home?
15. A. Do you advertise?   a. Yes ☐   b. No ☐
B. Where has advertising benefited most? _____
How else do clients and customers find out about you? _____
_____

16. How many hours per week do you work?
a. in your business at home_____ b. outside the home_____
17. How many paid employees do you have?
a. Full-time_____ b. Part-time _____
18. How many volunteers (including family members)? _____
19. What is your date of birth? _____
20. Are you   a. married ☐   b. never married ☐   c. separated ☐
                    d. widowed ☐   e. divorced ☐
21. Ages of children
a. living at home_____b. living elsewhere_____
22. Do you have insurance coverage specifically
related to the business?   a. Yes ☐   b. No ☐
23. A. Are there local ordinances which create problems?
                                        a. Yes ☐   b. No ☐
B. If yes, what are they? _____
_____

24. Gross income last year from homebased business:
a.   under $5,000 ☐   f. $25,100-$ 30,000 ☐
b. $ 5,100-$10,000 ☐   g. $30,100-$ 50,000 ☐
c. $10,100-$15,000 ☐   h. $50,100-$ 75,000 ☐
d. $15,100-$20,000 ☐   i. $75,100-$100,000 ☐
e. $20,100-$25,000 ☐   j. $100,100 +   ☐
25. Net income last year from homebased business:
a.   under $5,000 ☐   f. $25,100-$ 30,000 ☐
b. $ 5,100-$10,000 ☐   g. $30,100-$ 50,000 ☐
c. $10,100-$15,000 ☐   h. $50,100-$ 75,000 ☐
d. $15,100-$20,000 ☐   i. $75,100-$100,000 ☐
e. $20,100-$25,000 ☐   j. $100,100 +   ☐
26. Have you completed
a. elementary school   ☐
b. high school   ☐
c. some college   ☐
d. college degree   ☐
e. some graduate school   ☐
f. graduate degree?   ☐
I give you permission to publish any or all of the above information,
except as indicated by brackets [   ].
Date_____Signature _____

NAHB
Membership Form

Homebased businesswomen will be delighted to know that a group of women operating businesses from their homes have formed the National Alliance of Homebased Businesswomen.

Your membership in the Alliance gives you—
■ newsletters
■ a support network
■ a resource for learning and earning
■ a showcase for goods and services

Membership in this professional Alliance is only $25 per year, $20 if this is your first year in business. Membership fees are tax deductible because NAHB is a not-for-profit organization.

I wish to become a member of the National Alliance of Homebased Businesswomen.

_____
Name   Telephone

_____
Street Address   City/State   Zip

Name and nature of business_____

_____

My check for $_____ is enclosed. I started my business in_____.
                                                                                              year

Make check payable to NAHB and mail to:
NAHB   P.O. Box 95   Norwood, NJ 07648

I wish to become a member of the National Alliance of Homebased Businesswomen.

_____
Name   Telephone

_____
Street Address   City/State   Zip

Name and nature of business_____

_____

My check for $_____ is enclosed. I started my business in_____.
                                                                                              year

Make check payable to NAHB and mail to:
NAHB   P.O. Box 95   Norwood, NJ 07648

WWH Press
Order Form

Suggested uses for
*Women Working Home:
The Homebased Business
Guide and Directory:*
Marketplace for products
and services
Resource information
Business guidelines
Idea catalyst
Textbook
Networking list

WWH Press   Order Form
P.O. Box 237
Norwood, New Jersey 07648

Name _____
Address_____
     City _____ State _____ Zip_____
Area Code and Phone Number _____

Please send _____ copies of *Women Working Home: The Homebased Business Guide and Directory* at $12.95, plus $1.25 postage and handling, for each book. N.J. residents add $.65 sales tax. Enclosed is $_____. For information on quantity orders, write to WWH Press. Allow four weeks for delivery.
☐ Check. ☐ Money Order.
Charge my ☐ Master Charge ☐ Visa.

Card No: ⬚⬚⬚⬚⬚⬚⬚⬚⬚⬚⬚⬚⬚ Exp. Date _____
Signature _____

    We are still hearing from homebased businesswomen who would like to be listed in our directory. Our next edition is scheduled for publication in 1983. If you would also like to be included, please print or type the following information as you would like it to appear in the directory. We will be contacting you again as our second edition develops, but this will help us in our planning.

_____
Name

_____
Company / Business Name

_____
Address

_____
City, State, Zip

_____
County   Telephone

Occupation _____

Description of work _____

_____

_____

If artist, media: _____